Creating Competitive Advantage using Traditional Feng Shui

Where Competitive Advantage can last for decades!

Dr Michael Oon

Creating Competitive Advantage using Traditional
Feng Shui
First published in 2012
Published by CompletelyNovel.com

This book is not intended to provide personalised legal, financial or investment advice. The Author and the Publisher specifically disclaim any liability, loss or risk which is incurred as a consequence, directly or indirectly, of the use and application of any contents of this work.

ISBN 9781849142816

Acknowledgements

I would like to thank Helen Doherty, Damara Diamond and Kathleen Koh for their vital comments on the drafts of the book. Also, Rachel McCombie for her painstaking work in copy editing the text, and Wikipedia, the online encyclopaedia, for the reference information. The cover design by "The Mule". Finally to Tom Evans, "The Bookwright" who gave me the inspiration to write the book.

Dedication

I dedicate this book to the Sages of Ancient China. They understood the rhythm of planet Earth.

Contents

Dr Michael Oon

Michael was born in Singapore, brought up in a traditional Chinese manner with an emphasis on education. He had a strict father and a loving mother. He read Biochemistry at the Imperial College, London and he did his PhD at the Institute of Psychiatry (University of London) on hallucinogenic drugs. With this expertise, he joined the research department of the Metropolitan Police Forensic Science Laboratory in London. His 20-year career at the laboratory included a period as court-going forensic scientist. He has worked on a number of high profile cases and was nearly shot at whilst working in Gibraltar.

His second career is in Chinese Philosophy, specialising in feng shui, the Chinese system of land management, which is focused on achieving the best conditions for the well-being of the people working and living in the built environment. He came to this subject out of curiosity, but was fascinated by the link between how the environment contributes to the quality of a person's life. But the information available appeared to him to be chaotic, as there were so many different versions of the same subject. Using methods from his forensic science background, he managed to work out how the established information was disseminated. An obstacle to this search was the Chinese love of secrecy.

He is now a member of Alliance Feng Shui[1], a team of consultants practising traditional feng shui in various parts of the world. Traditional feng shui in its current form originated in AD 1500 in the Court of the Imperial Palace of the Chinese Emperor. It involves

[1] www.AllianceFengShui.com

the selection of students, training in established methods, apprenticeship, working in teams and following strict rules. He has worked in North America, Europe and in the Far East. He specialises in working on buildings, business parks and residential estates. He writes a blog on various topics, including feng shui, buildings and current news topics, on his website: www.MichaelOon.com.

Introduction

Why competitive advantage?

We live in a free market society. We compete for clients with our rivals, people in the same profession or trade. We have always competed for our business, and this has been the way of life for most of British history.

In the Yellow Pages, businesses compete to be first in the alphabetic listings – they do this with business names such as AAA, Aaron or Aardvark. These days, most of the local listings have moved to the internet and businesses now want to be on the first page of Google by using search engine optimisation (SEO) methodology. Being on the first page for keywords such as "computer repairs + town name" gives you a competitive advantage over another business which is lower down the search results page, or on the second page.

Businesses seek to gain competitive advantage and spend enormous sums to acquire it.

Pharmaceutical companies spend billions on research to find a preparation that would have a therapeutic cure on the human body. The patent for a formulation gives the company twenty years of competitive advantage. After this time, the competitive advantage is lost and it becomes a free for all. Generic companies can then produce copies with no royalty or licensing payments. Currently, the research and development cost of each new molecular entity (drug) is approximately US$1.8 billion.

In 2012, a US$300 million cable is being laid across the Atlantic Ocean so that financial traders can save six milliseconds in receiving data. A one millisecond competitive advantage is said to be worth US$100m a year to the bottom line of a hedge fund.

Competitive advantage is defined as the strategic advantage that one business entity has over its rival entities within its competitive industry. Achieving competitive advantage strengthens and positions a business better within the business environment. As with most cases, the competitive advantage is eroded with time, as the competition works out how the advantage can be challenged.

Advanced technology is a highly competitive market. The market is changing constantly. I commented on my blog (www.MichaelOon.com) that corporates in this sector are one-product companies. After their moment of glory, they fade away unless their next product is a step ahead of the constantly changing marketplace.

The sequence of market leaders in mobile phone technology was as follows:

- Motorola (new technology of mobile phones)
- Nokia (cheap, consistently refreshing case designs, simple to use)
- Blackberry – smartphone (emails)
- Apple (iPhone) – a computer in your pocket.

In each step, the competitive advantage erodes with time.

In the case of Apple Inc., it is continually creating the next generation of products to keep a step ahead of the competition.

From the above examples from the pharmaceutical industry, financial services and advanced technology, we can see that gaining competitive advantage is both capital intensive and time sensitive.

The most important point is the time period to maintain the competitive advantage. How long before the competitive advantage is eroded? Advanced technology is characterised by rapid advances. The period to maintain competitive advantage is short. In other businesses, the changes are slower. The period to maintain competitive advantage is therefore longer.

The competitive advantage is lost when a competitor recognises the weakness of the product and creates a product that is cheaper, has more features, more advanced technology, faster delivery, and is better marketed, so that the competitive advantage is lost. The cycle starts again!

Suppose you use a service to gain competitive advantage. The service providers use methods that very few people know about and do not disclose the client's names. This will not arouse any suspicions with their competitors. The competitive advantage will therefore benefit the client for years or for decades. Perhaps this competitive advantage has been used by top Fortune corporations and FTSE companies?

This book is about creating competitive advantage. It is using traditional feng shui to help design the 'high performance' building. The identities of the clients and their buildings remain confidential. The features of traditional feng shui are so subtle that you have to be fully trained in that craft to realise that it has been applied in a particular building. Your competitors do not, therefore, realise the advantage that has been created. If nothing is said, it will not be known.

What is traditional feng shui?

Feng shui is the Chinese system of land management which started with the rise of the Chinese civilisation some 4,000 years ago. It is about getting the right conditions for the well-being of the people working and living in buildings. Feng shui was solely practised in mainland China until the Communist takeover in 1949. The Leader of the Communists, Mao Zedong, banned the practice. Feng shui was then practised outside mainland China, with the nucleus being moved to Taiwan and the other Chinese outposts of Hong Kong, Malaysia and Singapore.

It was at the end of the 20th century that feng shui spread to the West (North America and Europe), at which time more than 50 derivatives of feng shui appeared. The practices included the use of symbols (from the Chinese pantheon), jewellery, furniture, thoughts, paint, paintings, food, interior decorating and so on. There were new practices such as clutter clearing, and feng shui from different origins – Celtic, Balinese, Nordic and so on. Everybody was confused with the term feng shui. In my opinion, there was no definitive method or text available to give guidelines for the practice (like tai chi, martial arts, and traditional Chinese medicine) and hence we saw the proliferation of new methods.

There is a group of feng shui consultants who have continued the tradition of practising feng shui in the manner of the Imperial Court of the Chinese

Emperors, first established in the AD 1500. In the Emperor's court, all work was done in the name of the Emperor. This meant that all credit went to the Emperor, to whom allegiance was sworn. Consultants' first priority was the success of the project, and the Emperor's interests and not their own. There was absolutely no conflict of interest. The consultants worked on the Emperor's building or city projects using the established methods of feng shui.

This is known as Traditional Feng Shui. It is a practical art and science that has been developed and used in China for thousands of years. It is a method of observing the pattern and cycles of nature, and harnesses the beneficial energies from these natural forces to promote success, harmony and vitality. It is about how these three elements – the physical environment, the people, the element of time – interact with one another.

To this day, this group of consultants has maintained a low profile. The consultants raise their profile only when searching for new students or clients. Otherwise, they avoid any prominence or publicity.

The key points in traditional feng shui are:

- You have to be selected.
- You are trained in established methods.
- You serve an apprenticeship.
- You work in teams.
- You follow strict rules.

They do not work with clients who have casinos, or people who are drug dealers, gun makers, disreputable lawyers or people with criminal records, amongst others.

The other differentiator is in the practice. They work on the exteriors (outside of buildings), and hence have the capability to work on the design of buildings, businesses and residential estates, as well as on whole towns and cities. The procedures were established after more than five centuries of use and have been adapted to modern 21st Century living. Currently, the main clients are property developers, property investors, multiple retailers and hotel chains in their development projects. The identities of the clients and their buildings are not disclosed.

The three main problems for development projects are:

- Can the project be completed on time and on budget?
- Can it be sold at the asking price, and when?
- The business outcome of new commercial building is uncertain:
    - Will the office building get tenants?
    - What will the hotel occupancy rate be?
    - Will customers make purchases in the shops?

The advantage for the clients is created by using the methods of traditional feng shui to solve the problem. The procedure involves five steps which have been used repeated for the past 50 years.

- Select the best site in the interests of the client's aims and goals.
- Locate the exact position of the building as this relates to the ultimate success of the building's owners.

- Help in the design of the landscape, exteriors and interiors of the buildings for the benefit of the owners and the people working there.
- Work out the date and place to start the project so that it will be completed on time and on budget.
- Locate the sales office to get the best sales and ascertain the best time to start publicity for maximum effectiveness.

What are the results?

- The projects were completed on time and on budget.
- The properties were sold at a 5% premium and about six months ahead of schedule. This gave the clients an increase of 5% gross profit for the project.
- If the building was a hotel, the occupancy rate was about 80%.
- Shopping malls and stores do exceptionally well.
- A number of top UK and US corporate headquarters, whose design incorporated traditional feng shui, are still at the top of the business sector after more than 50 years.

How do the clients feel after using the feng shui consultants?

They feel totally cared for. Their first priority of the consultants is the success of the project and the client's interests. They are with the clients from the inception to the completion of the project. No other service provider spends this amount of time with the client.

Have you considered how the environment affects you and your business?

Feng shui is about the environment and how it affects people. I will go through some examples.

In any residential area where all the houses have the same design along the street, the experience of the people in different houses will be different. However, there are occasions when, in a particular house, the outcomes of the different families who have lived there over the ages can be frighteningly similar. Could this be the environment affecting the outcome of people's lives?

In any residential area, there will be examples of the following:

a. An ordinary family move into a house. After a while, you keep seeing cars replaced with newer models, and regular improvements on their house. After a period, they move out. Another family moves in and the same process occurs.
b. An ordinary family move into another house. After some time, instead of the 'normal' two cars parked there, there is only one car. Sometime later, the house is put on the market but it takes time to sell even when the market is good. You hear that the family is broken up as the parents have divorced. They move out and another family moves in. The same process occurs.
c. Families do not stay long in some houses. They move in and move out soon after. You hear on the grapevine that they have encountered

financial problems. Another family moves in and the cycle repeats itself.

d. There are some houses that are difficult to sell even when all the house designs are the same. They just take longer than others to shift.

In most cases, families move in and stay there. But why are these particular houses different? This can happen in a housing estate with the same house design and on the same street. For every family that moves into these particular houses, the same process happens. These are the types of properties:

- The prosperous house,
- The divorce house,
- The financial difficulty house,
- The house that is difficult to sell.

A similar analogy happens on the high street.

There are some locations that do extremely good business and others that do poor business. A typical example is a café. One day, you will see an owner opening a café with the very best of intentions. Soon after, it closes down and a new owner comes in and reopens the café. It then closes after a brief spell. This happens continually over the years. Why?

Another example is the sub-post offices in the Woking area. One particular sub-post office always has a queue to get served. But you can get instant service in the other five sub-post offices. Three sub-post offices have recently closed in this area. Why?

When we look at the high street in the London area, the young ladies' fashions shops are on streets that are aligned East-West. Examples include Oxford Street, Kensington High Street and Guildford High Street.

Restaurants tend to congregate in clusters, and on roads that are aligned North-South. Examples include Charlotte Street and Queensway in London. Coffee shops located at street corners or junctions do particularly well. In the UK, examples of these are Starbucks and Costa.

There are towns and districts which are unknown and suddenly, out of the blue, they are areas of development and prosperity. Conversely, prosperous towns and districts suddenly lose their shine. Since the 1980s, the Thames Valley (Reading, Swindon, Basingstoke) has been the centre of economic activity, in which the high technology companies have been establishing their offices. The area west of London also had growth from the establishment of new offices and services.

However, since 2000, there has been a rise in prominence of the areas North East of London. Firstly, we have seen the regeneration of the east side of London with the Olympic site, the establishment of Tech City (also known as Silicon Roundabout) in London's East End, the prominence of the county of Essex in the media and business, and finally, new technology coming up in the area around Cambridge and Stansted Airport. Then, prosperous towns in Surrey such as Leatherhead, Reigate and Dorking are not as prosperous as before.

London: this is the capital city of the UK. London, and the rest of the South East of England, is the most prosperous part of the nation. London has continuously been a trading post since Roman times some two thousand years ago. It is now one of the world's three main cities for finance, the other two being New York and Tokyo. London was also credited for raising the money for the European wars during the Napoleonic era, and it became the central hub for goods from the British Empire. The question is, which came first?

- Was the business environment created by the geographical features?
  or
- Was it people going there repeatedly which created the business environment?

Moving to new premises

It is a common observation that, when a company moves to a new location, it faces a number of new challenges. In most cases, there is no change to the company's business structure. However, I would like to show three examples in which the company moved and significant changes happened. This is particularly significant if you are in a sports business, in which results matter.

1. Abbey Bank had established its headquarters at Baker Street over the decades. In 2002, it moved its head office to Euston. Its days as an independent bank did not last long, as in 2004, it was taken over after a financial crisis and a death in the building.
2. Arsenal Football Club had a magnificent run in collecting trophies until 2007, when they moved to the new Emirates Stadium. No trophies have been won since.

3. Williams F1 is one of the most prestigious teams in F1 motor sport; it won nine constructors titles between 1980 and 1997. What happened after 1997? It is a sad story of decline. They had move to a new factory in 1997, where they have remained since.

What is the topic in this book?

It is about the influence of the environment on man. It is a methodology that was established some forty centuries ago. It is now used to help property developers, business owners and people get the best out of their property.

The book starts with the history of feng shui, from its origins right up to the present day. It describes the how feng shui was practised only in mainland China and then thrown out of that country. After moving from Taiwan, it has spread to the four corners of the world. There is a chapter on social economic trends. It is these trends, the 20-year cycles, that catch the majority of the people out. There are two chapters on case studies. The first one covers the small cases, mostly remedial work, and the second one is about development projects. This illustrates the type and scale of work we do. There is also a chapter on common objections, in which I have provided an answer to each objection that I have encountered in my work.

This book is my journey from a forensic scientist to a feng shui consultant, and my search for a particular Master who could train me in my passions. This is also a story of a group of consultants who travel the world and work on various building sites. They do not seek fame, nor do they seek glory. They work for the benefit of their clients and do not seek acknowledgement for their contribution. These consultants work in the field of traditional feng shui to create competitive advantage for their clients.

This is my story.

Chapter 1
What is Feng Shui?

Feng shui, meaning 'wind, water', is derived from the ancient practice of KanYu. This is the Chinese system of land management, which governs how the land is used, where buildings are placed, where and when crops are planted, where wells should be dug for water, how to use roads and rivers for communications, and so on. It even governs how to defend a settlement from invaders, and yet it also allows that settlement to expand for growth and prosperity. These principles were based on empirical observation and tested with the history of time in the rise of the Chinese civilisation, which began 4,000 years ago.

There is much speculation when the term 'feng shui' started to be used. It was first mentioned in the *Book of Burial* (300 BC) –

"The energy that rides the wind stops at the edge of the water and is retained."

Energy, time and space.

Feng shui is all about the energy in the environment. It is about the movement and settlement of this energy. It is about the changes in the characteristics of this energy with the passing of time.

Feng shui is about Energy.

Feng shui is about Time.

Feng shui is about Space.

Types of feng shui.

There are two main branches of feng shui: ying house and yang house feng shui.

Ying house feng shui relates to the selection of burial sites for one's ancestors. This is part of the Chinese tradition of ancestor worship, which is part of the Confucius heritage. It is about having and showing deep respect for one's elders by choosing the best locations for their graves. This is believed to provide the descendants with good luck during their lives. The more auspicious the grave site, the better the luck for the future generations.

In ying house feng shui, we are dealing with energy going under or through the land; this branch of feng shui will not be covered in this book. yang house feng shui is about the living, and the energy that moves on the surface of the earth.

In the past fifty years, interest in feng shui has grown dramatically, and the number of people claiming to have this knowledge has increased manifold. More importantly, this knowledge is no longer exclusive to people in the East, but is now available to the rest of the world outside Asia – Europe, North and South America, South Africa and the Middle East.

Feng shui is always about space and time involving the environment, but after its dramatic growth in the last fifty years, new derivatives of feng shui have been published. These include spiritual, jewellery, interior design, gardens, kitchens, food, symbols (from the Chinese pantheon), watches, furniture, household items, lighting, paintings and many more. With all these variations, the public has without a doubt become confused.

This book is on traditional feng shui: how feng shui was practised at the time of the Imperial Court of the Chinese Emperor in Beijing from AD 1500 onwards.

Feng Shui is one of the Five Arts central to the ancient Chinese body of knowledge:

The Five Arts includes the following bodies of knowledge:

Ming: Destiny – BaZi (Four Pillars), ZiWei DouShu, Iron Plate, TanXin

Xiang: Reading – Face, Feng Shui, Seal (body), Palmistry

Shan: Meditation, Tao philosophy, Pugilistic Exercises (Martial Arts)

Xi: Medicine – Traditional Chinese Medicine, Spiritual Therapy, Acupressure, Acupuncture

Pu: Divination – MeiWah TiShu (Plum Blossom), Da LiuRen, Tai Yi, QiMen DunJia; Yi Jing

There were associations that practised this knowledge, some of which had the patronage of the Chinese Emperor in his Court.

Feng shui was considered to be extremely important in the development of China, being about the external environment affecting the buildings and the people who worked or lived in them. The prosperity of the country and the well being of the people is part of the Emperor's mandate, or purpose of his rule. As the Chinese civilisation grew, feng shui was used to design cities, towns and buildings not only within China but in the bordering nations as well. It was carried out by teams of specialists.

These associations were very much like the businesses of the present day in that their services used by clients. The principals in the association were the Masters, who were like the directors of a modern company. They provided leadership but also worked with their members. Recruitment based on a rigorous selection process, because just as today, demand depended on the reputation of the organisation. Training was equally as rigorous.

Even though there was much similarity to the Western businesses of today, there were a number of differences. Members felt extreme loyalty and respect for their elders, and particularly to the person (or Master) who trained and mentored them. The Master did not treat his employee like an employee, but like his child. The main aim was to develop the person to be as good as or better than the Master. This involved an incredible amount of time spent bonding and developing the personality. The Master passed to the next generation everything he knew and did. But the knowledge and application aspect was only part of the process.

Once the student had passed the training procedure, he was given a name. This comprised two parts – a generation name and his personal name. This became his professional name. Just by looking at the name, a potential client would know which organisation the man belonged to and which Master trained him. This gave him credibility, with an expected standard of work. However, should the work be done badly, the client would know where to get redress from – the organisation and the Master. Should the reason be the 'student', there were various forms of redress, including expelling and the withdrawal of the use of the name.

The Chinese have an expression – "Loss of Face". For an interpretation, change the term 'face' to 'honour' or 'prestige'. This is one of the most serious insults that any Chinese person could suffer. Should a 'student' give the Master or the organisation a bad reputation, the Master or organisation would do everything they could to stop that student from practising.

However, when a good job done, the client knew to which organisation they belonged, and who his Master was. Everybody, especially the Chinese, love the praise they would receive when told that their students have done well.

To prevent negative incidents from happening, the procedures for selecting new students were extremely rigorous. The student treated as a member of the family, in which everything was shared. This included spending time and living with the Master. There was much time and effort spent in getting the student 'better' than the Master.

An important aspect of the training was teamwork and discipline. Feng Shui is unique in the Five Arts in that the consultant has to move to the location of the development. There are many occasions; the size of the project requires a team of consultants. Teams increase workflow, involving specialist skills and innovative solutions to problems from the experienced pool of knowledge. Some projects could last ten or twenty years. Should anything untoward happen to the lead consultant, having a team in place ensured a smooth and seamless transition to the next leader.

Discipline is necessary for two reasons:

a. For smooth teamwork and professionalism.
b. The first priority is always the success of the client's project and their interests. There should be no conflict of interest.

Chinese naming system part 1

I will use my name to illustrate the system.

My Chinese name is Oon Chong Heng. It can be broken down to:

Family name: Oon. This is derived from the Hokkien dialect, but in Chinese (or Mandarin) it is Wen.

Generation name: Chong. All my male cousins have this name to indicate the generation.

Personal name: Heng. This is my name.

The village that my grandfather came from in Fujian province is WenCuo SanDo, in the District of HaiCheng. In this village, all the people have the family name of Wen.

As mentioned earlier, the Chinese have great respect for the elders. By knowing the person's generation name, you know exactly where the person stands with respect to you. Is he your senior or your junior? These generation names are inscribed on a village in stone. As I understand it, there is a list of 77 generation names on this stone tablet.

- My grandfather's generation – **Boon**
- My father's generation – **Khye**
- My generation – **Chong**
- My younger generation - **Jin**

There is a lot to be said for this system because of its simplicity. If a person with the name 'Wen' pleased the Emperor, the District chief or has just passed the Imperial Examination, this person brings the family honour. People with that family name would be held in high esteem. Conversely, if a family committed a heinous deed, all the Wens would be in disgrace – hence the great family pressure to behave well and to uphold the family name.

This illustrates the importance of family lineage to the Chinese. If your ancestors were considered to be great people, you would also be held in high esteem.

Chinese naming system part 2

In general, for a function or job, you are given a name.

Let me give you an example:

In my case, I am perceived in a number of roles.

Son to my parents, brother to my sister, cousin to my cousins, husband to my wife, and so on.

In each role, I have a different function. As a son, I was called 'Mike', as an elder brother, I was called 'Ko' and so on.

In a professional organisation, your name reflects your role within the organisation, and also the standing of the organisation to the rest of the world.

I worked as a Forensic Scientist at the Metropolitan Police (Scotland Yard). It was held in high regard as:

- The Metropolitan Police is the largest police organisation in the UK, and is known throughout the world. It is a high profile organisation.
- Forensic scientists are well regarded because they solve difficult crime cases, and feature heavily in television series such as *Silent Witness* or *CSI*.

The reaction I receive is very different when I say I am a feng shui consultant. The image this draws up is of someone who is somewhat mystical and hangs wind chimes in various parts of the house. That is why I am writing this book to clarify the situation.

So, once your Master has decided that you have finished the training programme and completed the project tasks to their satisfaction, you are allowed to represent the organisation and you are given a new name; a generation name and your own individual name. This is your professional name and it shows your status.

Chinese training system

The training system in AD 1500 was at a time when many people could not read or write. We are dealing with practitioners or artisans and not scholars or authors. The training was based on oral transmission of knowledge. The main system of remembering the key parts of the knowledge was the use of 'trick songs' poems with 'codes' within the text, and the key part was the correct interpretation of the 'codes'. All this information was kept within the association, and it was very much like the propriety information of business organisations.

The system was built around learning directly from a practitioner. As previously mentioned, it was the aim of the practitioner to enable the student to be as good as or even better than the teacher.

Trinity of luck

This is one of the tenets of Chinese tradition, and it says that life is governed by three factors:

1. Your Destiny
2. Your Environment
3. Your Self.

Your Destiny

Your destiny is like the roadmap of your life and is based on the date and time of your birth. This unit of time (hour, day, month and year) is unique and is converted to the Chinese system of five elements. From there, the roadmap is set up. There are two Chinese systems used for destiny analysis.

1. BaZi (Four Pillars)
2. ZiWei Doushu

BaZi means 'eight characters' but is commonly known as Four Pillars. Each Pillar is a unit of time (hour, day, month, year) and this consists of two characters – a 'stem' and a 'branch'. The Four Pillars thus has a total of eight characters.

A BaZi analysis provides a roadmap of a person's life. It points to the person's varying fortunes, such as difficult, tough, lean, plentiful, productivity, romance and fame. It only indicates, because two other variables (your environment and yourself) are also part of your life. This will be discussed later. The analysis also provides information on the characteristics of the person, such as appearance (tall, short, big or small), career (technical, creative, good with people, a drifter), predispositions for illness and so on. BaZi is based on the time of the birth of the person.

The information from BaZi is therefore only a guide with a time element. It is a very useful way of looking at the 'big picture'. More information on the 'small picture' is provided by Da LiuRen. This system can predict of result of events with a very high level of certainty. The result is based on the time at which the question was asked.

In the Western systems of astrology and horoscopes, readings are based on the relative positions of the stars in the heavens. The Chinese and Western methodologies are very different.

ZiWei DouShu is based on the relative position of the stars and is more an astrological system than a traditional Chinese system.

There are many people who are more interested in the accuracy of the result rather than the methodology, but one method has been outstanding in the preciseness and accuracy of the results in Da LiuRen. It is considered by the aficionado that you are a true Master when you can practise this subject well.

In the West, there are true believers in the use of these astrological systems but there are also many sceptics. Yet data from the Office of National Statistics (UK) has shown empirical data that people born in different times of the year tend to go to various occupations. For example, dentists are more likely to be born in the month of December, medical doctors in January and pilots in March.

Your Environment

In the West, there is no name for this body of knowledge of how the environment directly affects the person. Speak to a farmer and he will tell you which part of the land is good for different purposes; he works the land accordingly. This body of knowledge is very similar to feng shui, involving understanding the characteristics of the land.

Here are some examples of the environment affecting the person, using London as a case study.

1. One of the biggest steps in public health in London was the building of the sewage system by Joseph Bazalgate in the mid-1800s. Before that time, the River Thames was an open sewer

and epidemics of cholera were a common occurrence. No more outbreaks of cholera have been reported since, but more importantly, the general health of the city was greatly improved.

2. The areas of the slums in the inner city were redeveloped in the 1930s to the 1950s. People were moved to new suburbs and their lives changed significantly with the new environmental conditions of open space. This is well documented.

3. In the 1960s, the government started to re-house people into massive, badly designed tower blocks. This was a numbers game for political expedience rather than caring for the welfare of the people. What could be said for this expensive exercise, however, was that the old slums were removed. But new sorts of issues resulted with these new tower blocks. These problems of the tower blocks included the deterioration of the structure, facilities and the rise of crime.

Here are some examples some examples of how the environment affects the person.

1. If you work in a room that is totally mess or untidy, your thoughts and actions will reflect your environment. Your life will be messy and disorganised.

   If you work in a tidy room, your thoughts and actions will reflect it. Your work will be well organised, and so your life will be.

2. If you work in a small room, your thoughts and actions will reflect your environment. Your mindset will be of a 'small mind', thinking of minor issues and small goals. Of course, with a larger room comes a bigger mindset, larger issues and bigger aims.

3. If you live on a small island, the people of the island will have a 'local' mindset and an insular attitude. Conversely, if you live in a large country, your mindset will be totally different.

Your Self

Different people have different actions. Some people 'go for it', others 'think about it', others 'don't do it'. Some people are always positive while there are those who are always negative. When you look at how people behave, it is all different. That is why only some people achieve their goals.

For people who want to achieve a goal but find it difficult, there are ways to get help and one of the most effective ways is to use the services of a personal coach. For example, all the successful sports people I know have a coach to guide them. A coach has an overview of the person's strengths and weaknesses. The person himself is too close to his own situation and cannot see ways to make significant improvements. The coach uses his skill and experience, using the various methods he has developed to get the best out of the person so that he can achieve his goals in a meaningful way. There are many personal development methods available, but the methods used depend on the coach's expertise and matching it to the person and their goals.

How does the trinity of luck affect you?

Suppose you let life pass you by. You are just average in everything you do. One day, however, you decide to make a big improvement in your life. You want a more fulfilling life. How do you do it?

You can work on yourself; for example, changing your mindset to a very positive mode where you believe you can achieve your stated goals. Initially, you may think your goals are way above what you think you can ever achieve. Getting to the goal requires a continuous series of small incremental 'wins' which all add up to a big 'win'. After a number of big 'wins', the goal is within your grasp. It is about being persistent and following your chosen direction.

The results, in most cases, are quite predictable. Improvements will only come when you really want the results. It is always up to you.

You add in the second step by making sure that your environment is right. Working in the right location, in an ordered and tidy office, you will find opportunities presenting themselves to you. Instead of a 'No', it is a 'Yes please'. The door is opening to you.

In this example, we are improving both yourself and your environment, allowing you to reach your goals faster.

In the following examples, we will involve your destiny. The three elements – destiny, environment and self – each have an equal weighing of about one third each.

Suppose you have reached a stage in your life where everything goes against you. You get a 'No' for everything you do or propose. It could be that you are having a bad time with your 'destiny' element and that you want to get out of the situation.

The modern way to overcome this is by getting both elements (environment and self) to overcome the destiny element that is working against you. You do this by improving yourself and organising your environment to work with you. This has been used successfully on countless occasions. It is simply using two of the elements, environment and self, against the destiny element.

Just imagine when your destiny element is in your favour. When you get the other two elements working in harmony, everything just works. You will be consistently experiencing big gains.

The trinity of luck shows the big picture, or puts everything into perspective. You might find that at times, everything becomes a problem. All that you might need is a positive mindset, or to get your working and living conditions right and the problems just get solved one after another. Another scenario is when you move to a new house or office; you have an average performance before the move, but suddenly, everything takes off. Wow! This is because of the change of environment.

The point is that every little bit of your life matters – your destiny, your environment and yourself. They are all interlinked.

Traditional feng shui knowledge

The basis of traditional feng shui, like all the other topics in Chinese Philosophy, is energy or 'qi'. As feng shui is about space and time, we are referring to energy in the environment. So what is this energy?

One aspect of this energy in the environment is the result of the rotation of the earth. This results in energy movement in nature – the movement of elements such as weather systems, tides and so on.

As you can see straightaway, this energy changes with the different positions of the earth.

- The changes that happen in a day (24 hours). Half of the Earth is in daylight and the other half is night. There are different characteristics in various parts of the world as the day goes by. As the sun rises, people wake up and activity starts. The busiest period is when the sun is up in the sky. The activity decreases as the sun sets. A new type of activity starts, it is quieter as people prepare for a night's rest.
- The changes that happen in a month (about 30 days). This is the effect of the relative positions of the moon.
- The changes that happen in a year as the Earth revolves around the sun (365 days). This includes the four seasons in the temperate countries, but there are also changes in the wind and weather systems for equatorial countries.
- There are other longer-term cycles in nature, such as solar activity, a cycle of 12 years.

In feng shui, we are interested mainly in the energy movement that happens on the surface of the Earth. Therefore, this energy flow depends on the topography of the land.

This energy behaves very much like a fluid.

When the land is on a steep incline, the energy moves quickly down the slope. When the land has a gentle incline, the energy moves slowly along the slope. This energy flow would eventually have to stop at the bottom of a valley or basin, and this is where energy can accumulate.

Energy flows along the paths of least resistance, such as roads, pathways or rivers. When there is an obstacle, it bends and turns to get around it.

When it flows quickly, there is turbulence in its flow – it is not smooth. When it is moving slowly and gently, the flow is smooth. When this flow hits a small obstruction like a pole or a tree, it goes round it but there is turbulence after passing this obstruction.

Water

The properties depend on whether the water is static or moving.

In a lake or pond where the water is stationary, the energy is absorbed or held by the water. This is illustrated when a predatory animal such as a wolf or tiger is tracking its prey by smell. As soon the prey passes water, the trace of the prey is lost. (This assumes that there is no visual contact.)

In a river or stream where there is flowing water, the water absorbs the energy as it flows and can release it when it changes direction. More detail on this in Chapter 7 (Case Studies - Part 2).

Cities or settlements of people

These are usually places where energy can settle. The more pathways for the energy to flow into the location, the more energy it will get. A river brings in even more energy. For this energy to accumulate successfully, there have to be restrictions on the outflows of this energy from the settlement. For a settlement to be successful, the inflow has to be greater than the outflow of energy.

Let us look at London. Central London is in a basin, with the River Thames passing through it. Energy is allowed to accumulate here. London has been a successful city and trading post since Roman times, some 2,000 years ago.

Then, if you look further out, there is a much larger area bordered by the South Downs (in the South and South East), in the Chilterns (North and West) which surround London. These hills form a larger basin in which this energy can accumulate. This explains the success of the South East of England as an economic hub.

Timings

If you look at the activity of London with respect to time, different activities will occur within a typical day. In the morning, people come into work. Business activity starts, at the office, shops and coffee shops. Then at midday, the restaurants and cafes open for lunch. Later in the day these places wind down and other activities begin to start up – those preparing for the night-time activities. At the end of the business day, people go home but a new part of the city comes alive – the theatres, restaurants and pubs/clubs (that is, the nightlife). After all that, the city has to be cleaned and shops and restaurants restocked. As different activities happen throughout the day, the energy is changing along with them. At the weekends the city is much quieter, as most of the offices are closed, but it is the shops and nightlife that do the most business for the week. Nightlife is also at its most active.

From this, you can see at least two cycles operating the daily cycle and the weekly cycle. There will also be the monthly cycle, which depends on the people's pay packets and other business cycles. Another noticeable change is the yearly cycle. In summer, there is an influx of visitors to London. At the end of the year there are Christmas and New Year sales. It is different all the time. There are other longer cycles that occur.

I could illustrate the cycles in Nature – in the day (24 hours) – different animals do different things; birds sing in the morning, some animals start feeding. In the afternoon, they rest. At dusk, another set of animals make their appearance – bats, owls and other nocturnal animals go out in search of their prey. There are even more cycles – monthly (menstrual cycle in women), yearly (breeding cycle of animals), and the list goes on.

This point illustrates that in Nature, the cycles of time are a common occurrence.

The activity of man

In addition to the natural cycles present in nature, there is the effect of man – the movement of people and their peripherals – cars, buses and so on. All this equates to energy as well. Movement is energy.

The quantity of energy

Form feng shui (also known as landscape feng shui) is about understanding the flow of energy in the environment. In the exteriors, it is the consultant's job to get this energy into the target building. He does this by designing various elements (landscaping) to focus the energy flow into the building. As for the interiors, it is the consultant's job to design the elements to distribute this energy evenly to the various parts of the building. The third aspect of the design is to ensure that the energy is retained within the building, with leakage minimised. There is an old adage: there can never be too much energy. The more the better.

Form feng shui is about understanding the flow of this energy. This flow is determined by the form or shapes of the land. The main flows are in channels, such as rivers and roads. It is blocked by obstructions such as mountains, hills or buildings. This flow can be disrupted by trees or signposts.

The quality of energy

The flow:

The energy flow has to be smooth with an even flow. It should not be too fast or turbulent.

There are two additional variables in Nature: the presence of man and the passing of time. In feng shui, formulae are used for this purpose.

1. Eight House feng shui – this formula states the relationship between people and the compass direction. In feng shui, the main compass directions are the major cardinal points of North (N), South (S), East (E) and West (W), and the minor cardinal points of North East (NE), North West (NW), South East (SE) and South West (SW).

2. Flying Star feng shui – this formula relates the eight compass directions to the standard cycles of hour, day, month and year. There is an additional cycle of 20 years, which relates to the conjunction of Jupiter and Saturn.

The Selection of the Formulae

This is down to the skill of the consultant. It is a balance of the quantity and the quality of the energy. The quantity of energy can be determined by the physical landform in which the building is located. The quantity of the energy is very much the core of this Chinese philosophy – it is the 'cake'. The quality of the energy is determined by the formulae. The quality of energy is very much the icing of the 'cake'. If there is no energy at all, there is no point in determining the best possible quality of energy for the property.

The main point of choosing these two formulae is that they comply with the requirement that they follow the three main rules of feng shui. The use of these two formulae are minor to the main consideration of the flow and holding of energy.

The three main rules of feng shui

1. Ying and yang
2. Five elements
3. Eight trigrams

These are covered in more detail in Chapter 4.

Summary

What is feng shui?

Feng shui is about energy in the environment.

Feng shui is about how the environment can affect the person.

In the West, there is no subject relating the environment and the person.

Feng shui is essentially the rules or guidelines on how to use the environment to the person's benefit.

Feng shui is about both the quantity and quality of energy.

Feng shui is about both time and space.

Chapter 2

The Origins of Feng Shui

The Chinese civilisation as we know it had its origins some 4,000 years ago. People had just started to settle on the land; they had to work and live on it. KanYu (a system of land management and a former term for feng shui) grew out of this need for survival, especially when the civilisation moved from hunter gathers (nomads) to permanent land settlements.

It was from observations of Nature, including the terrain of the land, that the rules evolved for settlement. The basic rules covered where to build a safe shelter, provisions for water and wood, shelter for people, areas to plant crops and the keeping of animals.

The cradle of the Chinese civilisation was in the Yellow River Basin. It has a temperate climate and it made the establishment of life even more challenging because of the change of seasons. Whatever rules they developed for their civilisation, they had to have the extra resilience to cope with the changes in the seasons.

The early settlers studied how the land and Nature behaved. They appreciated its benevolence but respected its extremes. Nature could easily turn on the people with such extremes of heat and cold; it could also be too wet or too dry, or experience strong winds. The Chinese made a point of understanding the mechanics of Nature with the aim of working with

Nature. In other words, they learnt to utilise the power of Nature for their own benefit. It was this necessity to understand the rules of Nature that was the key to success for the race to survive. If you look at the Chinese Five Arts, they are all about analysing the situation to get the desired result.

In acupuncture, the needle is inserted at a point in the body to correct the imbalances in the flow of energy. It is using the action of the needle to get the body to 'heal itself'.

In martial arts, an analysis of the strengths and weaknesses of the opponent is carried out. An attack is made on the weak point. The 'fall' is done by using the weight and strength of the opponent.

Feng shui is about understanding the rules of Nature. Where there is energy, there is life. Feng shui is about getting energy into the buildings. Feng shui is about getting life into the buildings.

As the Chinese civilisation evolved from land settlements to communities, to villages and to towns, observations were made about the communities that succeeded or failed. The rules of land management were established, based on the successes and prosperity of the successful settlements. This is very much akin to the land management used by modern day farmers – they know where the arable land is, know how to look after the land, where to put the animals. This can be related to the modern idea of "location location location". It is knowledge, based on observation and experience.

These settlements grew with time, with some villages collecting together to become "kingdoms". In many cases, the "leader" of the new nations had always had advisors who were familiar with this knowledge. There were battles (particularly at the time of the Warring States) between these nations, but a dominant 'nation' emerged. The first Kingdom of united China was in the Qin dynasty (221-206 BC); the remains of the 1st Emperor – Shi HuangDi – can be seen in the Mausoleum of Terracotta Army near Xian.

The creation of the Calendar – a notable development.

There is evidence of a twelve-month lunar calendar in the Shang Dynasty (1766-1122 BC). There were many versions of the lunar calendar, and it was in use by the general populace until the mid-20th century, when it was replaced by the international standard, the Solar (Gregorian) calendar. However, the dates of many Chinese festivals and events are still based on the lunar calendar.

However, the feng shui Masters have always used a solar calendar. This information is available in the 'Tong Shu', or Chinese Almanac, which provides accurate information on events such as the arrival of spring, and when to plant crops and harvest them. The Chinese solar calendar has always included information on the dates of the summer/winter solstice and the equinoxes. This necessary and reliable information can only be obtained from the solar calendar and not from the lunar calendar.

This solar calendar also contains the Stems (ten Chinese characters) and Branches (twelve Chinese characters), which are related to the five elements (wood, fire, earth, metal, water). This forms the basis of the time aspects in Chinese Philosophy. The applications are: Destiny (BaZi), Auspicious Timings (QiMen DunJia), Prediction (Da LiuRen), and of course feng shui.

Feng shui grew out of the need to survive. Living at one with Nature, the people got their food, shelter and everything else from it. However, if you got on the wrong side it, Nature can turn against you. Too much or too little of anything can lead to problems. For example, too much water leads to floods, which will cause the destruction of land and crops; too little of water, and drought will lead to famine. Hence, feng shui is about getting the balance.

Feng shui is literally the understanding of how Nature works in the environment and its interaction with the built environment and man. It comes from the need to survive. It is about working with Nature. This is very different from the Western or Modern approach of either conquering or challenging Nature by using technology. Yet it has proved successful; China has the longest continuous civilisation in the world.

The way the Chinese have interpreted the working of Nature is centred on energy. All the mechanisms in Chinese philosophy are about energy. For example, when a person dies, it is believed that the energy has left the body. In the environment, the energy that is around us matters. Firstly, there is the energy from the rotation of the Earth and the winds. Then the natural terrain – mountains and hills, valleys, rivers, lakes and sea – mould the flow of energy. Human activity, such as buildings, roads, ponds and canals, all alter the natural flow of energy.

Feng Shui is about understanding the workings of Nature. Therefore, a building designed with the basic principles of feng shui would be about receiving the flow of the energy – the energy of Nature. It would be 'alive', and the occupants of the building will have greater well-being.

Other civilisations, such as the ancient Egyptians, Incas, Mayans and Ancient Greeks, have appeared and then disappeared. We do not always know why they disappeared. But the Chinese must have done something right, as their civilisation is still in existence today. Throughout the history of China, there have been huge problems – famine, floods, draught, strong winds – but the Chinese civilisation is still there. The Ancient Chinese read the rules of nature correctly and have developed the resilience to withstand the extremes of Nature.

A short history

The acknowledged 'founder' of feng shui is Yang YunSong, who is reputed to have left the Emperor's Court (Tang Dynasty, AD 618-907) in disgust, as feng shui was only being used to help further the Emperor's aims. He earned the name "Yang the Saviour of the Poor", as he left a legacy of many of the classic feng shui texts and is considered the founder of 'Form feng shui'.

The Chinese compass was invented in the Qin Dynasty (221 to 206 BC). It was a magnetic spoon floating in a bowl of water, which would point either to the north or to the south. One of its applications was the Eight House feng shui formula, which is based on the eight trigrams. It relates the person's date of birth to the eight compass directions.

It is said that during the Tang Dynasty (AD 618-907), the 'King' of a neighbouring vassal state had requested from the Emperor the secrets of the prosperity of China. The Tang Dynasty was one the most prosperous periods in China's history, and the request had put the Emperor in a 'tight spot', as it had hit a raw nerve for the Chinese. He had to accede to the request by the King of the vassal state, because had he not agreed to the request, it would have been seen as a 'loss of face', or an embarrassment. Secondly, he did not want the national secret to be passed on to another state.

The Emperor then commissioned a high priest to embellish the Eight House feng shui formula and present it to the King. The King was presented with the fake version and everyone, including the Emperor, was happy with the situation. As a result, there are two versions of the Eight House formula, and both the original and the 'fake' versions of the Eight House formula are in the public domain to this day. The original and true version of the Eight House formula relates only to the person. The 'fake' version is about both the person and the building.

In the Qing Dynasty (AD 1644-1922), the Flying Star formula (Xuan Kong flying star feng shui) was popularised by Shen ZhuRen. Shen was a writer but did not have formal training in feng shui. He studied the placements of tombs positioned by a number of feng shui Masters in his region. The placement of tombs and the burial of the deceased is part of yin house feng shui. This formula is currently used by consultants in countries such as Hong Kong. Flying

Star feng shui is derived from the method of QiMen DunJia and was originally used to form military strategy and tactics. It is related to SunTzu's Art of War. SunTzu's treatise is about the philosophy of the 'Art' and QiMen DunJia is the actual underpinnings. It is able to predict the most favourable times to attack, stay put or retreat together with the compass direction, and was used at the time of the Warring States to the Qin Dynasty (474-221BC). It is believed by a number of scholars that it was used in the Battle of the Red Cliffs (AD 208-209); by Liu Ji (AD 1311-1375) to secure the throne for a Ming Emperor; and, speculatively, in the defeat of General Chiang KaiShiek by Mao ZeDong (AD 1949).

QiMen DunJia uses many of the same elements of Chinese philosophy as feng shui, namely ying and yang, the five elements, the eight trigrams, the ten Heavenly Stems, as well as the twenty-four solar terms. To use the elements such as the eight trigrams and the twenty-four solar terms at the time of the Warring States, the Chinese compass and the solar calendar must have been commonly used at that time.

Over the centuries of Chinese history, QiMen DunJia grew in popularity and today includes contemporary applications, most notably that of business and finance. Today QiMen DunJia is especially popular in Taiwan, Hong Kong, Singapore and other nations of Southeast Asia.

Modern history

The defeat of General Chiang KaiShek by Mao ZeDong signalled the end of an era. In mainland China, Mao

ZeDong banned all these traditional practices when he gained power. However, it is said that he used these techniques for himself during his time of political leadership. The practice and knowledge of feng shui and related subjects was eliminated in the Cultural Revolution of the 1960s and 1970s.

Chiang KaiShek went into exile to an island off the Chinese coast – Taiwan. He built it in the hope of one day taking over mainland China. He had brought with him the academics, the practitioners, the books, the treasures and the practices from the Chinese Court, including the Associations of Five Arts from Beijing. This knowledge, while the practice of feng shui was previously restricted to the Imperial court and other important state projects, was then disseminated to the rest of the world. He built up relationships with his regional neighbours and allies throughout the world to enhance his credibility and secure political relationships by sending these teams of experts. Feng shui was used on many corporate buildings in the West, usually headquarters, and especially in North America and Europe. These corporations are still the backbone of business in the West.

Chinese methods of handing down information:

The Chinese have a reputation to have the following traits:

- They are very secretive. When they are teaching you, they will teach you to say 80% of the necessary information.
- They have pride and act to 'save face'. They do not want to be seen to 'lose face'.

- They are inscrutable. Their behaviour does not reveal much.
- They have great respect for their elders.

The obvious question that follows is: how can a great country like China create all that necessary knowledge and then maintain continuity for subsequent generations?

The excessive secrecy characteristic of the Chinese is a result of scarcity. Therefore, when any new information is published, pirate copying is carried out quickly. Authors of original information, to protect themselves, intentionally miss out sections of vital information or have deliberate mistakes in their published work. As a result, there is a secondary market for information to cover the 'missing areas' or 'mistakes'. There is also a big trade in information passing off as 'secrets' or 'vital or key interpretations'. It is, therefore, not surprising to see contradictory information on the same topic.

In the old days, not everyone could read and write. Practitioners were artisans who had the knowledge but did not have the writing skills. Not all authors were practitioners. Would a practitioner give all the knowledge to an author to write a book? Of course, it would be the author who gets the credit.

In pre-Mao ZeDong China (before the 1950s), there were three types of people who claimed to have the knowledge of feng shui.

The travellers or wandering minstrels.

They would turn up at a village, sing and do some acts, which established their credibility to the populace. The acts could include a glass-eating scene or an arm being dipped in boiling hot water. These acts were shown in the BBC television series 'Mind Body & Kick Ass Moves', which featured Chris Crudelli. It is difficult to give an opinion on these. My father used to say that they were acts of street entertainment rather than serious practitioners of the Chinese Arts.

The independent consultant.

There are many practitioners of the Chinese Arts and these include the herbal or acupuncture practitioners.

As always, some were credible and some were not. If they learnt their craft from a practitioner, they would know how to deal with many of the feng shui issues. However, there were those who got their knowledge from books.

With the lineage system, the teacher would only hand the name down only when he was sure that the student was credible and could maintain the teacher's good name. Secondly, a good student would be searching for a credible teacher in the first place so as to be the best in his field. As mentioned in the previous chapter, there is a Chinese tradition of a close relationship between the Master and the disciple. This is the result of a long training period, which could last as long as ten years.

Associations for the Five Arts.

These are organisations for practitioners, and there would be many topics of interest in the organisation. Each Association would therefore have a speciality, such as Traditional Chinese Medicine or feng shui.

The association was run very much like a modern-day corporation. It has its aims and purpose. Depending on its reputation, it would be selective in its students, but once in, there was no lack of knowledge. One of the aims of the Association would be to prepare the next generation to be better than the present generation. There was a free flow and open discussion of the teachings.

Again, there was a close bond between the Master and student. The training period could be long as ten to fifteen years, and this could also include living with the Master.

Summary:

The Chinese made it a point to understand Nature in order to survive.

It is part of Chinese culture to utilise Nature

The Chinese civilisation is the oldest continuous civilisation on earth.

Feng Shui is the understanding of Nature.

The knowledge of Chinese Five Arts moved from Beijing to Taiwan in the 1950s.

The use and knowledge of feng shui has grown dramatically since.

Chapter 3

Modern Day Practice

1950-1990

China

In 1949, under the leadership of Mao ZeDong, the Communists took over mainland China. Mao banned many cultural practices, as they were at odds with Communism and modernity. This ban was totally enforced in the Cultural Revolution of the 1960s and early 1970s. All expertise and documentation were destroyed, yet it is said that Mao's house was designed with the aid of feng shui.

There was a dramatic change in the practice of feng shui. Instead of being kept within the borders of mainland China, the main areas of practice moved outside its borders. Initially, feng shui was practised by the overseas Chinese, but later there was considerable interest from the non-Chinese – Europeans and Americans.

Taiwan

The previous leader of modern China, Chiang KaiShek, sought refuge on the island of Taiwan. He brought with him the whole Imperial Court, together with the national treasures. Chiang's China had also fought a long war with the Japanese (1928 to 1945), and all the treasures from the national museums, as well as the contents of the Palaces, had been packaged for safekeeping. These treasures were sent off to his new capital, Taipei in Taiwan.

Chiang built up Taipei as the capital city. He also developed Taiwan as an economic centre. In both cases, he used the feng shui specialists who were part of the Associations of Five Arts that he had brought over from the Palace in mainland China. He made their expertise available to many other Governments and Corporations through the world, not only to Asia but also to Europe and North America – the USA and Canada. Many of the corporations are still market leaders in their fields to this day.

Taiwan experienced tremendous economic growth, particularly in the field of electronics, personal computers and telecommunications. It is also one of the world's richest countries on a per capita basis.

Hong Kong

Before the Second World War, Hong Kong was a sleepy British Colony at the southern end of China, near the estuary of the Pearl River. However, after the fall of China to the Communists, it grew as trade with mainland China was closed. This small port expanded with people fleeing Communist rule. Among these people were the business community and those who were motivated to get themselves out of poverty.

Hong Kong, with thousands of willing workers, grew and grew. From a sleepy port, it became a key economic hub for the region. Initially, the major companies were the established British trading companies, but soon they were challenged by many Chinese businesses. An important business sector in Hong Kong was property development, as the availability of land on the island was limited. With buildable land a scarce resource, buildings grew upwards in both residential and business sectors. The feng shui practitioners were particularly innovative. The buildings had already been designed with feng shui, but these practitioners started working on an entirely new area: the use of feng shui in the interiors of the buildings. This brought the availability of feng shui to consumer level. With the continual and dramatic growth of Hong Kong, so the use of feng shui grew. Today, it is said that nothing moves without the aid of feng shui. Feng shui practitioners on the island developed their skills on interiors because there was very little they could do with the exteriors, which were already defined by the buildings. It is said that in the development of buildings, the property developer would call in the expertise from Taiwan, where practitioners are much more conversant with building design and the landscape.

Malaysia and Singapore

As with the Chinese, feng shui was used as part of the way of life in Malaysia and Singapore. Initially it was applied to single properties, but as the economies grew, specialists in larger developments grew in demand.

When Singapore became independent in 1965, a feng shui Master called Hong Chuan was involved in its master planning, including the infrastructure of this island nation. He used his skill to minimise the impact of a global downturn on Singapore in the 1980s. He came to national prominence when a newspaper article of his work on a Hyatt Hotel in Singapore appeared. The hotel was struggling, but after the renovations, the occupancy has remained very high to this day.

The awareness of feng shui grew exponentially from then on.

For Malaysia's sizable population of ethnic Chinese, feng shui was part of their way of life. There are a number of reputable practitioners.

Philippines and Indonesia

The Chinese population in the Philippines and Indonesia is a distinct minority. Feng shui was mainly a Chinese activity, and until the successes of the Chinese business community, feng shui was perceived as the Chinese 'secret' weapon. The local business community has begun to use this Chinese methodology.

South East Asia

During this period in the Far East, there was nascent but local growth in the knowledge of feng shui. If the local practitioner did not have the necessary expertise for the project, this expertise would be obtained from Singapore or Hong Kong. The practitioners based in Taiwan were for the really large projects. These Taiwanese practitioners had started to work on many projects in the West. From the 1980s onwards, they started to relocate themselves nearer their clients in the West and to train the next generation.

Journey to the West (1990s onwards)

In the early 1990s, a book called *Feng Shui* by Sarah Rossbach became an international best seller. It was based on the work of a Buddhist monk called Lin Yun who lived in Hong Kong. This knowledge was rapidly accepted by the New Age community and Self-Help

Groups. This was about improving yourself by altering your living environment.

In 1997, a Malaysian business woman, Lillian Too, authored the *Complete Illustrated Guide to Feng Shui*, and a number of other titles, which have sold more than six million copies worldwide. This explosive growth indicated the acceptance of this Chinese philosophy to an international market. There are more than 300 books relating to feng shui published in the late 90s and early 2000.

A glossy magazine – *Feng Shui for Modern Living* – was published in London but had an international circulation. There was a Chinese language version distributed in the Far East.

Then there was a new medium of communication: the internet. All this helped to spark the explosive growth of feng shui throughout the world.

Then came the next stage. Teachers of Chinese ethnic origin taught the various aspects of the feng shui formula. They jetted to various parts of the world, where they taught various students. Some names include Joseph Yu from Toronto in Canada, Raymond Lo from Hong Kong, and Joey Yap from Malaysia. They built up their following throughout the world. It was different with Lillian Too; students came to her hometown in Kuala Lumpur, Malaysia. As with many Chinese teachings, there is variation in the interpretations.

Sarah Rossbach described Lin Yun's feng shui formula as part of his religious practice. This was the triple gate method, in which the interior layout was of a set pattern relative to the main door. This was leapt upon by the 'New Age Movement' and adapted and incorporated to their other practices. Feng shui had become a label for a collection of practices that not only dealt with interiors, but also such things as: Symbols (the Chinese pantheon), jewellery, furniture, thoughts, paint, paintings, food, and so on. There were new practices such as clutter clearing, and feng shui from different origins – Celtic, Balinese, Nordic, and so on.

Then interior designers got into feng shui: it had become a 'style'. It was seen as Eastern and 'zen'. There was a spiritual angle, such as the worshipping of gods in the various parts of the property. Feng shui had become a verb that nobody could understand, but it was used to mean something Chinese. No wonder it was confusing and getting discredited.

With all that information coming out, there was no consistency. There were so many variations of the technique that the public became confused. Literally anybody could be an expert on and practitioner in feng shui. In the UK, the situation got so bad in the public perception that the Feng Shui Society introduced an 'accreditation system'. This was to introduce standards to the practice of feng shui, to establish credibility and stability in the industry. However, the established feng shui Masters did not subscribe to this Western system.

There were two issues. There were the so-called 'practitioners', whose behaviour was questionable at the best of times. Then there were the various types of practices that fell under the term feng shui. Different interpretations of the same formula were commonly observed.

A similar situation developed in both the USA and Australia: self-regulating bodies grew to accredit the practitioners.

After 2003, the wave of interest in feng shui cooled down. Feng shui was widely promoted as a Chinese system to enhance relationships, wealth and health. People were not consistently seeing the expected results, and not surprisingly, their interest waned.

This has allowed the true knowledge of feng shui to gain a firmer footing. It was not to be associated with the modern versions of feng shui. There were people who had argued that feng shui, like many Eastern disciplines, has been around for a few thousand years, so it must have worked or else it would have been discarded and forgotten ages ago. But we keep on hearing about the results of feng shui. There must be some truth in it. Yes, the true knowledge and established practices of feng shui exist, but the practitioners adopt a very low and quiet profile.

Far East

During this period, there was tremendous awareness by the public, particularly by the non-Chinese readers. The demand for consultations grew dramatically.

Hong Kong established itself as the "World Capital of Feng Shui". This city lives and breathes feng shui. No big development or refurbishment is carried out unless it has been examined by a feng shui consultant. The Hong Kong Tourist Board promotes a free half-day feng shui course as part of its tourism programme.

In Hong Kong, there is a constant demand for consultants on many residential and business projects.

However, the top entrepreneurs in Hong Kong and in the region use the consultants from Taiwan. Taiwan has carved out a reputation for top-notch feng shui that is both effective and enduring.

My search for knowledge

My background

In my childhood days in Singapore, there was a common belief that all Chinese are selfish in the sense that, when they teach or tell you something, there is always some information missing, and sometimes, there was even misinformation. There was a reputation for secrecy. This was not about the secrets of Chinese Philosophy, but about information as simple as cooking recipes or simple tai chi exercises. This is a scarcity mindset, which I discussed earlier. I was educated in English and accepted that people were being more honest and truthful with me by presenting complete information.

In my career as a forensic scientist, I would be constantly and consistently asking the question: "Where does this information come from?" This is part of the credibility check for the source of information. This is imprinted in my mind.

The recruitment process in the forensic science laboratory was quite interesting, and counter-intuitive to the outsider. Each vacancy had more than 3,000 applications, even before television programmes such as *Silent Witness* or *CSI*. The appointment board would therefore have the pick of the bunch, so to speak. They would be looking for the most suitable candidate and not necessarily the most qualified candidate. As you would expect for a job in a high profile forensic science laboratory, the best qualified candidates had a Masters degree in forensic science. But these highly qualified candidates were actually at a disadvantage compared to the other candidates. It was not until fifteen years after the forensic science courses started that a Masters graduate in Forensic Science was employed in the laboratory.

The question that came up was: where did they learn their forensic science knowledge? Lecturers prepared their lectures from books. Who wrote the book? Was it an ex-forensic scientist or an academic looking into forensic science? A teacher's knowledge is only as good as the information he can get. He might not have the right mindset for the subject or the 'gist' of the subject. A teacher is rated on this teaching skills and his presentation of knowledge.

The laboratory was looking for suitable candidates who have the discipline and focus but who were also good at problem solving. They were then trained in the skills and the mindset of a forensic scientist. They did not care whether you had a PhD, Masters degree in forensic science or a 1st class first honours degree. You need a university degree to be a forensic scientist because you would be appearing in a Court of Law. It is the person that matters.

Right tools for the job

Both forensic science and feng shui involve problem solving. These are practical subjects. You can learn the theory in the classroom, but the core of the subject is in the practice. The best place to learn this craft is by seeing, understanding and doing it. The most suitable environment to learn the craft is therefore with an experienced practitioner. No amount of theory is a substitute for actually doing the work.

Forensic science is slightly different from other aspects of science. The results have to be reported to a court of law and are subject to cross examination. The opinions expressed have to be credible. There is nothing worse than a discredited scientist in court. The lawyers will never allow you to forget it.

The methodologies will therefore be specific to forensic science. It is from experience and ability that a practising forensic scientist knows the most suitable tools for the job. A teacher or a university professor would not know the right combination of tools that is best for the job in order to get the most suitable result for the purpose. Their mindset is about teaching the latest or most spectacular developments in that field, or having the greatest student interest.

Both forensic science and feng shui are practical subjects. The best way to excel in the practice of these two subjects is to learn from a practitioner rather than a teacher. It was therefore my aim to find and learn from a practitioner rather than a teacher.

Team work

It is well acknowledged that working in teams has a synergic effect; it is more productive. The same number of people working as a team will do the job faster than the same number of people working individually. However, the team members have to be well disciplined and organised. Badly led and poorly trained teams are worse than a collection of individuals.

My travels to the East

My wife Helen and I travel to Malaysia, Singapore and Hong Kong regularly. We got to know a number of feng shui Masters very well. We would talk about buildings, their owners and the successes they had. These could be hotels, resorts, head offices and any other buildings. They would make comments on the feng shui that was carried out and on who carried out the work. Many a time, they would be consultants from Taiwan. They had a team who worked very quickly and professionally. However, they either did not know the names of the Taiwanese consultants or would not reveal them to me.

I had informal discussions with a group of these feng shui Masters. In our discussions, I had asked them about the variation of the knowledge and the practices of the various groups of practitioners. They had said that as long as it worked and the client was happy, that was what mattered. They disagreed on many of the technical aspects and methodologies. This is a common occurrence in many professions throughout the world.

I also asked them, as there are a number of formulae in the sphere of feng shui knowledge, which set of formula they would use. They replied that they would use a set procedure, as this was their expertise and was what they were most comfortable with. It did not matter what the application or type of building it was. I was always asking the question of how all these formulae fitted in with each other. I did not get a straightforward reply.

In some instances, they would comment that particular buildings had the involvement of Taiwanese consultants. They recognised some of the feng shui features used, but could not see how it all fitted together. The main point was that the building was very successful for the client.

I also asked them who should I study with. As this was an informal discussion, a number of them had said that I was asking too many difficult questions (for them) and they preferred me to learn from someone else. Some had suggested that I should learn from the Taiwanese masters. They also repeatedly pointed out to me that the source of the original knowledge and practice is in Taiwan. As you may recall, Chiang KaiShiek had brought over the Imperial Court, treasures, knowledge and people to Taiwan. They practice the 'original' feng shui and it was "really powerful". As I was so inquisitive about this knowledge and about the practice, they suggested that I go and learn it from a Master from Taiwan. This could be taken in many ways – a brush off, a hint or a challenge. They knew that very few people in Taiwan spoke English and that I did not speak any Chinese.

Lineage

It was interesting to see how these Masters formed an opinion of the various practitioners in the Chinese Arts. These feng shui practitioners in the East had expertise in, for example, tai chi or martial arts, wu shu or kung fu. When there was someone who was new on the scene, they would ask who his teacher is. From their opinion of the teacher, they would give an opinion of this new person. It was practitioners from the better recognised or older organisations that had the proper lineage naming system.

I was really privileged to be able to have these informal discussions with these feng shui Masters in such relaxed conditions. In a formal situation they would not admit to their limitations (the Chinese trait of 'face saving' again), or admit that the original knowledge was retained in Taiwan, or ask me to find a teacher from Taiwan. In general, Chinese elders do not like to be questioned, as it can be perceived as a challenge to their authority. This comes from the other Chinese custom of 'Respect of the Elders'. Of course, I followed the usual Chinese way of asking questions by starting a discussion rather than asking direct questions.

Assessment of practitioners in the Chinese Arts

When a new practitioner appears on the scene, the very first question the elders ask is who their teacher or Master is, or where he learnt his knowledge. The second question is how does he behave? Is he a credit to his teacher or association? This was refreshing to me. In the West, it is the person who is the focus. In the Chinese mindset, it is not only the person but the teacher or the association. To the Chinese, 'saving face' is so important that the teachers do their best to have their students uphold their names. The last thing they want is students who bring them a bad name. If there was a lineage name system, they could then trace the lineage of the names.

Further discussions would ensue. The frankness from the elders was really mind-opening, and they have a different persona in these discussions. A point would arise in the discussions: they would note the discipline or the behaviour of the members. Did they show respect to the senior members, or were they just a group having a good time on a vacation?

In the West, there is a similar system – by asking which university or company employs you. Your social ranking is different if you graduated from Oxford or Cambridge Universities compared with, say, a college of further education. The other similarity is asking whether you are working in a prestigious company – Google or Apple, or a company that has past it, such as Yahoo! or AOL. You are perceived very differently depending on where you work. I was held in high esteem when I was working as a forensic scientist at Scotland Yard. But the person is still the centre. The Chinese have taken it a step further with the use of lineage names as part of their society.

In my discussions with the elders, they would ask for my opinion. I would reply that I wanted to understand more of the basis or mechanics of feng shui and apply the knowledge. This was compatible with my scientific background. A number of them would tease me and suggest that I go and find a teacher from Taiwan. These Taiwanese Masters have the full knowledge, whereas they did not have the picture in depth. They knew that I did not speak Chinese and teased me that I should find out more from a Taiwanese Master. In general, English is not spoken in Taiwan, and it would be extremely difficult to identify and learn from a Taiwanese Master. They perceived me as not a proper Chinese person because I do not speak Chinese. They surmised that I had only a minimal chance of finding a Taiwanese teacher, let alone learning from one. As a result, they were brutally honest in their views about the learning of the Chinese Arts and assessment of people. They also teased me about my aims of learning from a Taiwanese Master, knowing the challenge I had in front of me of climbing this high and insurmountable mountain. A number of them had had their further education in Taiwan and were familiar with the situation.

My aim

Based on the various pieces of information that I had obtained, my main objective was still to help improve people's lives by changing their environment.

My aim was to learn from a practitioner rather than a full-time teacher, as feng shui was a practical subject. The most suitable practitioner would be someone from Taiwan, as the 'complete knowledge base; and teachings were only carried out there. It was therefore my aim to find a practitioner from Taiwan who spoke English. This practitioner would also offer a lineage name after qualification, and the knowledge taught included the design of towns and cities.

It was quite by accident that I found a series of open lectures by an English-speaking feng shui practitioner from Taiwan in Los Angeles, USA. Questions were encouraged, and they would be answered with clarity. The elders that I had previously met do not encourage questions. You had pay them if you wanted to get them answered properly.

What I found

The lectures were different to any previous talk that I attended.

An overview of the feng shui in the environment was given. The knowledge was presented from the mechanistic point of view but from a Chinese perspective rather than a Western one. An important point was that she answered questions willingly, without hesitation. Her viewpoint was that of a practitioner rather than a teacher. This was from the detail of the practice of feng shui rather than the slickness of the presentation. This was also the first time I had had a sensible reply to my perpetual question: how do these various formulae fit in together?

There was an invitation to become indoor students, where the information was proprietary. The indoor class would consist of the applications of the knowledge and would include many field trips to many parts of the world. This knowledge was not about how to improve people's homes, but about how to have the capability to design buildings and cities, so that people have a chance of a good life. This was a thorough training programme that would take years, in keeping with many training programmes in the Chinese Arts. The practitioner had a lineage and a lineage name that would be passed on when the student satisfied the certification criteria.

The aim of this training programme was to create a professional team of feng shui consultants to deliver an efficient and effective service for its clients.

I was accepted and these are the following elements of the programme.

It is a training programme to develop a team of world-class feng shui consultants. The main part of the training programme is developing the ability to function as a professional team, serving the client effectively and efficiently, solving the client's problems with a full and remarkable service.

The knowledge and its applications

This was not only about sitting in the classroom listening to the various aspects of feng shui, from first principles to the use of the formula; it was about how the formulae fitted together in the bigger picture. It was not just about knowing and understanding each feng shui formula. It was this understanding of the characteristics and how they fitted in with the other formulae for the job. This can only from practical experience. In fact, the knowledge of the Chinese Arts is integrated; they all come together when you have sufficient knowledge. However, to learn it, you have to start from somewhere.

There were numerous field trips to various countries, cities and buildings. Only by being present at the site could we really read the true subtleties of the location. This could not have been explained in a classroom. The situation could only be analysed by someone who has long experience of this subject. It is this analysis, together with this on-site experience of the various situations, that forms the proprietary knowledge.

One of the challenges in the training is the interpretations. Even though the knowledge might be in the public domain, the interpretation can vary. The purpose of the training was to ensure that the interpretations were consistent within the training group.

Other subjects in Chinese philosophy were taught alongside feng shui. This included techniques like QiMen DunJia (auspicious dates for particular actions), Four Pillars (destiny Analysis) and Da LiuRen (a prediction system). The crucial part of the training is for the students to get the right answer.

The development of the person

The training included personal development. You can only help other people when you know yourself well. You have to know how to handle your strengths as well as your weaknesses. You cannot do the work credibly if you have a bagful of personal problems and issues yourself. A training coach started with issues such as comfort zone, positive mindsets and goal setting. He then delved deeper into the person's past to sort out the present, in order to provide the correct template for the future. It was a painful experience for all.

Secondly, to work in teams, you need to know your own personality and those of your team members. All ideas of selfishness are gone; it is all about having a team mindset. The emphasis of the training was on 'We' rather than 'I'. Teams have been shown to be more effective and efficient in delivering results to clients. But the team members have to work well together. This was developed during the training, when we spent much time together, literally living together and calling each other 'study brothers and sisters'. We would even know how our study siblings would react to changes in the situation, the stress and the challenges. This all boiled down to understanding each other. The end product was a cohesive team that was both effective and professional.

An added element was the respect to the 'seniors' and other members of the team. Discipline within the association and the team is paramount for effectiveness and harmony. This training is not of a few short lectures; it takes years. There is a code of behaviour; how we behave to our clients, and applying the code of client confidentiality.

Team structure

We are part of a family. The parents or teachers are the seniors, and the students are the up-coming generation. The aim of the parents is to prepare the students as future consultants by providing us with the tools and attitudes to become better than the previous generation. This is just like all parents. This has more significance to the Chinese, because as we have already seen, 'face saving' is very important. Only the students who have passed the necessary criteria will be given the lineage names. The teachers, to save their reputation, will want the next generation to be better than them, but will also want them to make them proud to the other people in the industry.

This knowledge was established many centuries ago and many changes have developed to adapt to this modern age, from the modern transportation system – cars, trains or planes – to high-rise buildings, from electronics – mobile phones, microwave or electric ovens – to indoor plumbing. Change happens all the time – like business and social trends. As a team resource, the seniors are monitoring the constantly changing environment. New interpretations of the ancient wisdom have to be applied – how do you handle all this electronic equipment, cars, aeroplanes? What is the appropriate solution for these new situations?

This is very much like a corporation – the accumulation of experience, knowledge and history. This expertise was designed to help us get the best results for our clients.

The interaction with the client is paramount. After establishing the aims and goals of the project, the focus is delivering the client the remarkable value that we give. However, should the client keep changing the aims or goals, or not following our instructions, we are expected to walk away from the job. At all times, we maintain client confidentiality.

Summary:

Before 1950, feng shui was practised within mainland China.

After 1950, in the Communist rule, feng shui was practised outside mainland China, in Taiwan, Hong Kong, Malaysia and Singapore.

In the 1990s, it spread to the countries in the West, namely North America and Europe.

Many new derivatives of feng shui have been published.

The practitioners of traditional feng shui maintain a very low profile, but occasionally raise their profile.

Chapter 4
Methods and Applications

1. What is energy?

For the Chinese, the central tenet is of life is energy. When the Chinese are discussing life, they are referring to the flowing of energy. When death has occurred, it is about energy departing from the body.

It is integral to the Five Arts – be it medicine, divination, feng shui, astrology, martial arts – the central mechanics are energy with the five elements, together with ying and yang.

What is energy? Wikipedia gives the following list:

- Thermal energy; thermal energy in transit is called heat
- Chemical energy
- Electric energy
- Radiant energy, the energy of electromagnetic radiation
- Nuclear energy
- Magnetic energy
- Elastic energy
- Sound energy
- Mechanical energy
- Luminous energy (light)
- Mass ($E=mc^2$)

The major source of this energy in our environment is from the spinning of planet Earth. The movement in this energy comes from the various aspects of the Earth's movement.

1. The earth rotates once every 24 hours. There will be heating and cooling of the Earth's surface as it rotates around its axis.
2. The Moon orbits the earth once every 28 days. The gravitational effects of the Moon can be visually observed in the ocean tides.
3. The Earth orbits around the Sun in 365 days. The Earth rotates with an axial tilt of 23°, which creates the four seasons in temperate countries, the hot and rainy tropical countries and the dry desert belt across the world. This tilt and movement is primarily responsible for the planet's weather and climate systems. The changes in the weather, climate, ocean currents and tides all relate to the movemen^{t} of energy on the Earth's surface.
4. The core of the earth is molten rock. It gets hotter as you go down beneath the Earth's surface. This is another source of energy.

An interesting source of energy is mass. Mass can be converted to energy by Einstein's equation of

$$E=mc^2$$

when E is energy, m is the mass and c is the speed of light, which is squared (a multiple of itself). The point of this equation is that it shows the interchange of energy and mass.

2. Quantity

In feng shui, there is no established way to measure energy, but here are some guidelines on its behaviour for the purposes of analysis.

1. It behaves like a fluid and it flows downwards.

2. It flows along the path of least resistance. Energy therefore flows best on paths, roads and rivers.

Observations:

1. There is more energy lower down a hill than near the top of the hill, as energy moves downhill.

2. The nearer you are to the flow of energy on a road or river, the more the energy influences you. The further away you get, the less the energy influences you.

3. The energy flow is blocked by physical obstacles, though it will find a way around it. Hence, there is less energy on the blocked side of the obstacle.

4. At the top of the hill, the energy is moving all the time. In a valley, the energy is static (or held). There is therefore more energy in a valley than on top of a hill.

5. If you stand at a bottom of a road that has a very gentle slope and no traffic, you will feel the energy coming down to you. This energy is continuous, 24 hours a day.

6. When there is human and road traffic coming down the same road with a very gentle slope, you will feel both the energy coming down the hill together with the energy of the people and the road traffic. This combined traffic (energy and mass) is considerable.

This only occurs when there is human and road traffic. It is not continuous but periodic.

7. Let us consider a river. The amount or mass of water that the river carries can be converted to energy. Secondly, the water in the river flows continually, 24 hours a day. There is considerably more energy flowing in a river than a road, as it is continuous.

Hence it is better to have the landscape bringing the energy to you, rather than relying solely on human activity. Many feng shui Masters are skilled at using roads and rivers to bring the energy to the client's property. There needs careful positioning of the buildings on the property, as both roads and rivers can also draw the energy away. It is very much a double-edged sword.

3. Quality

There are two parts to this section. One is describing the 'quality' of energy directly. The second part is describing the quality through a feng shui formula.

3a. The description of the quality of the energy

Energy flow that is smooth, with no turbulence, has a good quality compared the energy flow that has turbulence.

Turbulence is caused by an obstruction (such as a pole, tree or small obstacle, or the corner of a building) in the flow of the energy.

Using the ying/yang criteria, the smooth flow is yang whereas the turbulent flow is considered to be Ying.

Another example of using ying and yang in the quality of energy in the environment. In a virgin forest or in a well-maintained park where the air is fresh and clean, the energy is yang, whereas energy at the rubbish tip or a blocked sewer is ying.

The terms of ying and yang are a means to describe opposites or polarities.

3b. Quality of energy by using feng shui formula

I have skimmed over the details of these formulae. A series of books on the Methods is being written and further details will be posted on my web site: www.MichaelOon.com when they are available.

Eight House

This formula relates to the person. Each person has four beneficial directions and four not beneficial directions. These directions are determined by the year of birth of the person.

This formula provides practical and extremely useful solutions to improve children's behaviour or one's love life. In many cases, it is about the re-positioning of the bed or the desk.

There is no time aspect to this formula.

Table1: Kua Numbers and Years

Year	Kua Number		Zodiac Animal
After 4th Feb	Male	Female	
1936	1	5 (8)	Rat
1937	9	6	Ox
1938	8	7	Tiger
1939	7	8	Rabbit
1940	6	9	Dragon
1941	5 (2)	1	Snake
1942	4	2	Horse
1943	3	3	Goat
1944	2	4	Monkey
1945	1	5 (8)	Rooster
1946	9	6	Dog
1947	8	7	Pig
1948	7	8	Rat
1949	6	9	Ox
1950	5 (2)	1	Tiger
1951	4	2	Rabbit
1952	3	3	Dragon
1953	2	4	Snake
1954	1	5 (8)	Horse
1955	9	6	Goat
1956	8	7	Monkey
1957	7	8	Rooster
1958	6	9	Dog
1959	5 (2)	1	Pig
1960	4	2	Rat
1961	3	3	Ox

Year	Kua Number		Zodiac Animal
After 4th Feb	Male	Female	
1962	2	4	Tiger
1963	1	5 (8)	Rabbit
1964	9	6	Dragon
1965	8	7	Snake
1966	7	8	Horse
1967	6	9	Goat
1968	5 (2)	1	Monkey
1969	4	2	Rooster
1970	3	3	Dog
1971	2	4	Pig
1972	1	5 (8)	Rat
1973	9	6	Ox
1974	8	7	Tiger
1975	7	8	Rabbit
1976	6	9	Dragon
1977	5 (2)	1	Snake
1978	4	2	Horse
1979	3	3	Goat
1980	2	4	Monkey
1981	1	5 (8)	Rooster
1982	9	6	Dog
1983	8	7	Pig
1984	7	8	Rat
1985	6	9	Ox
1986	5 (2)	1	Tiger
1987	4	2	Rabbit
1988	3	3	Dragon
1989	2	4	Snake

Year	Kua Number		Zodiac Animal
After 4th Feb	Male	Female	
1990	1	5 (8)	Horse
1991	9	6	Goat
1992	8	7	Monkey
1993	7	8	Rooster
1994	6	9	Dog
1995	5 (2)	1	Pig
1996	4	2	Rat
1997	3	3	Ox
1998	2	4	Tiger
1999	1	5 (8)	Rabbit
2000	9	6	Dragon
2001	8	7	Snake
2002	7	8	Horse
2003	6	9	Goat
2004	5 (2)	1	Monkey
2005	4	2	Rooster
2006	3	3	Dog
2007	2	4	Pig
2008	1	5 (8)	Rat
2009	9	6	Ox
2010	8	7	Tiger
2011	7	8	Rabbit
2012	6	9	Dragon
2013	5 (2)	1	Snake
2014	4	2	Horse
2015	3	3	Goat
2016	2	4	Monkey
2017	1	5 (8)	Rooster

This table shows the relationship between the person's date of birth and their Kua Number. The relationship between the Kua number and their best compass direction and sector is shown below. This is the best direction to face for physical well being.

Kua Number	**Compass direction**
1	South East
2	North East
3	South
4	North
5 (2- Male)	North East
5 (8- Female)	South West
6	West
7	North West
8	South West
9	East

Flying star: the time dimension of feng shui

Flying star is the time dimension of feng shui. It involves a number of cycles that follow the numbers in the movement of the Lo Shu Square.

4 (South East)	9 (South)	2 (South West)
3 (East)	5 (Centre)	7 (West)
8 (North East)	1 (North)	6 (North West)

The Flying Star chart comprises the Lo Shu Square with the compass directions. It is in the Chinese Convention to have South at the top of the diagram.

The movement of the energy follows that of a cycle. It starts off in the North (1) then to the South West (2), then to the East (3), South East (4) and so on, and it repeats itself.

20 year cycles and predominant energy

There are a number of different time periods in the cycles. There are hourly, daily, monthly, yearly and 20-year cycles. The 20-year cycle relates to the Jupiter/Saturn conjunction. Take for example the daily cycle; the energy coming from the North (1) lasts for one day before it moves onto the next direction, South West (2), and so on. These cycles are moving continuously and concurrently at this very moment.

When the energy comes from that direction, the characteristics of the energy from that direction are shown in the social and economic trends. The next chapter (Chapter 5) is a description of the effects of the energies from two different time periods. In Period 7 (1984-2004) the energy comes from the West and in Period 8 (2004-2024), it comes from the North East.

Period Number	Pre-dominant direction	Years (Period)
1	North	1864-1884
2	South West	1884-1904
3	East	1904-1924
4	South East	1924-1944
5	-	1944-1964
6	North West	1964-1984
7	West	1984-2004
8	North East	2004-2024
9	South	2024-2044

The time periods of the 20-year cycle. As 5 sits in the centre, it does not have an influence from any particular direction. Therefore, the time period 1944-1964 and be divided into two; 1944-1954 has the influence from the South East direction, 1954-1964 has the influence from the North West direction. To put it succulently,

- Period 4 lasts for 30 years and has the characteristics of the energy from the South East.
- Period 6 lasts for 30 years and has the characteristics of the energy from the North West.

This table also describes the direction of the predominant energy. For example, in Period 8, the predominant energy is from the North East

The description of this method can be extremely long-winded, and I have kept it as simple as possible.

Afflictions

There are three types of afflictions as they affect the construction or renovation of property.

Grand Duke Jupiter (also known as Tai Sui): a 12-year cycle, which is related to the complete orbit of Jupiter around the Sun. The relative location of Jupiter is marked by the Chinese horoscope animal, which includes rat, ox, tiger and so on. That compass direction has the Grand Duke Jupiter affliction. The affliction relates to the surface of the Earth or below it; great care has to be taken when digging the Earth in that particular area for that year.

The other two afflictions relate to the positions of particular numbers of the Lo Shu square. They affect the digging of the earth and give untold delays or unforeseen problems to the progress of the project. The afflictions are known as:

Five Yellows: this relates to the energy above the surface of the Earth in that specific compass direction for that year. No renovation or heavy vibration activities should be carried out in this area.

Two Blacks: this relates to illness or mishaps in that specific compass direction for that year. No renovation or heavy vibration activities should be carried out in this area.

Traditional feng shui recognises these afflictions and there are specific remedies for each of them.

4. Description of the energy

There are three fundamental methods to describing energy:

- Ying and yang
- The Five Elements
- The Eight Trigrams

Ying and yang

This is a comparative tool. Many books state that it is about male and female or hot and cold. But it is actually about the comparison of two states.

For example:

On a bright summer's day, let us look at the shade beneath a small plant. The plant casts a shadow on the ground. The area of shade under the plant is 'ying' whereas the area next to the shade, but getting the direct sunlight, is 'yang'.

On a winter's day in the forest, there are specks of sunlight coming through the forest cover. The areas on the ground that are bright by being lit up from the sun are 'yang', and the adjoining areas covered by the forest cover are 'ying'.

A summer's day is considered 'yang' when compared to a winter's day, which is 'ying'.

This illustrates the comparative terms of ying and yang.

The Five Elements

This is one of the fundamentals of Chinese Philosophy – the Five Elements. They are symbolic rather than actual physical material.

They are wood, fire, earth, metal and water. They are interlinked by three types of cycles. Each element has a unique set of characteristics.

The cycles: there are three different types of cycles.

a. The productive cycle.

Wood is burnt by fire to form earth. Earth then produces metal, which then liquefies to form water. Water aids the wood in the plant growth.

b. The reductive cycle is the reverse of the productive cycle.

Fire goes back to wood, which goes back to water, back to metal, then earth and then finally back to fire.

c. The control cycle.

Metal cuts wood, wood controls the earth, earth stops the water, water quells the fire and the fire melts the metal.

Other properties of the elements:

	Wood	**Fire**	**Earth**	**Metal**	**Water**
Colour	Green	Red	Beige, Orange	Silver	Blue
Shape	Rectangular	Triangular	Square	Round	Wavy
Actions	Spreads out	Upward	Static	Circular	Downward

The Eight Trigrams

This is one of the key fundamentals of feng shui.

	Kua No.	Family	Colour	Element	Job
North	1	2nd son	blue or clear	water	sales
North East	8	3rd son	orange	yang earth	organisation
East	3	1st son	dark green	yang wood	director
South East	2	1st daughter	light green	ying wood	marketing
South	9	2nd daughter	red	fire	publicity
South West	2	mother	black	ying earth	HR
West	7	3rd daughter	silver	ying metal	communications
North West	6	father	gold	yang metal	CEO

This is the accumulation of information from four different sources.

- The Five Elements
- The Lo Shu square

- The compass directions
- Ying and yang

The Lo Shu square is also known as the magic square. It is a square with nine cells – three rows of three columns. Each cell has a specific number, from 1 to 9. The order of numbers produced is unique and produces a number of interesting combinations.

4	9	2
3	5	7
8	1	6

The Lo Shu square

The characteristics of the Lo Shu Square

- The sum of each row or column always totals 15.
- The corner numbers are all even. The odd numbers form a cross through the centre of the square.
- The number on the opposites always total 10. This is the same as point one, as the centre is 5.
- Subtraction of these two numbers always equals 5: 9 - 4; 7 - 2; 6 - 1; 8 - 3.
- The numbers are the positions of the Lo Shu Square. The number 5 refers to the centre.

Compass directions

The compass directions are in the eight directions – major cardinals of North, East, South and West with the minor cardinals of North East, North West, South

East and South West. When we refer to the direction, it includes both the direction and the area that is in that direction from the centre or point of reference. For example, if we are referring to the North West, it means the direction of North West as well as the area or sector that is North West from the reference point called the centre.

This is the key tool in feng shui. It not only links the five elements, but defines the properties of the various compass directions.

Characteristics of the Eight Trigrams

The Eight Trigrams comprise a family: two parents (father and mother) and with a total of six children (three male and three female).

Characteristics of the family

- Father: the head of the family
- Mother: the carer, looks after the family
- First son – serious and studious
- Second son – travelling
- Third son – playful
- First daughter – organisation
- Second daughter – cooking and enjoyment
- Third daughter – young and playful

These are some examples of the use of the Five Elements and Eight Trigrams in the placement of various objects and personalities. These are exercises to illustrate the point.

Example 1.

Placement: the 'ideal' shape for the South West (element earth) is a solid square object. Therefore, a filing cabinet (element earth) is suitable for the South West sector (element earth) of the room. Extending that principle to the exteriors, a building that has a regular shape – square or rectangular (element earth) – is suitable for the South West (element earth) part of the city.

Colour: a suitable colour for a room in the East is green (element wood). Another favourable colour is blue (element water). The element water feeds wood.

Entrance: the door is in the South East of the property and faces South East (element wood). A suitable placement is having flowing water, as this element feeds the wood. Therefore, having flowing water in the form of a water feature would be appropriate. It would not be right to have objects of spherical or cylindrical shapes in metallic colours (metal element). The element metal destroys the element wood.

Buildings: a triangular-shaped building (element fire) can be located in the South (element fire) or the South West or North East (element earth) of the city. However, it is not appropriate to locate it in the South East or East (element wood) of the city. The element fire destroys wood.

Suppose a triangular-shaped building (element fire) was located in the South East (element wood) of the city. The element fire is destroying the element wood in that area. There would be problems within this building when it is operational.

Example 2.

A bedroom is a place to sleep; it is therefore a ying place.

Colours: should it be painted blue (water element), it will be more ying. The people in the bedroom will not want to leave the room. They will feel very comfortable in bed and will want to stay there.

Should the room be painted red (fire element), it will make the bedroom more yang. The people in the bedroom will feel restless and will not have a good night's sleep.

The ideal colours for a bedroom are the neutral colours – preferably earth tones to settle the person in bed and have a good rest.

Call centre: offices are yang places where people work or are in an activity. The walls are normally painted a neutral colour, but this was painted blue (water element). There was inactivity and performance targets were missed. To correct this, the managers decided to redecorate the room bright yellow and red (fire element). People became more active with the new environment but staff started to leave. The environment had become too yang and staff could not stay there for too long.

Example 3: building shapes and roofs.

The established building shape is square or rectangular. The roof is a standard triangular shape so that water can easily drain away.

With modern technology, there are now many different shapes in buildings. There are even triangular (fire) or round (metal) shapes or irregular shapes.

Have you ever noticed the number of parliamentary buildings, including town halls, that have round or circular building shapes? A circular shape represents talk with very little action. Politicians feel comfortable in this type of building architecture.

- London City Hall (round building)
- Toronto City Hall (round building)
- Reichstag (German Parliament, with a circular roof)
- United States Capitol (Congress building)

Politicians are good at communicating or talking, but we should be judging them by the results.

5. The fit

This is a very brief summary of the methods used in this practice.

As with all things in Chinese Philosophy, feng shui is all about energy. The main analysis is therefore about the flow and capturing of the energy in the environment.

It is about identifying the quantity and quality of the mix of energy going into the property. Then, it is the building design required to capture and retain this energy. It is the design of the interiors to distribute this energy.

The formulae described above are the additional minor component added to the mix for enhancement for particular purpose. It is up to the skill of the consultant to use what is available in the interest of the client. An analogy is that the consultant is like a chef. The main ingredient is the energy. The formula is like the seasoning. The seasoning is a minor component but can add considerably to flavour the dish.

Finally, a property is built to last at least a hundred years. As mentioned earlier, the predominant energy changes direction every twenty years. The location and design of the building need to take into consideration these changes, or else the prosperity of the inhabitants will change with time. The consultant has to design this factor into the solution.

6. Applications

Traditional feng shui is about understanding the flow of energy in the environment or exteriors. It is about getting this energy into the building through the vital positioning of the doors. The design is to retain this energy and distribute it around the building.

There are four main applications in the traditional feng shui:

1. The design of new property – buildings, estates or town and cities.
2. Finding a location for a new property.
3. Improving a property or refurbishment.
4. Selecting for a property portfolio.

1. The design of a new property.

This is for the design of buildings (such as offices, shopping centres, hotels, resorts, spas), business and residential estates, towns and cities.

The purpose of using traditional feng shui for

- Property developers – to complete the project on time and on budget, and also to sell the properties at a 5% premium and six months ahead of schedule.
- A multiple retailer or hotel chain – to have properties that are consistently doing an extremely good level of business. Hotels have an occupancy rate of about 80%.

2. Finding a location for a new property.

This is for multiple retailers or hotel chains who want the best locations in which to do their business. The methods include the tracking of the energy flows. The main aim in this property search is therefore to locate a suitable property as near as possible to the energy pathways. When there is the correct mix of energy in the building, the business will consistently do exceptionally well.

3. Improving the property.

There are occasions when the property is close to the energy flow but it is not possible to get the energy into the building. A modification such as locating a door or building an extension to get this energy is one option. There is also the option of a complete refurbishment of the building. This is to bring an underperforming building to the level of a high performing building.

4. Selecting for a property portfolio.

There is nothing better than having a group of relevant but high performing properties in the portfolio. It could be derived from the purchase of an undervalued property and improving it with the methods of traditional feng shui so that the property performs in an outstanding manner. The other method is to develop a new property.

Chapters 6 and 7 are specific case studies using the methods of traditional feng shui to correct energy problems. The case studies illustrate various types of properties that benefit using this methodology.

Summary:

Methods

The aspects of energy:

Quantity – the amount of flow.

Quality – two aspects:

- The quality of the energy flow – too fast or too slow, going round obstacles, and so on.
- Direction and time. These are described by the formulae – Eight House and Flying Star feng shui.

Descriptors:

- Ying/yang
- Five Elements
- Eight Trigrams

Applications:

1. The design of new property – buildings, estates or town/cities.
2. Finding a location for a new property.
3. Improving a property; major and minor modifications.
4. Selecting for a property portfolio.

Chapter 5
Winds of Change

Trends, by their very nature, come and go. They appear quietly for no particular reason and then disappear. I had always been curious to find out what was coming around the corner (so to speak). But it was only when I started seriously studying feng shui that it occurred to me: the answer was directly in front of me in the feng shui methodology. This chapter is my interpretation of the current trends.

As stated in the previous chapter, there are a number of cycles running concurrently. These cycles have time periods of an hour, a day, a month, a year and 20 years. In this chapter, I will be discussing the 20-year or long-term trend cycle that we experience but never consciously notice. It just creeps up on us and then gradually fades away. It is so subtle that we do not take notice of it when it comes or when it goes.

What is it?

There are nine numbers or energy types in the Lo Shu square. The predominant energy characteristic is the reigning number of that 20-year period. The characteristics of the numbers are defined in the 'family' in the previous chapter.

Let us take the example of Period 7 (1984 to 2004).

Characteristics of the number 7.

The element is metal and it is personified by the third and youngest daughter in the family. She has little education and works as a barmaid or actress; she enjoys life and is fun to be with. She loves to talk and have a discussion. She enjoys the material aspects of life, spends money easily and is extremely proud of her appearance.

Her personal characteristics define the Period 7 1984-2004.

The interpretation:

Prominence of Women

During this time, we saw the rise and prominence of the woman, especially the young woman. Margaret Thatcher became Prime Minister in the UK (1979 to 1990), and there were increasing numbers of women graduating from university and entering the professional workforce. There was also the marked rise of female medical practitioners and young women as celebrities.

Communications (talkative)

The industries that grew were in communications; both in people and in technology. There was a tremendous rise in the mass media, in print and wireless services – radio and television. There was a wide range of newspapers – national or local, paid or free, daily, weekly or monthly. There was the introduction of new colour printing technology to newsprint with the *Today* newspaper in 1986. The other national newspapers soon followed suit.

The other medium of mass communication – radio and television – expanded. The BBC expanded both its national and local radio. On national television, there were originally three channels: BBC1, BBC2 and ITV. Channel 4 became operational in the 1980s and Channel 5 in the 1990s. Satellite television introduced a plethora of channels of varying niche interests – documentaries on history, wildlife or nature; old motion pictures, 24-hour news channels. Although the population of the UK has been fairly steady, at about 60 million, the introduction of the new radio and TV channels have caused a significant decrease in the viewing figures per channel but the overall total remains the same.

With the need to communicate in the media, PR (public relations) and advertising agencies grew. The humble 'press officer' in corporations became the 'director of communications'. Institutions of further education began offering courses in mass communications and schools started offering 'media studies'. In the 1980s, the Thatcher Government brought a communications specialist (Bernard Ingrams) into the heart of the Government decision-making process. It was about the presentation of the news to the people.

On television, a new concept of show started: reality TV, in which ordinary people take part in the programme. A number of celebrities came out of these programmes, such as Jade Goody. They did not have much talent, but they were famous for being famous. Another celebrity of this era was Katie Price, who started as a glamour model and then developed to become a celebrity in her own right, with five autobiographies, television shows and a few celebrity weddings.

Communications (technical)

We have also seen rapid development in high technology – personal computers, mobile phones, digital cameras, GPS navigation devices and telecommunications, together with the development of the internet. This has dramatically increased the personal capability of the individual; for example, rapid personal communication through e-mail, increased accessibility of an international telephone, the availability online of a large reference data collection uploaded by anybody and everybody on the web. This has led to a big leap in the technical ability to communicate.

Websites such as eBay allow you to bid for the best price of goods being sold by the individual. It is communication or networking. E-commerce is the new way to shop. Many retailers started up websites with discount prices, as they had lower overheads and far greater choice. Amazon became the clear leader in the sales distribution of books, much to the chagrin of the existing book retailing specialists. The other important consequence was the depth and variety of products that could be offered on the web, as the ability and cost of disseminating this information was minimal. There is a phenomena that is known as the long tail. Let us take the example of a physical book store. Because of the limitation of space, it can stock, say, 10,000 different titles. An e-commerce store such as Amazon or iTunes can stock (have available) more than a million different titles at very little additional cost, but with the titles readily available to the customer. This gives the customer a multitude of choice.

A new term came into being – information technology (IT) – and the people who supplied the skills became known as IT specialists.

Materialistic, Possessive and Spendthrift

A whole new industry grew to service people buying houses. The banks and building societies, together with agents, opened new offices to lend to potential new house owners. Then there were the estate agents and the legal services which accompanied such purchases. With the availability of such funds, house prices went up. People went on a house buying spree, buying their second or third homes or even more. These homes were made available for rent to other people. Then the ancillary services, such as the house builder, kitchen and bathroom fitter, landscape gardener, electrician and plumber, grew in numbers. People were buying homes both in the UK and also in foreign countries. Real estate developments such as part ownership or holiday lets became part of the ownership mix for the people of the UK.

In turn, banks borrowed to expand their own growth. It was an era of borrowing; new cars and foreign holidays were also growth areas that used borrowed money. The other fad was the public buying shares on government privatisations – British Gas, British Airways and so on.

Another area of expansion was in retail stores. Not only were there new shopping centres, but also the growth of shops specialising fitting out new homes with furnishings, 'do it yourself' and electrical appliances. People spent their money and the shops devoured it. People became more materialistic, and presentation or appearance was what mattered, not the content or substance. People were judged based on their appearance and possessions, and not themselves. People had become materialistic and possessive, and most important of all, selfish. They cared for themselves and not family and society.

Enjoyment and morals

It is not surprising that the vices of wine, women and song reappeared. The phenomena of binge drinking appeared on the streets of towns and cities. Sexual morals declined with the increased presence of pornography and increased sexual promiscuity. The taking of restricted drugs continued with its climb. With the increase of reported crime would come the increase in the prison population.

Consumption

This was a time where people were encouraged to consume: to read the print media and books, view the television, listen to the radio and to consume from the retail shops, where products are neatly presented for purchase.

Argumentative

Another industry that grew was the law profession. People grew more contentious, fighting for their rights and compensations when wronged. Law firms grew way beyond what the original owners thought possible when they started. Lawyers were being employed to work within the corporate structure as the required legal safeguards for indemnity became more important.

Property

As metal is the element of this period, the buildings that are characteristic of this period are round, the metal shape. Also, the cladding of these buildings is in metal, or a metallic colour of silver or gold.

Examples of these in London are The Gherkin (30 St Mary's Axe), The London City Hall and the McLaren Technology Centre in Woking, Surrey.

The pre-dominant energy is from the West direction. The areas of prosperity will be where the energy can flow from the West easily. There is a West to East 'corridor' for the energy to flow in the South of England. This is from Bristol past Bath, through to the Thames Valley to London. There has been the development of new industries, particularly in high technology, around the Reading area. London's Heathrow airport is also in this business corridor. The head offices of the major technology companies such as Hewlett Packard, Microsoft, Dell and Oracle are all located here. Around this area are more British software development houses, such as Electronics Arts (games). Other centres for high technology business are in Swindon and Bath. The element of these businesses is metal.

The areas of prosperity in London are the western side of London, such as Uxbridge and Chiswick; Harrow in the North West, Kingston and Richmond in the South West. The development in business grew faster in these areas, and consequently, so did the house prices.

The Characteristics of Period 8

The next timeframe is Period 8, which is from 2004 to 2024. The element is earth. The mood of this period is totally different based on the model person: a creative young man who is very good with his hands, or an artisan. He is shy, quiet, spiritual and learned, careful with money, develops a community of people having a common interest, has high moral standards and standing in the community. This entails a shift from the services towards the sciences and engineering. The main style of buildings will be rectangular or regular-shaped. They could possibly be clad with earth tone – orange or yellow.

Creativity or productivity

This era is very different; it is more about creation rather than indulgence or consuming. The celebrities will be mainly men who have become famous for their skills and who have created products or developed something significant. The newly created products will be of value rather than based on appearance. It will be more of substance than of style. In period 7, there was a mainstream and a number of niches. The public are demanding their own choice, specifying exactly how they want the products. A case in point is toothpaste. Colgate used to have just one type of toothpaste, with the only choice being the size of the tube. At the last count on their website, I counted 34 varieties of Colgate. Consumers demand choice.

The mainstream is becoming a series of niches. The series of niches will become the mainstream. Every person will want their own version of the product.

Personalisation or craftsmanship will be the order of the day.

Artisan or craftsman

There is a continued interest in celebrity chefs and the way in which they create their dishes. This is seen in the numerous books, endorsed products on the supermarket shelves and the television exposure they get, both on the mainstream channels and dedicated food channels on satellite television. There is continued interest in the eating of foods in multicultural London. This widening of interest in other types of foods saw the Michelin Star being awarded to Atul Kulcher for his work on Indian food. This is the broadening of interest of the Michelin Awards from Western food to foods from the various parts of the world.

There has been the acknowledgement of industrial designers like Jonathan Ive of Apple and James Dyson who have both received knighthoods (KBE). There has been more emphasis on the teaching of science and technology in the education system. Likewise, there has been a raft of science and technology programmes on television and an extremely popular following of one presenter in particular – Professor Brian Cox, who presented a series of science documentaries on the nature of the Universe.

There is a new generation of products. This can be very small products, some of which can be used within the body. These are produced by natural systems from the body to develop new replacement organs for the human body. This is also known as stem cell technology. Other methods of nanotechnology include working at the atomic particle level. An interesting technology currently being developed is 3D printing. This involves the production of custom-built parts. There are going to be significant changes in the system of mass production. Mass production is the assembly of standardised parts. This system was started in Venice in the 16th Century with the production of the cannon and then developed by Henry Ford into the mass production of cars in the early 20th Century. This was fined tuned by car manufacturers to make different cars, but using the same mass produced parts (the VW group). We are going back to the age of craftsmanship where objects are specificity built for the person. Each object produced is different.

Integrity and accountability

This is the era of the craftsman; people have pride in their work and in themselves. They have pride in their achievements. Both honesty and integrity are perceived as important virtues. Everything has to be worked for; nothing is free. There is no expectation, and failure is accepted to be a means to improve.

Caring and Sharing

The other attitude that is developing is the care of the environment in which we live. Previously, it was just taking or using what was around us in Nature. Now, with natural resources being used up at an irreplaceable rate, people are caring more about what is happening to our environment. There is a concern that we could be destroying ourselves. This is shown with the global warming debate. The other concern is the welfare of people in other countries, or people who are not as fortunate as us. The term 'social development' is being used. The old way of giving is no longer viewed as viable, but rather, it is preferable to help people to help themselves. An example is the 'Fair Trade' range of products. These products are from sources which give the producers a fair price for an agreed quality. It is sold at a premium price in the UK market. This branding of 'Fair Trade' has been readily accepted by the mass market and is commonly seen in the supermarkets.

Personal and Spiritual development

People want greater personal fulfilment. They want to know more about themselves and how they can get the best of themselves. They are no longer satisfied just to work for an employer for the rest of their lives, as their grandparents did. There is a new genre of courses for the person – personality training or personal development. This is to develop the person.

Leasing or sharing

Materialism and possession will not be in keeping with the mood of the era. People will prefer to use and share the facilities. As there are continual changes in technology and in the marketplace, people will not want to own a product; they would prefer to share or lease it, and return it after use.

Life-long learning

Learning will be carried out at all stages of life. Previously, it was only at the education stage in early life, and one employer for life. The business world will experience constant change. There will be uncertainly because of these changes, and there will be a reluctance on the part of employers to give long tenure of employment. There will be a tendency for the highly skilled to work as contractors and move on when the job is completed. People will have to establish their own skills in the marketplace and move from job to job. As a result, there will be a continual and life-long necessity to keep up with the changes in the market. Course providers in both training skills and personal development will have plenty of opportunity.

There is also the spiritual side to fulfil. Previously, people would have turned to religion, but with the decline of state organised religion, people are turning to other religions or faiths. Others take a different but personal route of seeking their spiritual side themselves.

Networking and groups (communities)

In Period 7, networking was the order of the day. People met, talked and perhaps did business. Success came to organisations such as BNI, where people who ran small businesses could meet and do other things. Another example of this was eBay. People met to do business because of the low price and never spoke again. In Period 8, people will want to stay in a group because of a common interest. This group can be in any part of the world, but they are linked by the internet. For example, there could be a group with the common interest of vegetarian bodybuilding. Its members can be in any part of the world. We could take this further. We live in countries with defined borders. The government is there for protection and to provide the people with basic infrastructure and needs of care. However, with the presence of accessible communication and common interests, people could have allegiances to their common cause rather than to the country they live in. There will therefore be people moving away from countries that they are not comfortable in. They will move to another country that they feel will be more welcoming to them. There will be a huge movement of the people. People will be able to work in one country and live in another. This is already a common phenomenon in the European Union, where people work in the UK but spend the weekends with their families in Southern Europe, where the weather is warmer. People will not need to stay in their own country should they disagree with the views of the Government. People will move readily because of economic opportunities and because of their personal interests. It is people who are equipped or talented who will benefit from this mobility. The opportunity is there for the taking.

Social media

This development on the internet is about building up relationships with people. It is not simply networking or social communication where you talk or contact each other. It is above that: it is about social interaction, with the web as the communications conduit. Facebook is the prime example of a group of people being held by common interest. People not only communicate but share experiences. LinkedIn is another example, but for business. Communities, organisations and groups are held together by communication.

The Areas of Growth in the UK

The predominant energy of Period 8 is from the North East. Therefore, areas which allow this energy to pass through will benefit from it. The first and most obvious area is the Fens and the areas to the North East of London. The relatively flat lands allow the energy to move past it easily. The centre of this area is Cambridge, which, as I see it, will be the hub of the new technology – nanotechnology, for instance. This area will see more new development and therefore more new jobs than other parts of the UK.

It the North East and the East of London would have most to gain from the energy from the North East. This area will see the most development. This can be seen in the Olympic Park near Stratford. Another area will be East London, north of the River Thames. One significant area is known as 'Silicon Roundabout' or Tech City, which is a hub for new technology and supporting industries.

The other area which will benefit from the North East energy is the area South West of London, in the Guildford area of Surrey and the Fleet area of Hampshire. The other areas of England are Cornwall and Devon, and also some seaside towns on the South coast of England.

The changes from Period 7 to Period 8

Like everything, trends have to come to an end. But how does a trend end?

It ends with excess!

Financial Crisis

Let us take the example of house prices. House prices increased because of the readily available amount of money for house purchase. Owning a house or a number of houses was seen as a status symbol. This ended dramatically with the sub-prime crisis in 2008. Loans were given to high-risk borrowers on their property. These loans were subsequently sold on as 'high quality' debt to purchasers of these loans. It was actually revealed who the borrowers were. They were high-risk borrowers, and they could not keep up with their monthly instalments to service the loans. The subsequent value of these loans decreased dramatically. As the values decreased, the confidence was broken. Nobody wanted to lend any money because of possible default. The money flow stopped and the whole system went into a crisis. Rumours of trouble at the Northern Rock Building Society caused queues to form at the banks as people withdrew their savings to safer locations. Banks in the UK such as RBS and Lloyds TSB, who had acquired the troubled HBOS, required Government cash for a bail-out. Confidence was lost, and many people withdrew from doing business deals. Almost overnight, all confidence evaporated and growth in the development of the new trends crashed.

The UK will experience contraction of the excesses of borrowing. The size of bonuses of the investment bankers has been a hot topic for quite some time. It was this part of the banking industry that brought on the crisis in the first place. The banker, once held in high regard, very quickly became a derogatory term, as shown by the jokes made by comedians. House prices will start to decline as loans for new properties are difficult to obtain. The credit worthiness of people will change. There will be less confidence to borrow money in uncertain economic circumstances.

News International Group, controlled by Rupert Murdoch, came into prominence when Margaret Thatcher was Prime Minister (1979-1990). He helped to 'destroy' the excessive practices of the print workers by building a new Editorial and Print factory in 'Fortress Wapping'. In exchange, Thatcher allowed special access to her Government for this newspaper group. Later, both Tony Blair (1997) and David Cameron (2010) had the support of the News International newspapers in their election campaigns to gain victory over the incumbent party. It is widely acknowledged that these two party leaders had lobbied for the papers' support in exchange for favourable access to the Government. In the meantime, these newspapers became more confident or arrogant with their behaviour towards any person who expressed views that were disparaging to them, publishing unfavourable information about that person. For example, when the former MP Clare Short spoke out against the Sun newspaper on the portrayal of woman as sex objects on page 3, she was branded "fat", "jealous" and a "killjoy". Methods such as illegal phone hacking or interception of voicemail messages were used to gather information for stories. When the activities were uncovered, there was a great reluctance by the other media, government and the police to investigate these activities. It was the persistence of one MP, Tom Watson, and the Guardian Newspaper to disclose the phone hacking activities surrounding the case of a murdered teenager, Milly Dowler, in 2002, that led the Government to start an inquiry in July 2011. The consequences of the unfolding of the cover-up has led to the closure of The News of the World, the world's best selling paper, together with the resignation of many senior executives from the News International organisation. The fall-out has also included the resignation of senior officers of the Metropolitan Police, including the Commissioner and one of the deputies. The tone and behaviour of the media is now less arrogant.

The newsprint media is also suffering the consequences of the changes in communication from the internet. As the news can be distributed on the internet free of charge, the newsprint media has to charge for its content unless it can get advertisers to cover the costs. It is a difficult fight when you have to charge and your competitor is free. Newsprint media has been cutting down on their budgets but have to retain their paying readership. It is tough.

Both music and book publishers have had to take the consequence of the effects of the internet. Music downloads were free from pirate software sites such as Napster. Apple had come up with iTunes for downloading music for a fee, and there are now also music streaming sites such as Spotify. Both these methods have slowed the sales of physical music (CDs). In the field of book publishing, there is a new range of publishers with self-publishing. Traditional book publishing is at a crossroads, trying to handle the closure of high street book stores in the face of the online book store, which is dominating book sales, and the new publishers which embrace self-publishing and the electronic formats.

The use of media by the government is a double-edged sword. It can be useful in informing us of the situation, but extremely distasteful when it is used to commit a country to war on the basis of false information. This is known as 'spin' or 'spinning' of information. The Blair Government used spinning excessively during its time in power, which has resulted in the distrust of information from the Government and from mainstream media. The most prominent example is the case for weapons of mass destruction in Iraq. Out of this, we have seen the growth of information on the internet and conspiracy stories.

Age of Accountability (Politicians Expenses Scandal)

A major scandal showing the abuse of MPs using their expenses for frivolous claims such as the cleaning of the duck moat or house repairs triggered public outrage. A number of MPs have had to serve prison sentences for false accounting. There were public apologies, sackings, resignations, repayments and retirements in disgrace. The Speaker of the House, who had repeatedly tried to stall the accountability process, had to resign 'under a cloud'. As a result of the scandal, the public now expect clarity in due process and cannot accept public officials spending public money in an unaccountable manner.

A trend continues until excesses take over. The excesses can be seen as a 'bubble'.

This happened with the 'Stampede' for the buying of houses during 2005-2008. When everybody agreed that house prices would rise, everyone rushed. Of course, house prices rose, but this bubble was stopped when mortgage-holders started to default on their repayments, which sparked the sub-prime crisis. This in turn was one of the factors of the 2008 financial crisis. Mortgage lending is now restricted, with uncertainly over job security, and house prices appear to be on the downward trend.

Cosmetic surgery

In period 7, appearances mattered and not a person's personality. We have seen the growth of using cosmetic surgery to enable a person to look younger, to lose weight and to correct physical flaws. It is 'instant', but it does have some physical discomfort.

At the start of the trend, we had some role models having this surgery, but one or two took this technique to excess. For example, the pop singer Michael Jackson's appearance in his later years bore no resemblance to his teenage years, and it has been accepted that this was due to cosmetic surgery. As the trend develops, more and more people are accepting it and use the technique. The excesses of the trend appear when unsuitable people, such as teenagers whose bodies have not yet fully developed, want surgical enhancement. It has been reported that some have been given cosmetic surgery as a present for their 16th birthday. They want to emulate their idols, such as Katie Price, by achieving a curvaceous figure. At the other end of the age spectrum, older women pay for surgical procedures to tighten their skin so that they look younger. There have been images in the media of some people who look almost unreal because of the surgery they have undergone.

It has transpired that one of the suppliers of breast implants has been using industrial grade silicone rather than medical grade silicone as fillings. At the moment, there is uncertainly over how people having these substandard implants will fare. With all this uncertainty, many people will be discouraged from this procedure for purely cosmetic reasons.

From bling to integrity

People will start to realise that instant gratification is a false dream. Other examples of instant gratification include the consumption of recreational drugs and alcohol. I would expect these to decrease over time. With the decreasing use of recreational drugs, I would expect the concomitant decrease in crime, and therefore in the prison population. A decrease in alcohol consumption will also see a downward fall in violence and liver and related diseases. People will start to realise that everything has to be worked for. It has to be achieved. It is you who must work to create your own integrity.

Summary:

Period 7 (1984-2004)

Prominence of women

Communications – people and technical

Materialistic, Possessive and Spendthrift

Enjoyment and morals

Consumption

Argumentative

Possessive

Period 8 (2004-2024)

Creativity or productivity

Artisan or craftsman

Integrity and accountability

Caring and Sharing

Personal and spiritual development

Leasing or sharing

Life-long learning

Networking and groups(communities)

Social media

New areas of prosperity.

Significant changes from Period 7 to Period 8

Financial crisis

Age of accountability (media, politicians)

Cosmetic surgery

From bling to integrity

Chapter 6

Case Studies – Part 1

These two chapters of case studies relate to the application of traditional feng shui. They demonstrate the three types of work that we carry out after an assessment.

1. Looking for the best site for a new premises (usually on behalf of a client, such as a multiple retailer or hotel chain).
2. Planning and designing of remedial work to an existing property.
3. Assisting in the design of a developmental project – a new building, an estate or town.

This chapter relates to the first and second of these three points. The next chapter covers the main work that we do – project development, the design and building of new properties.

Alliance feng shui: ethos and mission statement:

"...is a global organization dedicated to the practice of Traditional Feng Shui with professionalism and integrity. We utilize proven methods to meet the unique needs of each client, enhancing opportunities for successful business growth, goal attainment, and personal quality of life." taken from "www.AllianceFengShui.com"

Members work specifically in the interests of our clients and want every success for them. This involves giving honest opinions on whether the project is viable and providing the best advice available for the success of the project. Secondly, we do not disclose the names of our clients and their projects, as we maintain client confidentially at all times.

After the assessment of the site

The assessment procedure is to prepare a report on the feasibility of the proposed work. It is straightforward if the answer is "yes, we can do as it was proposed."

There could, however, be a report in which we could state that the project, in our opinion, is not worth proceeding with, as the final result will not be of benefit to the client. For new clients, this would be a shock to them, as we are telling them that we are unable to help them. This can appear very unusual, as we appear to be turning down work. We are consultants and we give an independent opinion. Yes, we do turn down work regularly. We pride ourselves on our integrity and excellence in the service of our clients.

There are other occasions on which we state how we would help the client, but he disagrees with our recommendations. We are employed to get the best results for our clients, and they want us to do it differently. As before, we turn down such work, as we do not want to go into a situation where there is a disagreement before we start work on the project. Our aims are very specific, and we have to maintain our integrity to ourselves, to our team members and to our clients.

We have a reputation for giving our clients a full and remarkable service, and they get untold value as a result. These case studies are examples of the type of results we have been providing for years.

The Case Studies

Feng shui is used as a tool or a method. It can also be used to identify the strengths and weaknesses of the building. When a client has a business problem, the cause of the problem could be related to the building. This is the application of traditional feng shui: identifying the problem and remedying it. Not all problems can be solved. We work solely in the interests of the clients; we will be honest and say whether we can help or not. This is illustrated in the following case studies.

The case studies describe a fair cross section of the work that I, with my colleagues in the team, have done over the past few years. The work has been located in the UK, Europe, the Middle East, Far East, and North America. As stated earlier, we do not name our clients, and hence we are unable to give the location or building involved, as this would reveal their identities. I have therefore kept the background information of the case studies general, but described the situation.

This is meant to show the wide range of solutions that we provide, together with the results achieved. It is also an attempt to show the care, attention to detail and remarkable value our service offers to clients.

Selection and rectification

1. Shopping mall and multi-storey car parks
2. Hotel by the river
3. The unfocused hotel
4. To invest in a café or the chef?

5. Hotel and restaurant up the hill
6. Selection of retail shop in a shopping mall
7. Two restaurants and one kitchen
8. Tapas bar
9. Selection of house
10. Hotel with two sets of doors
11. Piling
12. Residential estate in a championship golf course

1. Shopping mall and the multi-storey car parks

The town used to have just one shopping mall, but a second one was being built. While the client's shopping mall was the only one in town, the shopping mall had the monopoly of the mall business and it was always busy. It was so busy that there were not enough parking spaces. He built a multi-storey car park directly in front of some of the entrances. Still the business was not affected noticeably, because this shopping mall was the only one in town.

The second shopping mall opened. It was new, it had space and everybody preferred to do their shopping at the new mall. The business in the old mall dropped. It looked tired in comparison to the new mall, and it was small and cramped. Initially he was not concerned, but when his tenants started talking of moving, it shook him. He had always counted on their loyalty because of the good business he had given them previously.

I was called in and identified that the problem was the multi-storey car park buildings that were blocking the energy to the entrances of the shopping mall. There was not a problem with pulling them down because there were hardly any cars parked there, even on weekends.

He said to me, "I thought that you feng shui consultants would come up with a cure and every problem would be sorted."

I replied, "I wish. If I could cure everything that I touched, I would be a multi-billionaire and retired in some tropical island after curing all the world's problems. I have come up with a solution that works. It might be painful, BUT it will bring back your customers and retain your tenants."

"Tell me."

"I suggest you pull down the multi-storey car parks and you will see the business come back in."

"But I just built the car parks two years ago for the convenience of my customers."

"Yes, the multi-storey car parks are destroying your business. No energy, no business."

"What happens if I refurbish the interiors of the mall. Will it help?"

"Refurbishing the interiors will help, but the real winner is the removal of the car parks."

Outcome: It was a battle. His prime tenants wanted to leave because of the decline in their business. He had given them extremely good business for all those years. Now they wanted to leave because the prospects over there were better. Where was the loyalty? It was the thought of his tenants leaving that was hurting his ego.

His prime tenants left for the other mall. He refurbished the interiors and spent a fortune on a publicity campaign – advertisements, PR and promotions. A new set of tenants came in but they were at the cheaper end of the market. The mall was never ever busy, even when they were dealing at the popular end of the market.

About a year later, I had a phone call from the owner.

"I remember what you said about the car park blocking the energy to the store. As the car parks are hardly used and there is no point having them, I would like to pull one down and would like your opinion on which one."

I told him that if he removed one of the car park, that particular area of the shopping mall would see better business. Similarly, the removal of the other car park would benefit a different area of the mall.

He then said, "I have thought about it. If I pull down this car park structure, as you said, the business in this area will improve. These multi-storey car parks are not being used and I have nothing to lose by pulling one down. I am not allowed to do other things with these car parks. Which car park building would you suggest pulling down?"

I made my selection.

About six months later, I had another phone call from the owner, but this time, there was cheer in his voice.

"You were right all along. It was the multi-storey car parks that were causing the problem. The business in the marked area has improved considerably. This really cheers me up. This leads me to the next issue I have. I have had an offer for my shopping mall which is difficult to refuse. I have an idea, another shopping mall. Would you come and have a look at the proposed land site?"

I said, "Hang on, before we do anything, will this town be able to take a third shopping mall?"

"It would not be a problem with your help."

We looked at the site for a shopping complex together with an entertainment centre, hotel and conference centre.

Comment: Many owners do not realise that one of the factors in the success of the business is the amount of energy going into the property. This is basic tenet of feng shui: the more energy going to the building, the better the business will be. If you are successful and you alter or change the entrance door, you are changing the flow of energy. As soon as you decrease the amount of energy going into the building, business will drop. It is that direct.

The owner was willing to try. He tried the industry standard procedure. Refurbish and re-launch. It did not make much difference to the business, other than a short-term rise because of the publicity. He recalled what I had said and gave it a try. He was open-minded about the approaches that he took.

2. Hotel by the river

A new hotel had just been opened in this city. It was by the river and was a tall building with eleven floors. It had become a city landmark. However, the general manager was complaining that the occupancy rate was only between 30 and 50%. The owners were just not satisfied with this performance. It was not good enough for a hotel in this prime location.

I was called in to have a look at the solution. The hotel faced the river bend, but there were no doors on the riverside. Therefore, no energy could be collected from the river. The energy was coming into the building from the main entrance (A) at the back, the land side of the building.

There is a workable solution: a new door at the front of the hotel, facing the river. This would collect the energy from the river.

The general manager replied: “We did not put the door in the front (riverside, B) as we did not want passing pedestrians to wander into the hotel lobby.”

I told him that if he designed the door appropriately, it would deter these passing pedestrians.

He thought about it and agreed with the idea. The design was commissioned. With the new door installed, the occupancy rate of the hotel shot up to a high 80% within a year. It is still in the top five performing hotels of that hotel chain. This is the leading hotel brand in the world.

Comment: This follows the basic tenet of feng shui: the more energy that comes in, the better the business. This was done by judiciously selecting a location for the door that could tap into the flow of energy brought by the river. The moving water of the river creates a considerable movement of energy. It moves energy towards a building or it can suck it away. Therefore, considerable care has to be taken when working near a river.

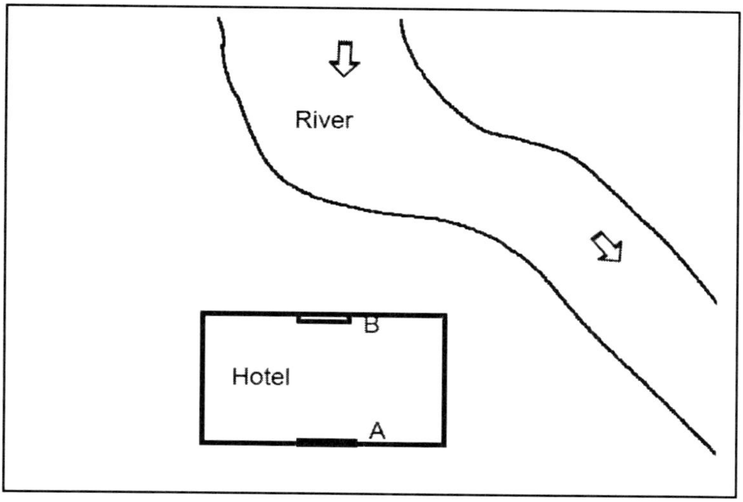

Diagram: Hotel by the river and the new door (B)

3. An unfocused hotel

I was invited to visit this hotel to check out why it was under performing. It is a small boutique hotel which wanted to be known as a cultural hotel. This hotel had three distinct features.

1. A whole series of antiques – valuable ones at that. They were not only in the public areas but also in the bedrooms.
2. It is a hotel with six rooms. The rooms have these antique pieces but the design is for style and not for practicality.
3. There are two fine dining restaurants and a rooftop bar. The two restaurants were modern

Chinese and modern Western, but the food was coming from the same kitchen.

I had a meal there and would you believe it, there was a fly in my soup! The food was an attempt and there were a number of wrong orders. They could certainly do better!

This hotel had three distinctive features that it was marketing. Most businesses just focus on one, and do it extremely well. If you are a hotel, you promote yourself as a hotel and you provide good service as a hotel. In feng shui, you only do one type of business from that particular property.

Comments:

1. There was no focus in this hotel. Was it a museum, Chinese restaurant, Western restaurant or hotel? Focus on just the one feature; at that time, the business was not doing anything properly.
2. Antique furniture – this is a tricky call. It is the older Chinese person who would have second thoughts in sleeping in the bedroom full of antiques. It is a old Chinese custom not to have furniture that you do not know the provenance of. The furniture takes on the energy of the people of the house. Suppose this the person had a chronic and terminal illness. This energy would be retained by the furniture. That is why the Chinese prefer to purchase new property and new home furnishings.
3. Restaurants – why have two different types of restaurants? What is the point of having both

Western fine dining and Chinese fine dining? It just confuses the kitchen.

Recommendations: Just focus on a particular feature, the core business of the hotel. The restaurant is a service to the hotel. Keep it to Chinese fine dining and no more. Keep the antiques to the public areas and do not have them in the bedrooms.

Focused business: Take the example of the internet: look how focused Google is. On the search page, it is simple and clean with only one line – "enter your search". This shows that Google does one thing – searching on the internet – and it is good at it. It has become the de-facto search engine for the vast majority of people. If you look at Yahoo!, there is a multitude of topics on its homepage. It looks unfocused. Would you want to use its services? It does not inspire confidence. Just look the business performance of both companies. The company that is focused is the world leader. The unfocused company appears to be in terminal decline, looking for someone to save it.

4. To invest in a café or chef?

A client requested that I look at a café. He had been invited to make an investment. The owner is the chef of the café.

The small café had twenty tables and some comfortable sofas. The café not only served coffee, but had an unusual collection of New York-style pastries and snacks. The chef wanted more capital so that he could expand his business into the events market as a specialist caterer. This was a good fit for my client, who was an events organiser.

I looked at the café.

I advised against investing in it. The kitchen was in the North West of the property. This indicated that the chef could be hot-tempered and unreasonable whilst inside the business, even if outside the café he could be most placid in his behaviour. There would be staff and inter-personal problems with my client.

"How do you know that?" he asked.

I replied that I knew this from the feng shui analysis of the café, nothing more. The chef looked really interesting, having come up with a collection of New York-style pastries and snacks which are not available in this quality in this country.

My client told me: "The chef had worked in New York for a long time and had won quite a few awards for his work. He has come back and has been looking for funding for his idea of a coffee shop with New York-style snacks. He could only get funding for this small café, but he has had incredible rows with staff and customers. He even used a knife to threaten them. However, he is an incredibly talented pastry chef.

"I want to nurture this talent, but I want to find out more about him. Can he work with people, or is his ego and aggression part of his personality? Can you help me look for a café where we can re-locate him so as to evaluate him from there?"

We found the chef a café in a good location where he could show his skills to the customers and the investor. He rapidly gained a loyal following for his work and his café. The most important result is that the chef did not exhibit any of the violent actions that he had displayed in the previous location.

I found out later that he was so busy and energised by the reception of the customers to his work that he has come up with an even greater selection of food. He was in his element.

Comment: My client had the time and money to back the chef. But from my point of view, he was willing to listen to me as to why the chef was behaving badly in the first place. Had he not taken my point, this 'talent spotting' would not have occurred, and the talent would have remained unspotted.

A different concept in cafes is being prepared. In a city crowded with coffee shops, it had better be good!

5. Hotel and restaurant up the hill

A building had become available. The client had requested that I go with her to the site to see her idea for the new hotel and restaurant in that existing building.

It was a magnificent site. It overlooked the city, which was on both sides of the river. However, the building was about ten metres from the edge of a steep slope.

My client commented, "Isn't this location magnificent? Just imagine having dinner at night overlooking the city and its lights. The rooms in the hotel will also have such commanding views. People swimming in the pool will also enjoy these views, very much like the Marina Bay Sands in Singapore. This is something to die for!"

I replied, "Yes, it would be a tremendous draw for guests and for the tourism industry. I have visions of this place being filled with people really happy with this hotel and restaurant.

"Despite this, I would not recommend this location. Your business will not do well and I do not expect you to stay here more than four to five years at the very most. Just have a look at the past history of the people living or the businesses here. I will bet you that they have not been here for more than five years and were relieved to have left."

"From what I understand about feng shui, there are cures which you could place and correct the situation?"

"I do not understand about the placement of cures. I provide workable solutions. In this case, I would recommend that you do not go ahead with the project because it is highly likely to end up in tears."

"Is there any workable solution that you could recommend me in this case? I have been thinking and dreaming about this project for the past two years."

"I have wracked my brain to come up with something to help you fulfil your dream. It is because the property is so near the edge of the steep slope. Do you remember the restaurant by the coast? It was on top of the cliff with magnificent views over the bay. It was one of the most beautiful restaurant locations that I have been to. It closed down. It did not fulfil its potential because it was too near the cliff."

"Oh yes, I recall that restaurant by the cliff. It closed. I will check on the previous tenants in this place and come back to you."

Comment: The client went back and checked the tenants who were in the building. At no time had any of the tenants lasted for more than five years. The only time this was exceeded was during and after the war, when it was a clinic. I have not heard back from the client.

6. Selection of a retail outlet in a shopping mall

A well known UK fashion house had been invited to open a store at a new shopping mall in another country. This new shopping mall was large, about 1.5 million square feet, and it had eight floors.

The brief was to find a location for the client's store. Of course, this store was to do good business and establish the brand in this city.

As I was in that country, I visited the sales office. After looking at the layouts, I found a location on level 2.

The client said: "Level 2 is a level below the established brands (Dior, Chanel, Mont Blanc and so on), where they expect most of the business to be."

"That is what they expect – people to go for the brands on Level 3. This floor (Level 2) will do more business, as it gets more energy because of the 'design layout' of the building. This location is probably the best around. I am sure that they will offer you a good price for the location, as is it is not perceived as 'prime'."

The client negotiated a very favourable rate for the property. After about five years, he is extremely pleased with the location.

Comment: In this shopping mall, because of the layout, all the energy goes down to the lowest two floors. Level 1 is a food court and Level 2 is for retail outlets. This is where the best business is done. The main floor (Level 3), where the brands are, is acceptable, but above that level, the tenants struggle.

7. Two restaurants and one kitchen

A restaurateur was doing well with just one restaurant. He wanted to expand, but he could not be in two places at the same time. The shop next to his restaurant became vacant and he thought that an easy way to expand was to take over the neighbouring location, convert it into a café, but supply the food from his existing kitchen. He loved this idea, as there were the economies of scale, and it meant that he did not have to be in two places at the same time.

He opened the café, and the overall business to both locations dropped. He could not understand the situation. He did not change very much of the original, but had simply added another outlet to the existing kitchen.

I visited the restaurant and looked at the arrangement.

"How long have you had this new café?" I asked.

"About six months."

"How is your business?"

"It was OK until I opened the café. The business has dropped. It has not risen as I would have thought."

"This restaurant and this café are in separate locations but have the same kitchen."

"Yes. But I do not understand the situation. It is not logical. I should be getting more business."

"It is very simple. One kitchen cannot supply two different outlets. One kitchen supplies only one outlet. In your case, the restaurant with the existing kitchen combination works. If you want to have a café, then you have to have a separate kitchen for your café. This will make space very tight in your café, so have you thought of finding a really good location for your café?"

"I agree about the existing restaurant and kitchen combination. Let me think about the café, either to add a kitchen or find a new location. I will get back to you."

We discussed the possible combinations on the phone. There is no point moving to any old location – you could be leaping from one situation to a worse one. After much thought and discussion, he built a kitchen in the café. He reduced the menu, but most importantly, the amount of business in both the restaurant and the café increased.

Comment: It is like many things in life. When you focus on a particular task, you will do it well. When you try to do too many things, you get unfocused. In feng shui, in general, one building should have one purpose for the business to succeed.

8. Tapas bar

An hotelier had a tapas bar in his hotel, but it was small because of the space limitations within the hotel. The demand for the tapas bar was high, and it was full to overflowing every evening. It was embarrassing to turn away potential customers. A new but larger location was necessary.

He called me to help him look for a location for this tapas bar. Based on the existing bar, I said that what he needed was a corner location and one that can fit a long bar. The food was to be prepared behind the counter.

“Why a corner location?” he asked.

“Simply because this is the best place for coffee shops, cafés or fast food outlets. Have you ever noticed that Starbucks are usually near a junction? In this country, virtually all coffee shops, cafés and food courts are at road junctions.”

“Point taken.”

He then went off to an estate agent to get a list of properties. Funnily enough, he showed me an old bar with a very long bar counter for people to sit beside. It was designed for people to come in, eat and drink and then move on. It had three sets of doors. They were all in the right positions; one was set up to harvest the energy from the junction, the other two doors were an extremely good combination when used together. This place was clearly originally designed with feng shui.

Instead of using just ‘ordinary’ staff to prepare the food, he brought in the staff of a multi-Michelin star chef to prepare the food. This hotelier does not do things by halves. I was there on the first night and wow, the food was fantastic.

Yes, the three doors were in the right position, but because it was air conditioned, a particular set of doors were designated to be the main doors. The property had been designed with feng shui previously. One set of doors were designed for use with the junction, with a particular formula for 'fast foods'. The other two sets of doors were to be used together, as it made a very good combination.

I made it very clear to the owner how the doors were to be used. There was not to be any random way of opening the doors.

Comment: Every type of business is different. The ideal location of a coffee shop would therefore be different to that of a pharmacy. Each type of business has its own type of ideal location. Most corner locations are ideal for coffee shops, cafés or bars. The ideal locations for a pharmacy or a retail store are somewhere quieter. This recognises that every business has different requirements.

9. Selection of a house

A client had a magnificent house near the top of a hill. It had such a conspicuous location that people from miles around would be able to see the house. It looked imposing because of its position. It was the only one in this location and had commanding views of the entire neighbourhood. This included the town by the river in the valley and the neighbouring hills. They had been dreaming of such a house for years, so why did they want me to help them in a new house search?

"We have had such a horrible time since we moved into our dream house. Within a year of moving in, we were served with a court order with regards our business. Our business partners left us because of this problem. Our business is just stuck, we do not have any income and the legal fees are draining us. Our marriage is strained but we believe that it was our stay in the house that was the cause of our problems."

"Why do you say that?" I asked.

"As soon as we moved in, we could feel there was no energy in the house. It was empty or hollow. We had the splendid views, but there is more to life than amazing views. We have never had so many problems since we have been in this house. That is why we want to move out as soon as possible."

The house is built into the hill. There are no doors at the back of the house. You have to go to the front to get into the house. The windows are all at the side or front. Everything is positioned for the view.

As they had decided to downsize, I asked them to go to the estate agents and look for houses in their price range in the areas that they wanted to live. I told them to shortlist the houses that they liked, but to ignore houses that are up the hill. I also advised them to avoid property that is near a steep downhill junction or road. I told them to try to get a house near a road junction or corner on nearly level land. With the shortlist, I would inspect the houses and make a recommendation.

I made the recommendation on which house they should move to. As soon as they moved in, life became normal again. The litigation died; the other parties stopped pursuing the claim. It simply disappeared into thin air.

10. Hotel with two sets of doors

A hotel had been refurbished. The modern expectation would be that a refurbished hotel would do better than a tired property. But it did not. The occupancy rate dropped like a stone, from 70% to 30%. There were expensive marketing campaigns, offering two nights for the price of one with dinner thrown in, and a half price room sale. The owner was at his wits' end. He had taken advice from established marketing and promotion experts in the hotel business. They were using the industry standard methods, but there was no change in the occupancy rate.

The hotel owner invited me to look at the property.

He said, "We took on the refurbishment with great optimism. A newly decorated hotel would attract more guests. It was not to be. Would like you to help me improve the occupancy rate. Also, to help me find out what the cause of the sharp decline could be?"

I asked him, "What were the previous arrangements of the lobby and the reception?"

"We used the other door (A). The interior designer said it would give a different perspective to the hotel should we use door (B)."

"Using this set of doors (B) is the cause of the hotel business dropping."

"Tell me more."

"There is a road directly in front of the door (B). There is two-way traffic, but the road slopes downwards. In other words, the energy moves away from hotel."

"The interior designer said that, in this location, you can see the road and that this gives a feeling of openness. An illusion of space."

"Well, you pay your money and take your choice. I would suggest that you use the first door (A) and that you keep the second door (B) shut. However, I have to give you a date and time to do the switch over."

"That is fine."

Needless to say, when the first door (A) was re-used, the occupancy rate went back to its original levels – about 70%. The owner was extremely happy, but more importantly, he was relieved. He was one happy man. The owner is now thinking of refurbishing the lobby again. This time, the desk faces the first door (A) so that the hotel will look more presentable.

Comment: Doors are extremely important in feng shui. They are the interface of the exteriors to the interiors. In other words, doors allow energy to come in as well as allowing it to get out. In a building with good feng shui properties, the doors let the energy into the building and the building retains this energy. There is a low leakage of energy out of the building. In this hotel particular building, the second door (B) allows the energy to leak away, thereby depleting the building of energy. Hence the drop in the occupancy rate after the refurbishment.

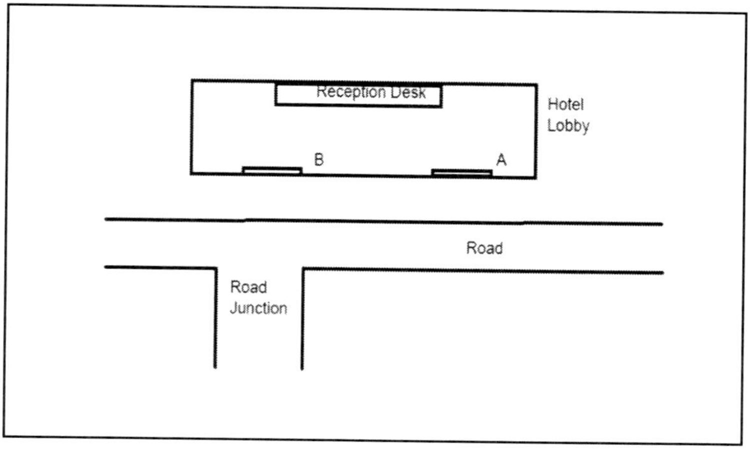

Diagram of the hotel lobby and the two doors

11. Delay in earthworks

A building site in the city centre had been worked on for more than two years. They had cleared the land and had been doing the piling for the past 18 months. I was contacted by the contractor.

"Can you help me?"

"It depends."

"We have been working on this site for the past two years and we have had no end of problems. We have had two deaths, a lawsuit from a neighbouring building, and we are extremely late in our contract.

"We have had an incredible number of technical problems. We have had issues with the machinery and with the earth underneath. Everything that can go wrong has gone wrong with us. I have been in this industry for the past twenty years and have never experienced anything like this.

"We are so far behind that we have to make payments to the property developer for the delays."

I told him, "Show me the sequence of the work that you have done. Both the excavation of the earth and the piling."

I studied the charts and saw that they had hit the Annual Afflictions for the first year and then for the second year in a different location. There are two different Afflictions in this situation, the feng shui terms being Tai Sui and Sui Po.

Annual Afflictions: Every year, a particular sector of land becomes an affliction when the soil in that area is disturbed. Problems occur in this area, known as 'Tai Sui'. The land that is diagonally (180 degrees) across is 'Sui Po' and problems also occur here. In the following year, the Tai Sui moves into a different sector of the land, followed by the Sui Po.

Let us take an example:

In 2010, the Tai Sui is in the North East sector of the plot. The Sui Po is in the South West sector.

In 2011, the Tai Sui is in East sector of the plot. The Sui Po is in the West sector.

In the first year (2010), they first started to excavate the plot in the North East sector. In 2010, this was the location of the Tai Sui. Problems started to occur.

In the second year (2011), they started to pile in East sector of the land first. This was the location of the Tai Sui for that year. Problems continued.

The Sui Po for 2010 was in the South West sector and for 2011 it was in the West sector. It so happened to have a building in that area. The supporting walls of the building started to show cracks. Apparently, the foundation of this building moved and blame was put on the earthworks at this site. It was a messy situation.

The client told me, "We have been allowed to restart the piling. Where do we begin?"

I told him, "I can provide a solution. You have to do the piling in a particular sequence to cover the area, but you will have to start at a particular time and date. You will not be able to deviate from this plan. Is this fine with you?"

As expected, the piling work was completed within three months of the start of the new schedule.

Comment: When digging or disturbing the earth, there are certain areas of the building plot that can come out with a series of unforeseen problems, as in this case – deaths, neighbours being disturbed and machinery malfunctions. By understanding the situation, we can plot the path for the piling or digging the earth. We also supply the time to start working for that part of the building plot.

12. Residential estate on a championship golf course

A residential estate of about twenty acres with 48 homes had a stated selling price of around €800,000 per unit. The estate was specially designed for golfers for the nearby renowned golf club, which had a championship course of 36 holes. The estate had all the modern conveniences and all latest amenities that a golfing enthusiast could want. However, there was a section of fifteen houses that just would not sell.

I was called in by the developer to help sell the unsold section of the estate.

After I had looked at the estate, the developer told me:

"I have not been able to sell any of the units in this part of the estate. This part has been on the market for the past 24 months. We had a sales campaign with special incentives, which included an incredible 10% discount. It just did not shift. The units in the other parts of the estate sold very quickly and there is a healthy market for the sold units. Why can I not sell these units? These unsold units are not only draining me of money, but also of my energy."

I asked him, "why do you have this strange road system going through the estate?"

"By accident. It just happened. The original road system did not work so we made this a one-way system so that the trucks used for the construction could get through easily. We also created some shortcuts to save time. We have never changed it since the completion of the construction."

"I suggest that you make the entire road system two-way. Block off the shortcuts so that everybody has to go all the way round the estate rather than just be kept in this sector. The area in which the unsold houses are located has no road traffic passing through. It is out on a limb, isolated. No energy is being circulated around that area. With no energy, it is not possible to sell the properties."

"OK, what do you want me to do?"

I suggested the following:

a. Re-route the road system and block off the shortcuts, as we had discussed earlier.
b. Re-paint the exteriors and interiors of the unsold properties. Tidy up the gardens together with the swimming pools.
c. Build the sales office at this point.
d. Start a sales campaign when you are ready. I will give you the starting date.

"What about prices?"

"I would suggest that you raise the prices to the current market prices of between €950,000 to €990,000. There are two units that would sell really quickly. I would suggest that one be priced at €1.2 million and the other at €1.1 million."

He did what I had suggested. The units sold at the asking price soon after. The higher priced units were sold at an even higher price than I had suggested, but they were the first two units to be sold. He was a happy man. He not only recouped his investment, but had a healthy return. Just a few months earlier, he had been prepared to write off the unsold units, thereby making a serious loss on the project. When I met him, he was emotionally drained. When the remaining units were sold, I could see the spring in his step. He was really invigorated with the completion of the sales of the remaining units.

Chapter 7

Case Studies – Part 2

This chapter deals with how traditional feng shui is used in the designing buildings for people to work and live in.

The primary focus of traditional feng shui is to save our client's time and money, to maximize revenue and efficiency, to ensure the project is completed correctly first time, to ensure that it works in harmony with nature, and to ensure health and well-being for the future residents of the building.

A team of traditionally trained consultants will be involved in the project from start to finish.

These are some of the steps taken with the client.

1. Assessment of the owner's goals and needs.

In the initial stages, the aims, needs and ultimate goals of the project are discussed in detail with the client.

2. Assessment of building site, including site selection.

The building site is inspected with the primary focus on landform (mountains, bodies of water, trees and so on) in order to assess the impact of the environment upon the future buildings.

Consideration is also given to how this environment will affect the construction phase, workers and management of the project.

3. Initial feng shui design guidelines for the architect.

When the initial building site assessment has been completed, we work with the architect on road access, building placement, building materials and outlay of interior design.

4. Initial landscaping recommendations.

This step deals with the construction and placement of waterways and other land features. Recommendations are made on the best location and direction, type of trees or flowering plants, as well as date selection for breaking ground. These are the most important aspects of the project, as anything done in this stage will have a direct impact on the other stages of the project and on the future residents.

5. Participation with design team and review of building and landscape plans. (Until the finalization of the plans.)

At every stage of the project, the consultant will review all building and landscape plans in order to minimize any negative effects and maximize potential profit for the client. In addition, it is every consultant's responsibility to ensure the well-being and harmony of the future residents. Constant review and attention to detail is necessary to ensure these objectives are clearly met.

6. Input into materials, colours, furniture and object placement.

The consultant makes recommendations as to materials, colours, furnishings and object placement within the homes or buildings themselves, as well as making recommendations regarding the use of materials, colours and objects surroundings the residences/buildings.

7. Assist in the sales process.

It is the consultant's job to make certain recommendations during the sales process. These recommendations will include the location and design of the sales office, including the placement of the boardroom, meeting rooms or offices and reception. In addition, recommendations will be made with regard to displays and sales materials (i.e. brochures, printed materials and media). The consultant will also provide date selection for the best time to start the publicity process.

8. Date selection for best time to begin work

As mentioned previously, date selection is an important part of the process and will be applied as needed. Primarily, date selection will be used for groundbreaking and certain decisions regarding sales, marketing and event planning.

Other considerations

Due to the size and complexity of this project, it might be necessary to employ a team of feng shui consultants to work on an ad hoc basis. Members will be selected based on the needs of a project at a particular time and the skill sets of the team members to fill that particular need. Each member has received the same training and will employ the same techniques to solve any issues that may arise.

Again, due to the size and complexity of this project, many unforeseen issues will arise that may need special attention from time to time (such as improper construction, acts of God, and so on), and it is the consultant's duty to assist in a quick resolution of these unforeseen issues.

Feng shui involvement

- Initial visit – to assess the owner's needs, assess the site, provide initial design guidelines and begin design meetings with the team.
- Possible second design stage visit – should issues arise which cannot be handled via phone and email. The consultant will determine whether this is necessary.
- Pre-construction visit – to verify that what is planned has been laid out accurately on the site and will be built correctly.
- Possible during-construction visit – should issues arise which cannot be handled via phone and e-mail. The consultant will determine whether this is necessary.
- Post-construction visit – final recommendations and adjustments.

In between the different phases of construction, the owner and the consultant can determine how many times are necessary for a visit, and exact an additional visit fee.

Large jobs

1. Factory park
2. City by the river
3. Multi-use apartment by the river
3. Water theme park
4. Hill residential estate
5. Pristine land by lake
6. Stepped condominiums
7. Small town with golf courses
8. Hotel at beach resort
9. Small plot of land in London
10. Development of shopping mall

The case studies below describe a fair cross-section of the work that I, with my colleagues in the team, have done over the past few years. The work has been located in the UK, Europe, the Far East, and North America. As stated earlier, we do not name our clients and hence, we are unable to give the location or buildings involved, as this would reveal their identities. I have therefore kept the background information of the case studies general, but described the situation.

This chapter is about the selection of sites for property development. In some of these examples, the land is next to water – be it moving water, as in a river, or static water, as in a lake, pond or swimming pool. Water has both a good and bad effect on the property.

The point of these case studies is to show that we will only work on a project that we can definitely help. If we cannot help, we will say so. This is our position and our tradition. In each project, we have to consider the welfare of three parties – the client (or the property developer in this case), the workers building the site, and the people who will be living in the houses that we are involved with.

1. Factory Park

A property developer had purchased a large tract of land (one square kilometre, or about 250 acres) to develop as a factory park. This is like a business park, but there are factories. He had built a show area for the 'model factories' of the various specifications. He would then build the factory to the agreed specification and location for the customer. After two years, despite a series of marketing campaigns and serious discounting, he had only made one sale.

He called for our help.

We explained the situation to him about the land on the east side of the lake. His plot of land (Plot 1) was not receiving any of the predominant energy from the West. It was being absorbed by the still water in the lake (see Comment below). He immediately understood the situation. He then told us that he knew of the owner of land on the West side of the lake (Plot 2), and would check whether it was for sale. It was available. He bought the new parcel of land and sold his old plot.

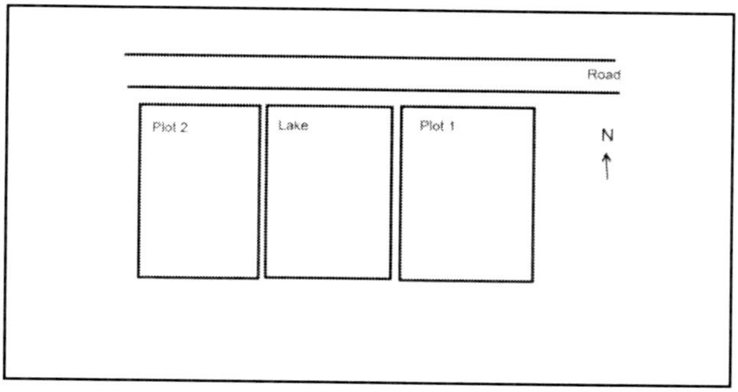

Diagram: the factory park Plots 1 and 2 on either side of the lake.

We then worked out a master plan for the development of the site. The aims were:

a. The sites were to be sold quickly and at a premium to the market.
b. The tenants of the various sites would not only do good business, but have a good relationship with all involved – the main site owner, the employees, their suppliers and customers.
c. The sales office was designed and located in the best position for the best results.
d. The infrastructure of services – electricity, water and waste – must be considered. The road was laid out so that the energy is distributed evenly and reaches the furthest points on the site. We also considered the future changes of direction of the predominant energies. The factories were to do well in the present and in the future.
e. The park was zoned for the various types of factories. The different specialisms or sizes were placed at specific areas to get the best conditions for the tenants.

Results

Within a year, all the plots sold, and prices were better than the client had expected.

Comment: Still water absorbs energy from a particular compass direction in a particular period of time. Conversely, energy from another compass direction can be reflected in the same period of time.

In the time period 1984 to 2004, the predominant energy is from the West. The land on the west side is good, as the predominant energy coming from the West is reflected back. The land on the east side is not good. It does not get the predominant energy from the West.

2. City by the river

An entrepreneur had acquired a large tract of land that was by a major river and adjacent to a new major international highway which passed through four countries. The land was next to a huge bridge, had easy access to the river for transport and an operational aircraft runway nearby. He was thinking of using this as a transport hub by linking it to other roads in the country.

We visited the site and made a number of recommendations. This area could be built as a city specialising in financial services, as well as a hub. The feng shui analysis showed that the river configuration with the bridge was very good for wealth generation. This totally expanded the scale of the project and it offered far better return, with lower risk for the client and his investors.

He was excited about this prospect and found that a 'tax free' status could be had for an investment of this size. We were working on the master plan whilst the client was with the local authorities and investors.

The proposed city was zoned with the important commercial areas for the financial services to be located alongside the river. The roads in the city were designed with the terrain so that energy would be distributed evenly throughout the city. It would also take into account changes in the energy flow in the coming decades. The roads were the heart of the transport hub and distribution network. There was land set aside for people to change their modes of transport (road, air and river) and for freight to be distributed.

Other areas were for the administration (City Hall) together with the social services (care services such as the hospital, and municipal services such as fire, water, electricity, waste disposal and police). Other considerations were the residential, shopping, commercial services and recreational areas. Sites for hotels were located in the city centre.

This is very much a work in progress.

3. Multi-use apartment blocks by the river

A property developer made an enquiry at the planning stage of the project (£5.5 billion). Three buildings (in three phases) were to be built on a prime site by the river. It was about two miles from the city centre and had good views of the river. Buildings in Phases 2 and 3 had stunning views of the city. These buildings were to have a variety of uses: retail outlets, offices and the other businesses associated with modern living, such as fitness centres, bars and restaurants. There was to be a range of apartments on the upper floors.

In the discussion with the developer, the Phase 1 building was to be completed and the proceeds were to be used to finance the development in Phase 2. I said that the units in Phase 1 would not sell, as the river is drawing energy from the site. If Phase 2 is built first, this building would stop the energy leaving the site. This retained energy would help in both the development and sales of the units on the site.

The developers maintained their view that Phase 1 was a very attractive proposition, especially the pricing. Phase 2, because of its views over the city and the river, would be priced at a substantial premium. I could not help them, as my advice was not taken. It is our policy that if we cannot make the project work or the client is not willing to take advice, irrespective of the size of the project, we do not work with the client and walk away.

I understand that these property developers are now under administration. This was their only project.

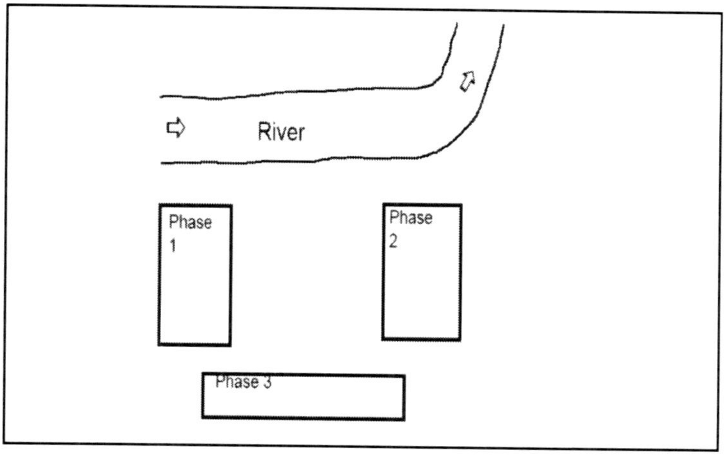

Diagram showing the three different phases. The building of Phase 2 first would stop the energy being pulled away by the river.

4. Water theme park.

An architect has a project of 100 acres which is about ten miles from the city. It has a man-made lake (100 by 20 metres) as a centrepiece, which offers water-based activities such as wind surfing using wind turbines, canoeing, kayaking, and a water adventure park with water chutes, luges and so on. Fifty houses have been built and put on the market on a sale and lease back scheme. Only one property has sold. Currently, the architect rents out these houses for visitors to the park. He raises revenue by renting these houses as accommodation for families wanting to use the park and by charging an entrance fee for day visitors.

In the plans for the next phase (Phase 2), the centrepiece will be a 20-acre man-made lake which will include a landing strip for sea-planes and water taxis

(Venetian style) to ferry people between the various parts of the park. Surrounding the park are houses and hotels suitable for family accommodation.

The architect has invested US$100 million on this project, which started five years ago. The architect is now seeking further funding for Phase 2. He had come to me at an inopportune time; the ideal time for a discussion on how to proceed would have been be at the very beginning of the project.

Description of the site and feng shui analysis

Phase 1. (completed) A man-made lake of about 100m by 20m, and houses built to the east of the lake.

Phase 2. (planned) Extend the lake to 20 acres, which would accommodate a sea plane landing strip with water taxis to ferry people to the various locations. A scuba diving area is also planned. There would be more houses, and the premium houses would be located on the peninsulae by the water. Most of the new houses are to be on the west side of the lake. A hotel with conference facilities and an entertainment complex are to be located at the end of the lake. These plans are ambitious.

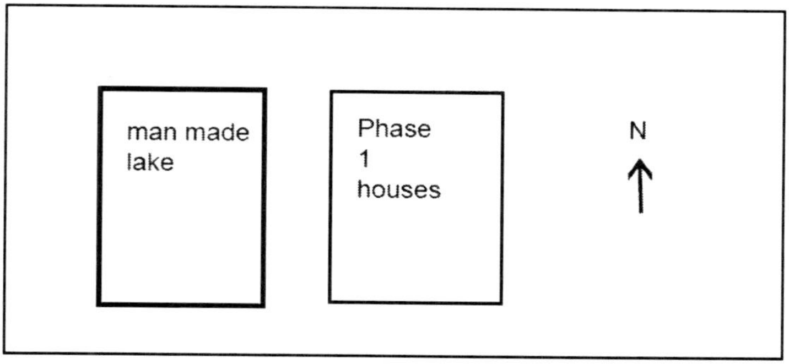

Diagram: Phase 1. (completed) – man-made lake and Phase 1 houses

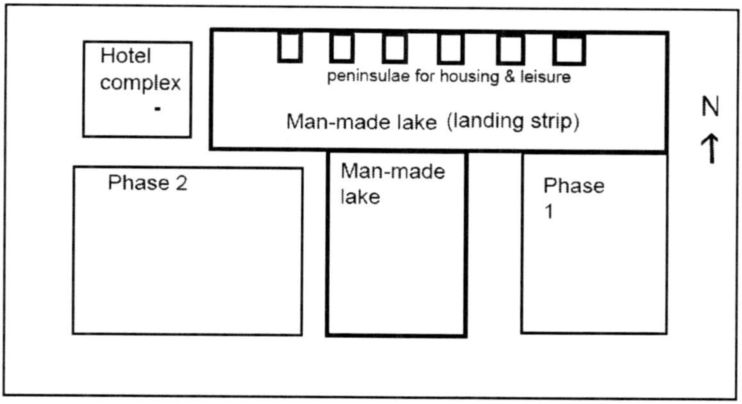

Diagram: Phase 2 – extension of the man-made lake and building and hotel complex. The small peninsulae are for premium housing and leisure facilities.

Phase 1 was carried out in Period 7 (1984-2004), when the predominant energy was from the West. The preferred side to build on is therefore on the west side of the lake. He had built the houses and the sales office on the east side. Hence the difficulty he had in selling the property.

We are now in Period 8 (2004-2024), in which the predominant energy is from the North East. The best place to build and sell property is therefore on the North East side of the water. He plans to build new property on the west side of the lake. The West side will not get the beneficial energy of the North East. He will encounter problems selling the properties, as before.

He did the right things but at the wrong time. In Period 7 (1984-2004), he should have developed the area to the West of the lake. Then in Period 8 (2004-2024), he should develop the area to the North East of the lake. The properties would have sold quickly. Hence the importance of consulting us at the earliest possible stage.

5. Pristine land by a lake (€200m)

An established property developer had acquired a 200 acre plot of pristine land by a lake adjacent to some mountains. This property developer specialises in preparing the infrastructure of the site then building and selling low to mid-priced houses. We were asked to make an assessment of the site.

The site was adjacent to a lake and the setting was really beautiful. This lake could be classed as a 'water dragon' because of certain features. This means that it is a really auspicious location. The beauty of the location would be spoilt by developing it into a housing estate.

We recommended that the area be developed as an estate for upmarket homes (more than €1 million) together with a hotel, spa and equestrian centre. With this set-up, the natural environment, including the trees, would be preserved. The houses were to be built around the trees.

The client baulked at this idea, as it was outside his comfort zone. He thought about it and then went for the idea of a joint venture with another developer who was familiar with upmarket houses, along with a hotel developer. The land could easily hold about a hundred exclusive homes, a hotel and spa, equestrian centre and other relevant amenities.

The environment there was really beautiful, and by this proposal, the properties would blend into the existing landscape easily because of the extremely low housing density. Each house would be individually designed, not only to blend in with the environment, but to be of benefit to the occupiers of the homes. The landscape feng shui of this site was incredible.

6. Hill residential estate (200 houses, detached and semi-detached)

A property developer, who had previously worked with us, had an option on a piece of land. He called us over to check whether it was suitable for a residential estate. This plot of land (nearly 50 acres) which included a complete hill, a lake and a stream.

After we carried out an assessment of the land, we discussed his aims for the project. He wanted a residential estate with facilities including retail outlets such as a grocery, bars, coffee shops and restaurants.

We agreed to a master plan for the site that fitted in with the aims and goals of the project.

In the master plan, the location of the entrance, the layout of the roads and the overall landscaping of the site were all taken into consideration, as were services such as water, electricity and a site for waste treatment facilities. The area was zoned for residential and commercial activities, such as retail units and the management and sales office. There were four types of house designs, and each design was then modified to the location for feng shui purposes, as well as the exact location of the properties and the pricing structure – the standard, premium and special locations.

The other important step in this procedure was the designation of the phases. Each phase was about allocating an area for the building and selling of the properties. But as each new building is constructed, it changes the environment, and this changes the pattern of the flow of the energy in that location. The phases were carefully planned so that whatever was built could be sold at the listed price. This maintains the vital cash flow for the project.

The site of the Sales Office was chosen and interiors were designed. The date to start the publicity, the groundwork and each phase were given.

We were in constant communication on the progress of the development. Checks were kept on the progress. The client sold all the property when about three quarters of the building work had completed. The pricing was about 8% above the market.

The client is completely satisfied with the success of the project. The project completed and there is ample return on the investment. He has his reputation enhanced and confidence strengthened.

7. Stepped condominiums on a mountainside

A property developer was proposing to build stepped condominiums, forty groups of ten units, on the mountainside. There was to be a business and entertainment area in the clubhouse of the golf course in the front or base of the mountain. The developer had noticed that a similar project had had difficulty selling the condominiums, so he called us.

The main problem with a development on a hillside is the downward flow of energy. It is job of the feng shui consultant to ensure that energy is retained in the development. When there is energy, the properties sell at the asking price and there is good well-being for the occupants of both the business and residential properties.

The original layout of the condominiums remained, but the following was altered to retain the energy.

1. The locations of the swimming pools were changed.
2. Roads were re-routed to minimise the downward flow of energy.
3. The business areas (restaurants, clubhouse and other public areas) were located in a position in which to capture the residual downward energy flow from the hill. This energy was used to the centre's benefit.

4. The Sales Office was re-located and a new entrance to the estate were found.

The properties in the project were completely sold at their asking price within two months.

8. Small town with golf courses

This €15 billion project was a 3,000 acre development that is a small town in itself, complete with a shopping mall, schools, hotels and residential areas (houses and condominiums), and a number of international championship golf courses.

We were originally hired to help sell two blocks of condominiums. We used the house selling formula to help sell the property. It completely sold within two months.

With the client suitably impressed, we were then asked to look at specific problems in the Business and Recreational zones in the central area. This included two hotels (a 3 star and a 5 star), offices, retail outlets and entertainment areas, which included bars, restaurants and clubs. The hotels were not getting the planned number of guests, nor were the other facilities getting sustainable business. There was some property that needed to be sold.

It was fortunate that this central area was not heavily built up. The layout of the roads were altered and the doors were re-positioned to accept the new pattern of energy flow. We changed the position of the road entrance to the town and altered the location of the sales office.

The business in the hotels and the business areas took off dramatically. This very much improved the finances and really pleased the client. The client told us that the residents of the 2,000 houses had been going out of the complex to facilities outside, because they were much cheaper. After the makeover of this central area, it became very attractive for the residents, even though the prices were much higher than the shops outside the complex.

This development was now in a good state. All the available residential property sold, the business and recreational centres, together with the hotels, were doing well, and the client wanted to move on. He then sold the remaining undeveloped land of this development project to other developers.

9. Hotel at a beach resort

The client, who had worked with us previously, had an option on a foreclosed building site for a hotel. She asked us for an opinion.

The building plot was an extremely well known beach resort, and the land value for the beach properties were astronomical. The beach-fronted properties were the first tier and were on the sea side of the beach road. The second tier were the properties on the land side of the beach road. The third tier were the properties behind the road side or behind second tier properties. It was really a 'lucky dip' situation, in which some properties in this location are successful and others are not. It is all about finding the energy flows, and then finding a plot for a building. We traced the energy flows. It so happens that the proposed building site receives this energy directly from the sea.

It comes through a small gap between two buildings, from the shoreline right to the building plot. We then checked whether the building plot included the land right up to the road; it did. The energy gap was on land that the clients owned.

The building plot had planning permission to build a 200-room hotel with conference facilities. So the question was: was it possible to modify the existing plan to utilise the energy from the energy gap? Unfortunately, it was not. New plans had to be drawn up.

We told the client that it was possible to build a successful hotel here, but the existing architectural plans for the hotel would have to be redrawn. She thought about it. None of the hotels nearby were doing good business. They were offering extremely high discounts, which lowered rooms rates in the area. This was very discouraging to our clients. The reason these hotels did not do well is because they did not get energy; the flow of energy was blocked by the other buildings which were nearer the sea. However, this proposed hotel would be getting a good flow of energy through that energy gap which was on her land. She knew that she had to keep the energy gap open at all times.

She had a new set of architectural plans drawn up based on our input. The main entrance could tap into the energy from the energy gap. There were subsidiary buildings behind the main block to trap and use the residual energy for the benefit of the business. The hotel was completed on time and on budget.

The interiors were laid out with similar care so that the energy could be distributed throughout the building, to the offices (management, sales, marketing, human resources), reception, bar, restaurant, café, gym and swimming pools.

The hotel is now operational with good occupancy rates, but charging a premium for its location. Its rates are way above the hotels in that location, but slightly higher than those of the second tier properties (hotels on the 'land side' of the beach road). She is extremely pleased with the results of the project.

The client said: "You have found a jewel in this cluster of buildings. I just do not know how to thank you for your contribution to this project."

10. Small plot of land in London

A property investor had made money in the rise of the property market in the UK in the 2000s. He just bought, refurbished and then sold property. He had a good return. He wanted to move up the league to be a real property developer, wanting to make even more money. He had found land that was previously occupied by a disused factory, but it was within a rectangle of existing properties. It had a narrow entrance, about four metres wide. He wanted to build three units of one-bedroom apartments, and he was looking for ways to improve the price. He had an option on the land. The planning authorities were willing to change the land use permit from an industrial site to a residential site. With the change, he would then have to get planning permission to build three apartments. He had done all the necessary homework, including the architecture fees and the construction costs. He wanted to get it right and justify the asking price. Having feng shui done was perceived as a method to justify the asking price. The main justification for the high price was the location near central London and easy access to the transport network. That would give the property investor a good return on his development.

I looked at the site and told him that I could not help him, as there was hardly any energy going into the site at all. There would be difficulty developing the site. The apartments would not be easy to sell and the occupants of these apartments would not have a good living environment.

He asked, "Is there any cure for this, or will you accept any payment to say that the site was designed with the aid of feng shui?"

I replied: "I cannot offer a solution, and it is best that I walk away from this project. Another feng shui consultant might have a different opinion, but this is my opinion. I only offer workable solutions."

I heard later that he had gained the necessary permission to develop the site, but that he had quite a few problems. He had problems in the construction of the building, but had even more problems trying to sell the units. As I heard, he is now renting out these properties. Obviously he did not get the quick return he wanted from the initial investment.

11. Designing a shopping complex

This project is from the shopping mall in Chapter 6. The client had problems with his shopping mall when a second mall in his town became operational. I had suggested that he pull down one of the multi-storey car parks that were blocking the entrance to his shopping mall. He did this and business improved. In the meantime, he received an offer for his old shopping mall and was interested in building a new one.

I asked him what the current situation was, and what the aims and goals of the project were.

“I have sold the old shopping mall and am planning to develop a brand new shopping complex for this town.”

“What sort of shopping complex do you want?”

“A modern design, but the business aims are very simple: to do good business for my tenants and for their customers. I want to target women and families. Men are not good shoppers; most of them do their shopping on the internet nowadays. I want it to be a shopping paradise for women, particularly young women from the middle market, very much like London’s Oxford Street, but ‘on steroids’.”

I asked him, “What type of design did you have in mind?”

“The modern design of a building by the junction. It stands out so that everybody can see it. The car parking is behind this building.”

“Have you any land in mind?”

“It is between two major junctions. It is large enough for expansion when the time comes.”

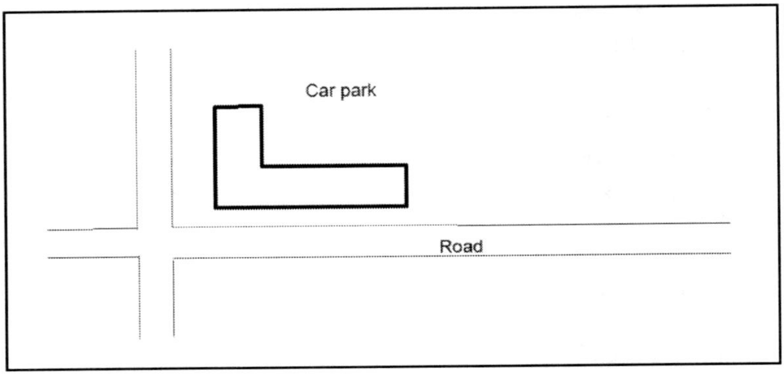

Diagram: initial layout suggested by the client.

I told him: “With your aims in mind, I would like to change the design of the building. You want it to be like Oxford Street in London ‘on steroids’; I will do that in the design.”

This design is a very simple building with the central hall running the East-West axis. The building would be about two-thirds of the way back, so that there can be a car park in the front and loading entrance at the back. We are talking about Phase 1, during which this building would cover half the plot and the remaining land would be used as a car park. Phase 2 of the development will cover the use of the remaining land, on which there could be an entertainment centre and a hotel with conference facilities.

The client wanted it to be like Oxford Street. The main shopping streets for the young and middle market are on streets that are on the East-West axis – Kensington High Street, King’s Road, Chelsea, Guildford High Street. The entrances face South, which will be capturing the pre-dominant energy from the South during the time period of 2024 to 2044. From the completion of this building to 2024, this predominant energy will be rising in quality. This shopping centre will be very busy for the next thirty years. It will give the client and his family a just reward for their investment.

The finer details of the positioning of the various types of shops would be considered – cosmetics, clothes, accessories, shoes and so on – as well as the management offices, grocery supermarket, food and beverages (coffee shops, café, restaurants and so on). Details of Phase 2 would be discussed later, but it was highly likely that there would be plans for car parks at the appropriate locations.

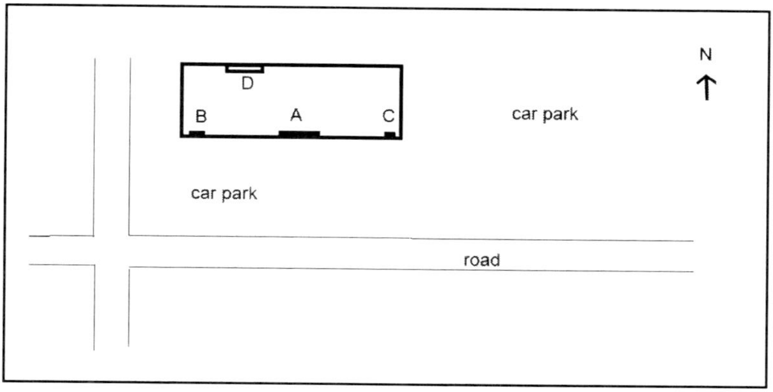

Diagram 2: the suggested layout of the third shopping complex. The doors facing the car park are A, B and C. The entrance for the loading bay is at D.

Work is in progress.

Chapter 8
Objections

Introduction

Feng shui only surfaced in the West in the late 1980s. The subject was warmly received initially, but scepticism set in when it spread to the main stream of the population.

1. *It is a method that has been used by the Chinese for centuries, but is new to people in the West. I will only use it when someone can explain how it works. I have to understand it in Western scientific terms.*

This happened when acupuncture was first introduced to the UK in the 1970s. There was a lot of scepticism. It is reproducible and it is now a standard procedure in the medical establishment, including the National Health Service in the UK, National Institute of Health in the USA, and the World Health Organisation.

We do not know the Western scientific version of how acupuncture works. Yet, based on empirical evidence or observation, it is now used extensively in the treatment of pain relief and often as a step in IVF (in-vitro fertilisation) treatment.

Science always starts with observations. When the observations are reproducible, a hypothesis is built around the observations and then tested. When all the tests have been verified, a theory is formed together with a mechanism for explanation. Western science is limited by its sphere of knowledge. If it is outside this sphere, if it cannot explain the reproducible observations, this does not mean it does not exist. Let us take the example of acupuncture. When you insert a needle at an established point in the skin, you get reproducible observation of pain relief. Because Western science cannot explain how it works, this does not mean that acupuncture does not work. Acupuncture works, but Western science cannot provide an explanation.

In my opinion, feng shui is in the unexplained stage as far as Western science is concerned. In my practice of traditional feng shui, I have found it reproducible and can explain the characteristics in terms of the energy.

2. There are so many versions of feng shui, I do not know which one to follow or believe. I am confused.

Yes, there are many versions of feng shui. This is part of a modern trend in which there is too much information; just look what happens to the debates on eco-conservation or climate change. There are so many opinions. It is the sign of the times. We have to deal with this by finding the truth and giving honest opinions.

This book describes the practice of traditional feng shui to create competitive advantage for our clients. I create advantage by helping design high performance buildings (superior or 'significantly above average performance'). These buildings provide far better returns for the owners than the average or industry norm. I do not disclose the identity of my clients and their buildings. Together, this creates a competitive advantage for my client.

Traditional feng shui was how feng shui was practised in the Imperial Court of the Chinese Emperor since AD 1500. These are five characteristic steps for practitioners of traditional feng shui:

- Be selected
- Trained in established methods
- Serve an apprenticeship
- Work in teams
- Follow strict rules

The practice of traditional feng shui is about using established methods that have been updated to cater for modern 21st Century living. Its forte is the selection of the location, design and building of properties, estates and towns.

3. *The New Age movement took the concept of feng shui to its heart as part of its philosophy. There are many Western people teaching and practising this subject, but where did they get this knowledge from? I have heard from Chinese friends that in the proper Chinese teaching system, training takes at least ten years to complete.*

Each to their own – hence there are so many variations of the practice of feng shui. It took me a long time to sort it out. I used my training as a forensic scientist and asked a very basic question – "Where does the information come from?" Is it credible, or is there some doubt? I had the advantage of being ethic Chinese, and I understand the Chinese mindsets and behaviour, which I outlined earlier. Hence the route of the learning that I have made.

I would not like to say where the 'New Age' followers got their information from, but there is a lot of similarity with the book *Feng Shui* by Sarah Rossbach, which is based on the teachings of Lin Yun. The Feng Shui Society in the UK offers a practitioner accreditation programme where they do basic checks on the person, their knowledge and their practice.

My training in traditional feng shui and Chinese philosophy has taken me more than ten years.

4. *Chinese practitioners and teachers of feng shui use different methods of feng shui. Is this confusing the market?*

What they practise and teach depends on which country they have learnt it in. The main countries, outside mainland China, that practise feng shui are Hong Kong, Malaysia and Singapore, and Taiwan. Each country has a different 'style' of practice, as it depends on the landscape or terrain and on the resulting expertise that comes from it.

Hong Kong has a very small land mass and the population is very dense. Most of the buildings there are high-rise buildings. The feng shui practice therefore concerns the interiors and the person's destiny (Chinese astrology). The practice is based on formulae (Flying Star feng shui and Four Pillars).

There is very little that can be done with the exteriors of a high-rise building that you live or work in.

In Malaysia and Singapore, where there is more outdoor space, feng shui practice is about exteriors together with interiors. As before, practice is based on formulae (Eight House and Flying Star feng shui) and some form feng shui.

In Taiwan, where the Masters had come from the Imperial Court in Beijing in the year 1949, the attitude is very different. Feng shui practice is based on form feng shui (or landscape feng shui). This feng shui is extremely difficult to learn and to get an interpretation correct initially. However, this type of feng shui can be applied in a wide variety of situations, from the interiors of property to the design of cities. Taiwan is the country where the various forms of Chinese philosophy (including feng shui) are taken extremely seriously. However, there are very few feng shui practitioners in Taiwan who speak English.

Are you saying that the feng shui from Taiwan is the best?

Not quite. Every methodology has its own characteristics. Some are specific for residential or business. It depends on the application. The main characteristic of Hong Kong, Malaysia and Singapore feng shui is that the property is dealt with in isolation from the rest of the city, whereas with the Taiwanese system, every building on the street, every street in the city is one large eco-system. Everything in the city interacts with everything else.

It was my aim to be a specialist in the designing of building and cities using established methodology which was reproducible and results oriented. Hence my search for a feng shui Master from Taiwan.

There are quite a number of feng shui teachers in the West (Canada, the US, the UK and Germany). It is possible to identify the country that is the source of their information from the type of feng shui they teach. Then again, some feng shui practitioners use Taoist practices. I do not know anything about these.

5. *Potential clients want to know whom I have worked for or see the buildings that I have worked on.*

We have a confidentiality agreement with our clients. We are very much like medical doctors and lawyers, who keep their clients' confidentiality a top priority.

When we start working with you, the confidential information of a lot of companies will surface in the conversation or the dealings. We will start to learn about your business and its workings, the function, the moving lines and so on. We will also learn a lot about you personally. This is all confidential information, very much like the medical or the legal professions. A doctor does not disclose a patient's information to others.

We just want to let you know where we stand.

6. *Why do you work in teams when everybody else works alone?*

The team structure consists of two seniors, who currently have more than seven decades of combined experience. Other members each have at least two decades of working in the feng shui business at various levels.

Working as a team on larger project, the workflow is faster; there is also continuity between the members. Should anything happen to the lead consultant, the project can be handed over smoothly. There are projects that can last from ten to twenty years.

A team also creates a pool of experience: solutions to problems that crop up can be solved quickly and correctly from this collective experience. The seniors are always available to give an opinion of the work done and provide a checking mechanism.

7. I have not heard of you, are you any good?

You might not have heard of us when compared to the high profile feng shui authors and consultants. We are specialists. We specialise in working on the design of buildings and cities, finding new properties and correcting a problem in an existing building. As in the medical profession, specialists do the more challenging projects. Members of our teams have been working on this in various parts of the world for the past 50 years. In fact, we are the only team in the world that is operational.

8. What happens if it does not work?

Do doctors and lawyers give guarantees?

It is our ethos to work to the client's best interests, but also to give the client remarkable value from the results of our work.

However, to achieve that, there is a strict procedure prior to doing any work.

- A meeting with the client to determine whether we could work together.
- Establish the aims and goals of the proposed project.
- Assessment of the site to the client's objectives.
- Discussion of the manner in which the work is to be carried out.
- Agreement and instructions on the work that is to be carried out.

Should the client state that the anticipated results were not achieved, our first reply would be, "Were the instructions followed precisely?" The most important instruction is the time and date to start digging for carrying out the preparation of the earth. If this is not followed precisely, we normally walk away from the project.

In general, the first time we work with a new client, it would be a minor project such as a remedial or selecting a new property. It is unlikely to be a project such as the design of a new building or city. We have to establish a relationship first, and to understand the ways in which both parties work.

9. Is there an additional cost, or can you prove that it can increase a client's bottom line?

Yes, there is an additional cost, but what is the return of this additional investment?

Our usual fee is between 0.5 to 2.0% of the development project.

We go through the procedure with you as described in Chapter 7. The main benefits of this procedure are:

- Help you avoid delays.
- Smooth the progress of the projects.
- Help you to keep within the budget.
- It helps move your inventory faster – four to six months ahead of projected sales.*
- Residential properties sell at a 5% premium in comparison to other similar property developments.*

*(Figures obtained from US clients on residential developments, landed and high rise development projects.)

This has given our clients an increase of 5% gross profit in spite of the 2% fee. This does not include establishing your reputation, and with the success comes less stress, more confidence and more time to spend with your family, for leisure or to create more opportunities.

Surely these results justify the extra costs?

10. Feng shui is Eastern mumbo jumbo or "only Asians use it".

I have used the analogy of algebra to answer this objection. The Arabs "discovered" it, but you do not need to be an Arab to understand or use algebra.

Traditional feng shui was established in China. It is a system of land management based on empirical observations of the interaction of nature and people. These are based on countless observations over many centuries. This is applicable to all parts of the world and to all people. In fact, it has been used by clients from all parts of the world, including Europe, North and South America, South Africa, the Middle East, Australia, New Zealand, and of course East Asia. The clients of the various nationalities made their decisions on business criteria. In fact, there are a number of Fortune corporations and major international retailers who use these methods.

Traditional feng shui originated in China; hence the methodologies are based on Chinese nomenclature. An example is traditional Chinese medicine – acupuncture and acupressure – which is used throughout the world.

11. Not many people use it, or I have not heard about it, or successful companies do not use it.

In the practice of traditional feng shui, the consultant or the team does not list or mention their clients unless the client chooses to do so. That is probably why you have not heard about the use of this practice.

I understand that a number of the largest corporations for the last few decades in North America and Europe have used traditional feng shui. However, it is common knowledge that Singapore had the city designed on feng shui principles, and so have a number of corporations in Singapore and the Far East.

12. It is not modern or I am very religious; I do not use superstitious activities.

Traditional feng shui is a Chinese system of land management. It is about the energies in the environment or the forces of Nature interacting with man. It does not involve religion, superstition or a belief system. It is about understanding the interaction of the forces of Nature and Man.

13. "I'm familiar with feng shui from other projects. It doesn't work."

There are many people practising feng shui. I personally do not know how many types of feng shui there are.

We practise traditional feng shui; this was how feng shui was practised in the Imperial Court of the Chinese Emperor since the 16th Century. We work in teams and specialise in projects that involve the design of buildings and development projects which include master planning, architectural and landscape design.

The practice of traditional feng shui has been around for centuries in China and for decades in the rest of the world. What we do is based on knowledge and practices derived centuries ago and updated to the modern lifestyle of the 21st Century. If these methods did not work, the practice would not be in existence today. All our team members are selected and trained in the established procedures.

14. It is just for homes; it is about placing trinkets and moving furniture around.

There are currently many people practising under the name of feng shui and they work specifically on people's homes. I have heard that some use the placement of trinkets and moving of furniture. I do not know much about their knowledge base and practices, and I am therefore unable to comment.

I am a specialist in a different sector of the market. I help companies solve their problems. This could mean helping them to find new locations for their properties, or to improve existing buildings. I work with property development companies designing new buildings or estates so that they can completed on time and on budget, selling properties at a premium to the market and ahead of schedule.

15. It's just for helping people who are having trouble in existing properties.

We can help clients who are having trouble with their existing properties, but this is subject to inspection of the property. But we also help clients in the selection of new locations for their businesses and in the design of buildings. Then, there are development projects that include master planning, architectural and landscape design.

16. Isn't feng shui just a type of interior design?

In the past 50 years, we have seen the dramatic growth of feng shui in the West. Many types of feng shui have evolved. These deal with interior design, symbols, spiritual, garden, jewellery, gardens, kitchens, food, symbols (from the Chinese pantheon), watches, furniture, household items, lighting, paintings and so on. Interior designers promoted the interior design

aspect of feng shui in an attempt to differentiate themselves in the market.
I concentrate on using traditional feng shui to create competitive advantage for my clients. This is the subject of this book.

17. My development projects are always successful. Why do I need to incorporate feng shui?

It depends how you define the word 'successful'. There is always room for improvement, and you always have the ability to do better. I can help to improve your bottom line and save you money. Let us take an example using information based on our work on residential properties (landed or high-rise) in the USA. Our client's properties sold at a premium of 5% to the other comparable properties in that area. The properties also sold four to six months ahead of projected sales. This yielded a gross profit of at least 5% higher than expected.

I can help smooth the progress of the project and avoid delays. I can also help avoid lawsuits, help make your employees more comfortable and avoid them having health issues. This does not include establishing your reputation, and with success comes less stress, more confidence and more time to spend with your family, or for leisure, or to create more opportunities.

Is this a major leap in the word 'successful'?

18. I believe that success is based on hard work – why do I need feng shui?

Do you drive a car? A car is a tool which helps your solve a problem. It helps you get from point A to point B faster and safer.

Traditional feng shui is also tool. It helps property developers complete their projects on time and on budget, and also to sell their properties at a premium and ahead of schedule.

Chapter 9

Conclusion

This is an overview of how the various problems we have encountered that can be solved using the techniques of traditional feng shui.

The Problems

Business in the building does not perform to expectation.

For example:

- Retail outlet:
    - Restaurant business is quiet, with few customers.
    - Shop is empty most of the time and customers do not make many purchases.
- Corporate office: the business struggles and has poor staff morale.
- Hotel: low occupancy rate with poor service.
- Office building: not filled with tenants.
- Shopping centre: partially occupied with tenants but with a number of vacant lots. It is not busy and hardly any shoppers are making purchases.

This is particularly apparent when all the adjacent or neighbouring properties are doing well and you are not. You are in a surrounded by a sea of prosperity.

Sales of residential and business properties:

The properties are difficult to sell, or have to be sold with a substantial discount.

The ideal situation:

Business: The business in the property does well. This business is always doing well irrespective whether the adjacent businesses are doing well or not. This is irrespective of where it is located - in the prosperous part of town or impoverished neighbourhood; in a successful city or a failing town.

Sales: The properties are sold at or above the asking price and ahead of schedule.

The solutions

There are three ways to solve the above problems.

- Select a building in a new location.
- The building may require either minor remedial work or a major renovation to bring it up to a high performance standard.
- Develop a new building with high performance characteristics. This starts with the selection of the site and the procedure is described below.

These are the steps to achieving a high performance property.

We normally start with an assessment of the project and the site. This gives the consultant clarity over whether we can help the clients or not. It is our unambiguous policy that the first priority is the success and interests of the client's project. We do not take on a job for the sake of taking on a job. It is our reputation that matters.

The services

1. Assessment of the project and site.
2. Looking for a property in a new location.
3. Minor remedial work.
4. Making major renovations.
5. Development projects.

1. Assessment of project and site

This is the first step in the relationship with the client. This allows the consultant to have a look at the site with regard to the aims and goals of the client. This will give the consultant an idea of the expectations of the client. It is also the opportunity to qualify the project and the client.

Examples in Chapter 6 (Case Studies – Part 1):

- Case study 1 – shopping mall and multi-storey car parks.
- Case study 3 – the unfocused hotel.
- Case study 4 – to invest in a café or a chef?
- Case study 5 – hotel and restaurant up the hill.
- Case study 7 – two restaurants and one kitchen.

2. Looking for a property in a new location

Not all properties are the same. Those that are near the flow of energy are of particular interest and have a high chance of business success. The consultant will work from a shortlist of six to eight locations provided by the client. These are properties deemed suitable by the client for their purposes. A suitable site is only recommended when it fulfills the criteria of the consultant, not because it is the best on the list. When no recommendation can be made from the first list, a second list is requested.

The property might need minor remedial work, such as the repositioning of an entrance, or creating a new door. There could be some alterations to the landscaping.

These are some of the steps taken with the client.

a. Assessment of the owner's goals and aims.
b. Assessment of the building.
c. Design guidelines for the architect or interior designer.
d. Date selection for best time to begin the interior work.
e. Date selection for the best time to start business in the new location.

Examples in Chapter 6 (Case Studies – Part 1):

- Case study 6 – selection of retail outlet in a shopping mall.
- Case study 8 – tapas bar.
- Case study 9 – selection of a house.

3. Minor remedial work

Remedial work is one of the appropriate courses of action when a building is not performing. This action will only be suggested when appropriate remedial work can be done to improve the situation, but not otherwise. This could be the creation of a door to allow energy to get into the building. It just depends on the location of the building and the flow of the energy.

These are some of the steps taken with the client.

a. Assessment of the owner's goals and aims.
b. Assessment of the building.
c. Initial design guidelines for the architect or interior designer.
d. Date selection for best time to begin work.

Examples in Chapter 6 (Case Studies – Part 1):

- Case study 2 – hotel by the river.
- Case study 10 – hotel with two sets of doors.
- Case study 12 – residential estate in a championship golf course.

4. Major renovations

A client's building is to be renovated to a new level of specifications and facilities as drawn up by the interior designer or architect in conjunction with the consultant. The purpose is to take the building to new levels of performance.

These are some of the steps taken with the client.

a. Assessment of the owner's goals and needs.

b. Assessment of the building.
c. Initial design guidelines for the architect or interior designer.
d. Initial landscaping recommendations.
e. Participation with the design team and review of building and landscape plans.
f. Input into materials, colours, furniture and object placement.
g. Date selection for best time to begin work.

5. Development project.

The consultant is involved from the start to the completion of the project.

The benefits of using the procedure:

- The development project completes on time and on budget.
- The properties have been sold at a premium of about 5% and six months ahead of schedule.
- The completed building will have high performance. For example, a hotel with an occupancy rate of 80%, office buildings that are occupied by tenants, shops that are filled with shoppers making purchases.

These are some of the steps taken with the client.

a. Assessment of the owner's goals and needs.
b. Assessment of the building site, including site selection.
c. Initial feng shui design guidelines for the architect.
d. Initial landscaping recommendations.

e. Participation with the design team and review of building and landscape plans
f. Input into materials, colours, furniture and object placement.
g. Assist in the sales process.
h. Date selection for best time to begin work.

The whole of Chapter 7 is devoted to examples of this process.

Competitive advantage – a service of exceptional value.

Competitive advantage is defined as the strategic advantage one business entity has over its rival entities within its competitive industry. Achieving competitive advantage strengthens and positions a business better within the business environment. In most cases, competitive advantage is eroded with time, as the competition works out how the advantage can be challenged.

As stated in the Introduction, using examples from the pharmaceutical industries, financial services and advanced technology sector, gaining competitive advantage is both capital intensive and time sensitive. However, in the case of using traditional feng shui, it is different; the advantage gained lasts as long as the competitors do not realise how the advantage has been gained. They only think along the standard industry lines and not outside the box. When you look down the list of Fortune corporations or the FTSE companies, some of the corporations appear to be fixtures, being at the top for more than seven decades. Whatever they do is right. There is a normal life cycle for these corporations, but the rules appear to be changed for these ‘special’ corporations. Then a new corporation comes long, seemingly appearing from nowhere, and their growth outperforms their competitors in that market sector. Many ask, “How do they do it?”.

In this case, the advantage is created by using the methods of traditional feng shui. There are different benefits to different types of clients.

1. Multiple retailer or hotel chain.

A building that has been designed with traditional feng shui becomes a ‘high performance building’, the definition of ‘high performance’ being superior or “significantly above average performance”. These building provide far better returns for their owners than the average or industry norm.

Retail outlet: there are more customers and more purchases (by value) per customer.

Hotel: I have observed the occupancy rate to be about 80%. This is considered by many experienced hoteliers to be the optimal rate between financial return, staffing levels and maintenance levels to the building.

2. Property developers.

The three major problems are:

- Can the project be completed on time and on budget?
- Can it be sold at the asking price, and when?
- The business outcome of commercial building is uncertain. Can an office building get tenants? What will the hotel occupancy rate be like? In retail shops, will customers make purchases?

What are the results?

- For residential developments, the project was completed on time and on budget, the developer sold at a 5% premium about six months ahead of schedule. This gave the developer an increase of 5% gross profit for the project.
- For commercial buildings, these have a reputation for the tenants doing extremely good business. The tenants stay and are willing to pay premium rent.
- I have found that hotels have occupancy rates of about 80%, office buildings are filled with tenants, and retail shops are filled with customers making purchases.

Competitive advantage

This part of competitive advantage is about information not being released to the public domain.

- The team that worked on the building will not disclose it.
- The clients, wanting to maintain competitive advantage, are unlikely to disclose it.
- Traditional trained consultants work on the project to identify the features in the building. Would they make this identification known to the public? It is unlikely.

For the first twenty years, this competitive advantage is maintained. This information is kept highly confidential within the corporation and no one realises the purpose of the key design elements required by the traditional feng shui consultants in the building. The buildings are upgraded to be in keeping with the current development of the corporation. These key design elements are forgotten and subsequently modified. As a result, the performance of the corporation deteriorates. In other words, it is the corporation destroying its own competitive advantage out of ignorance rather than anything else.

More about the advantage: traditional feng shui

Traditional feng shui in its current form originated in AD 1500, in the Court of the Imperial Palace of the Chinese Emperor. The main features are:

- All potential students are carefully selected. The Masters are looking for candidates who are good at working with clients and solving their problems. They will also have the mindset of putting the client's interests and project success above everything else.
- All students are trained in the established methods, which have been updated to the modern 21st Century lifestyle.
- The apprentice can learn and gain experience from a range of projects. He can also see how the clients are handled with our priority – the success of the project and the interests of the clients.
- Working in teams results in faster workflow, together with quick access to experience and expertise in any situation.

- Strict rules are enforced for discipline and maintaining our reputation for putting our priority into the success of the project and the interests of the clients.

Having seen so many projects blossom to highly successful buildings and businesses, I can see the benefits of using this methodology. It is exceptional value based on the amount paid for the services relative to the return of the project. However, the methods of traditional feng shui are not known outside the traditional feng shui community. Buildings designed with traditional feng shui do not appear any different from any other building. They are extremely difficult to identify. The features are very inconspicuous. Only a traditionally trained consultant will recognise it, after a careful study of the building. The names of the clients are always kept confidential.

Therefore, to sum up, these are some of the suggestions:

Multiple retailers

Multiple retailers are located in the high street, shopping malls, shopping parks or their own sites (where the supermarkets are located).

In the first three instances, we can help in the selection process, particularly the best possible location. The best results are for the shopping parks and their own sites, because we can design the necessary landscaping to bring the energy into the store.

Observations

I have seen so many examples of different types of shops being placed at their appropriate locations, and it works beautifully. An example is with coffee shops; they get the most business when they are at street junctions. This can be seen in London and other parts of South-East England. I noticed that when an American brand started here, it only had its outlets at street corners and it started to grow extremely rapidly.

At the other end of the retail spectrum, a (then second largest) retailer used traditional feng shui on its branches. Within a few years, it became the market leader. It still is.

Hotels

There are three options.

1. Taking over an existing hotel.
2. Refurbishing a hotel.
3. Developing a new hotel.

1. Taking over an existing hotel

The best time for the assessment is either before or during the negotiations on a hotel. The client will already have the hotel's details. This will add to the information on the hotel building. The assessment will give information on whether the hotel can be improved at nominal cost or whether it requires a total refurbishment. The assessment might come out with a negative comment. Do remember that our first priority is the success of the project and the client's interests. We do not take on a job for the sake of taking on a job.

2. Refurbishing a hotel

An industry procedure is to refurbish the hotel on taking over. There are a number of reasons and these include, updating the interiors and exteriors to the new requirements of the owners or management, improve the image particularly, particularly after the wear and tear over the years of hosting the guests. This is a good opportunity to check whether the performance of the hotel can be improved. Can new sources of energy from the exteriors be brought into the building?

3. Developing a new hotel

This is the method of choice, as all the right characteristics can be incorporated at the design stage. This is done at all levels: landscaping, exterior and interior design.

Observations

I have observed that hotels designed with traditional feng shui have an occupancy rate of about 80%. The owners of the building and the senior management are pleased.

I have noticed the systematic development of hotel chains from the Far East (Hong Kong and Singapore), which are extending their properties to the various countries outside their region to the West (Europe, the Middle East and North America). Some of the hotel chains have incorporated these methods in the development of new hotel properties.

Property developers

This methodology is the ideally suited to property developers. This method reduces your risk, as you can sell at a premium and ahead of schedule. Using figures from some residential projects, the properties sell at a 5% premium in comparison to other similar property developments, and sold four to six months ahead of projected sales, resulting in a 5% gross profit increase. The project completes on time and within budget.

Should you be in commercial property, and should you be able to provide buildings that have an excellent track record of tenants doing tremendous business, you will be constantly oversubscribed.

I have heard that a particular residential estate development in East London did not have feng shui incorporated in the site. Visits from prospective buyers from China are less than half the number of visits to other sites in London said to incorporate feng shui.

Property investors

We can identify the following to your benefit:

1. Underperforming buildings in which there will be no performance improvements after countless refurbishments.
2. Underperforming buildings in which there will be a significant improvement in performance after a refurbishment.
3. The design and development of buildings incorporating traditional feng shui features that will be perform exceptionally well.

Observations

This is one way to stand above your competitors. They will not know why you are getting such good results!

Facing Illness

Edited by
Nigel Collinson and David Matthews

EPWORTH PRESS

Proceeds from this book
will be shared between

*The Jerusalem Orphanage
in Addis Ababa, Ethiopia*

and

*The Special Care Baby Unit of
the John Radcliffe Hospital
Oxford.*

British Library Cataloguing in Publication Data

Facing illness.
1. Sick—Psychology 2. Adjustment
(Psychology)
I. Collinson, Nigel II. Matthews, David
362.1'96 R726.5

ISBN 0-7162-0427-4

First published 1986
by Epworth Press
Room 195, 1 Central Buildings,
Westminster, London SW1H 9NR

Typeset by Gloucester Typesetting Services
and printed in Great Britain by
Richard Clay Ltd
Bungay, Suffolk

CONTENTS

This book is the result of a series of meetings held at Green College, Oxford in 1985 and 1986. The participants and contributors were:

Dr David Birch	General Practitioner
The Revd Nigel Collinson	Minister of Wesley Memorial Church, Oxford
Dr Michael Davies	General Practitioner
Dr Adrian Grant	Perinatal Epidemiologist
Dr George Johnson	Regional Medical Officer
Dr Winifred Lloyd	General Practitioner
Dr David Matthews	Joan and Richard Doll Senior Research Fellow at Green College, and Honorary Consultant Physician
Sir John Walton	Warden of Green College, President of the General Medical Council and President of the Royal Society of Medicine.

PREFACE

by Sir John Walton

This book has the express aim of helping all of us who may, from time to time, become ill and who therefore need to seek medical help and advice. And it is also intended as an aid to those who may find the burden of illness in a loved one perplexing, demanding and perhaps even difficult to bear. Prepared by a group of doctors working in different branches of medicine, in collaboration with a minister of religion, it attempts to pose many of the questions which arise when illness strikes any one of us or a member of our family, either briefly, or over a longer period, and goes on to give answers to most, if not all, of them. Special attention is paid to chronic, progressive, or incurable illness.

The different chapters deal with topics such as the definition of illness, limits of medical knowledge, communication between doctors and patients, the organization and delivery of medical care in the hospital and in the community, and then go on to discuss the very special problems posed by illness and handicap in childhood. The approach to these complex and sensitive issues is enlivened and illuminated throughout by the Christian ethic and it is therefore proper that subjects such as miracles, prayer, death and bereavement should be considered.

While I have been involved from the beginning in the discussions which led to the initial concept and the subsequent emergence and development of this volume, I am not an author of any of the chapters and therefore feel able to say that the topics discussed here in depth are, in my view, handled with remarkable clarity, compassion and sensitivity but yet commendable objectivity. This book is a thoughtful, comprehensive guide to the personal problems and dilemmas

which illness often brings to individuals and to their relatives and friends. It will be especially helpful to committed Christians but even those lacking religious beliefs and convictions could not, I believe, fail to derive comfort and support from the advice it contains. It deserves a very wide audience.

Introduction

In the days when only rather primitive medicine was available, people no doubt developed a fatalistic attitude to illness. They accepted that it might rob them not only of their health but also of their livelihood and their home. They could not do much about it. Human growing and dying were accepted as part of the natural way of things.

Modern medicine has gone a long way towards prizing human life away from the cycle of nature. Men and women still get sick and die and serious illness is always significant. But it does not necessarily mean the end of everything. On the contrary, we get more and more used to hearing about the miracles of modern medicine.

But we are still working – and living – within limits. Illness can strike at any moment. Then we are faced with age-old questions. Then we show the best of which we are capable, and sometimes the worst! And it is then that we are faced with the down-to-earth problems of organizing ourselves, or helping others to cope with being in hospital or being 'on the sick list' at home.

It is to help those facing illness that this book is written. We have been concerned primarily with those who care for the sick – the parent, the son or daughter, the neighbour or friend. After all, these people bear a major part of the burden of illness and often are fearful, perplexed and alone.

But inevitably the discussion spills over into what it is like for the patient also. That is unavoidable in dealing with a subject like illness. Illness cannot be contained easily. That is part of its problem. The way illness affects the patient shapes its impact upon the one who cares, indeed upon the whole family. Likewise, the attitudes of the people who do the caring have a profound effect upon the way

the patient faces up to things.

Over a period of about a year, a group of us, seven doctors and a minister of religion, all members of the same Oxford congregation, met in Green College next to Oxford's Radcliffe Infirmary, to share our thoughts about 'Facing Illness'.

We offer this book, aware of its limitations, in the hope that it will be a source of support and some understanding to those who face illness. The Christian faith encourages us to bear one another's burdens. We believe that illness can be borne together, for all that it is a personal experience, and that out of that corporate burden can come joy and peace. At its heart, this book is about the way in which God heals, not by 'the extraordinary miracle', but through the miracles of modern knowledge and the capacity of ordinary people to respond to adversity with courage, openness and caring.

We would like to thank Miss Rachel Church for typing some of the script, Mrs Sheila Davies for her contribution to the chapter on Handicapped Children and Mrs Clare Matthews for editing the type-script and for substantial contributions to the text.

1 · What is Illness?

At its simplest level, the question 'What is illness?' does not need an answer. We all know what it is. We all become ill at times. We suffer from coughs and colds, from 'flu and chicken pox, from corns and ingrowing toenails. Illness is a natural process - it is a biological response to something going wrong and it is part of our biology. But although it is 'natural' in that sense, it does not mean that we therefore like it. We much prefer to be healthy!

But there is another level at which the question 'What is illness?' is much more difficult to answer. For illness is not just a state of our body, it is also a state of mind. We all know of those who will take time off work as being 'sick' with a cold, while others afflicted by the same germ will soldier on with daily life as though nothing were wrong. The difference between the two is that one actively suffers the unease or 'dis-ease' while the other chooses to disregard it. The borderline between what we regard as health or illness can change with our emotions or with our awareness of normality. There is a huge industry devoted to influencing our ideas of normality. Is dandruff a disease? When does being plump turn into being fat? When should you go on a diet? Should you exercise regularly? Can you eat E101 or E110 without developing allergic reactions? These sorts of questions are not trivial. General practioners may spend a lot of their time trying to reassure healthy people that the amount of sleep they are getting is 'normal' and that they do not have insomnia, or that the number of times they go to the lavatory is 'normal' and that they do not have constipation. We all get anxious about many things. When does this become 'an anxiety state'? To a large extent we have to define *for ourselves* what we are going to regard as illness. To take a trivial example, acne is a problem that afflicts many

teenagers. Which of us has got to twenty-one without a few spots? Only a few worried individuals will go to their doctor and ask for treatment, and then most doctors will need convincing that the acne is more than just a nuisance – that it is a 'problem'. But once convinced, the doctor will take it seriously. Acne, like so many illnesses these days, is treatable.

We may be too ready to define trivial problems as 'illness': but there is a converse side to this. For to be uncomplaining is one thing, but to be too stoical is also a mistake. We have to decide when a spot on our skin might need expert attention, or when our tummy-ache seems more serious than usual. One GP reviewed the cases that he had been called out to see at night time, and thought that as many as nine out of ten were trivial problems. But he also reckoned that he had only once ever been called out when the patient *knew* the problem was trivial. So we all have to educate ourselves to make a balanced decision. And that may not be easy for us or, indeed, for those around us, whom we can easily label 'neurotic' (i.e. goes to the doctor too often!) or 'cavalier' (i.e. does not go to the doctor when he needs to!).

Nor is it just a question of whether someone *takes notice of* their illness: it is also a question of what frame of mind they adopt towards it. A doctor tells of an ebulliently good-humoured man whom he saw in an outpatient clinic. This man had had both his legs amputated at the knee after an accident several years before. The doctor commented on his remarkable cheerfulness in the face of such a severe disability. 'Oh, it doesn't affect my life', the patient rejoined, 'and would it bring my legs back if I were miserable all the time?'

So although health is the desired norm, it is nevertheless possible to keep our essential 'wholeness' – the best of our personality – even if our bodies are not all they should be. If we can face illness without anger, recrimination, fear or bitterness, then we can minimize the 'dis-ease'. If we can find positive or humorous aspects to our afflictions, then, paradoxically, our wholeness may increase despite infirmities of the body. William Barclay, the famous Scottish theologian, became very deaf in his later years, but he pointed out that this was a great advantage in church when there was a boring sermon – he could just switch off his hearing-aid and think his own thoughts. Howard Booth has put forward the interesting idea that if health is really more to do with what we *are* than with what is

going wrong with our bodies, then it is actually possible to die healthily.

Indeed death must be regarded as part of our genetic make-up. We are 'programmed' to die, and the Psalmist made a good approximation of our longevity as three-score years and ten (Psalm 90) with an extension of ten years if we were lucky. The body is a self-healing organism, so that if you cut yourself it will heal in a few days. In theory, therefore, we ought to be able to live indefinitely, but we do not: ageing is inevitable and cannot be 'cured'. We live only within the bounds of a natural cycle of birth and death.

But illness can still be regarded as a taboo subject. It arouses many emotions – fear, resentment, passivity (the idea that 'it is God's will'), or even refusal to accept the reality of the illness. The sick person can become disorientated, tearful and difficult to live with. Relationships can become broken, or strained to the limit. There are new and great pressures on those who look after and visit the sick person – there are practical problems, emotional problems and even theological or philosophical problems to be faced. And it is to these problems that the rest of the book is devoted.

*

Near the Sheep Gate in Jerusalem there is a pool with five porches; in Hebrew it is called Bethzatha. A large crowd of sick people were lying in the porches – the blind, the lame, and the paralysed. A man was there who had been ill for thirty-eight years. Jesus saw him lying there, and he knew that the man had been ill for such a long time; so he asked him, 'Do you want to get well?'

John 5.2–6 (Good News Bible)

2 · *The Limits of Knowledge*

Introduction

Medical knowledge has expanded vastly in recent years. We have moved, in the course of half a century, from the most rudimentary understanding of disease to a state where most important functions of the body are comprehended in intricate detail by many specialist disciplines. Anatomy, histology, physiology, biochemistry, biophysics and genetic engineering have expanded our horizons, and intervention is now possible with highly sophisticated medical and surgical treatments.

'Modern medicine', as we know it, had its birth in the 1940s and expanded in the 1950s to provide a huge armoury of specific therapies for all common serious ailments: antibiotics for infections, steroids for skin problems and some 'rheumatic' diseases, anti-cancer drugs and surgery, control of the working of the heart by drugs, control of pain, and so on. Understanding of the body's hormone mechanisms led to the development of the contraceptive pill and understanding the electrical working of the heart led to pacemakers.

The result has been a change of attitude among both doctors and patients. Doctors began to expect that with careful effort it would become possible to diagnose all medical problems and that most would be treatable. Patients, in their turn, began to assume that all illness could be cured. Indeed, we live now in a society where there is an expectation of 'limited immortality' – we feel that nothing can go wrong with our bodies between the age of seven and a half minutes and seven and a half decades that cannot be rectified. We still accept accidental death, but death from disease we regard with horror, disbelief and anger. In the United States of America now, litigation from relatives may follow any 'unexpected' death or complication

of illness. One gynaecologist, early in 1986, announced that he was giving up his practice. He had been successfully cleared from five consecutive suits filed against him, but he was spending more time in the courts than in the hospital.

But medical science is not all-knowing, and vast gaps in our knowledge still remain. In a book such as this, it is well that we catch a glimpse of the doctor's approach to illness and at least try to come to terms with these gaps and with their implications. In this chapter we discuss some of the uncertainties that remain about disease, the problems associated with medical treatment, and the longer-term consequences for those who are ill and those who try to look after them.

Limited knowledge about the illness

Medical advice is usually first sought because someone is not feeling well or has noticed something unusual about himself. Doctors use any of three ways to try to find out what is wrong. They may ask questions about the problem – 'Where is the pain?' – 'What sort of pain is it?'; they may make a physical examination – 'Does it hurt here?'; or may organize special tests – 'I think you need an X-ray'. In some cases the cause of the illness is obvious – you have got an infection in your ear – your leg is broken – and appropriate treatment is organized. But in many cases the cause is not clear and on the strength of the information which he has collected the doctor has to decide whether it is serious or not. He may decide that there is no serious cause. Many feelings of being unwell – such as general tiredness perhaps, or backache – tend to disappear of their own accord without their underlying reason ever being known. Alternatively, further tests may be arranged or someone else's advice sought.

There are situations when even after prolonged investigation the true nature of an illness remains unclear. This may apply to non-specific complaints such as general malaise or persistent tummy-ache (where one cannot pinpoint the site of the illness or the cause of it) or more specific problems such as repeated miscarriage. There are times when little is apparently done in the way of treatment, and when doctors may find it difficult to discuss the problem with the patient or relatives. Some people – both doctors and patients – find it very hard to accept that a doctor 'does not know'.

At other times, uncertainty may exist about the extent of an illness rather than its cause. Without knowledge of this the choice of

treatment may be difficult. Heart disease and cancer are common examples. Doctors may advise many investigations for chest pains simply to delineate the extent of the problem, and even then may remain uncertain as to whether to advise surgery, medications or a different life-style. Cancer can spread insidiously in the body, and there are only limited ways of tracking its course.

Limited knowledge about the treatment

Many standard treatments, such as insulin for diabetes, are highly effective. Some may lead to complete recovery – antibiotics for infection, or removal of the appendix for appendicitis. Others, although the best available, may be less satisfactory: treatment for arthritis may give relief from pain and discomfort but will not get rid of the underlying reason for the inflammation of the joints. It may help some people but not others, and it may be impossible to predict which people are most likely to benefit.

Furthermore, all treatments cause unwanted side effects in some people, and therefore can do harm as well as good. Aspirin taken over a long period of time may irritate the lining of the stomach and occasionally cause bleeding. On the other hand, aspirin has many beneficial effects and we would be much poorer without it. It is found in many proprietary medicines for 'flu and the common cold because it counteracts pain and relieves inflammation.

Faced with all these uncertainties, a doctor has to assess the balance between good and harm when deciding what treatment to recommend. In such circumstances of incomplete knowledge there may be widely differing medical opinions and these in turn may be reflected in wide variations in the ways problems are managed. For example, pregnant women who have problems in early pregnancy and have a threatened miscarriage will be told by some doctors to take it easy and by others to carry on a near normal life. This difference reflects the fact that we are still not certain about all the causes of miscarriage.

Other variations in medical practice reflect differing interpretations of the knowledge that is available. None of us can escape some of these dilemmas. How does one balance quantity of life with quality? Is it better to live longer with increasing incapacity of one sort or another, or to die earlier when some dignity or independence is left? And what is quality of life? It is in these situations, which are probably more common than many people realize, that those who are ill

and those who care about them can play an important part in choosing between treatment alternatives.

For some illnesses no curative treatment is available. Doctors, especially, find this a particularly difficult limit of knowledge to cope with. They enjoy helping people to get better and their training tends to concentrate on illness which is potentially curable. They receive very limited guidance about how to talk to patients or relatives in cases where their medicine has little to offer. The feelings of frustration, failure and embarrassment that all this engenders may occasionally lead to seeming indifference or even apparent hostility from the doctor and feelings of isolation for the person who is ill. Support from family and friends is particularly important at such a time.

The outlook

Given all these uncertainties about the nature of many illnesses and about the effects of their treatments, it should not be surprising that predictions about the longer-term outlook for those who are ill are often guarded. Because of inherent differences between people, such predictions can often only be given accurately in statistical terms which describe an 'average person' or a group of people with the disease. Statements such as 'x per cent of women with early cancer of the breast will survive 15 years' can seem very impersonal and of limited usefulness.

Most medical predictions are based on a combination of statistics, experience and judgment. They are useful provided that they are recognized for what they are – informed guesses. But they cannot be an accurate forecast of what may happen in any individual case. The outlook is often stated only in terms of duration of the illness (the survival statistics), and not at all in terms of how one could use the hours and the days or how one can become relieved of fear and bitterness even when the disease cannot be stopped.

Doctors and limited knowledge

The days before modern medicine were often marked by dogmatic certainty and autocratic paternalism. Medical attitudes are quite rightly changing. This, in part, is a response to the growth of scientific knowledge. Now that doctors know that they can do some good in some situations, they are more prepared to acknowledge their deficiency in others. But we are in a transitional phase. And the discussion of limited knowledge needs to be a two-way conversation

between patient and doctor or relative and doctor. Because of the responsibility which all doctors carry, they are sometimes described as 'playing God'. Doctors generally find this description wildly inappropriate, despite the life and death decisions they are often called upon to make. They have no wish to be seen in such a light. However, many people do still expect them to play such a role and this is destructive of both truth and confidence. If the expectation is of certainties, then disappointment may follow; but if the expectation is of trying to solve problems together, then a bond of comradeship can be formed.

The change in the relationship between the doctors and their patients which this implies means a greater sharing of responsibility and a greater sharing of the limited but growing knowledge which is available.

Medical research

One response to these uncertainties is medical research. This all-embracing term covers a variety of medical activities aimed at pushing back the limits of knowledge. Some research attempts to discover the underlying causes of disease. Other research aims to assess the suitability of new treatments and then to compare them with current, standard treatments. All plans for research involving patients are considered by a hospital ethics committee to safeguard the interests of the subjects of the research. These committees, which usually consist of non-medical as well as medical members, consider the need for the research and how it will be conducted. They may also give guidance about what information should be made available to potential participants.

Trials of new forms of treatment are of varying kinds. New drugs are only tried on humans after animal testing. This in itself raises ethical questions which are outside the scope of this book, except to say that problems have arisen in the past when insufficient data were collected before drugs were tried on people. At first, human trials are restricted to healthy volunteers. If these tests prove satisfactory, the drugs are then tried on a small number of patients with a specific disease. For all new therapies the final phase is comparison with the best-available existing standard treatment.

In rare instances the advantages over conventional treatment are overwhelming. For example, tuberculous meningitis – an infection of the membrane lining the brain – used to be almost invariably fatal

until the introduction of anti-tuberculous antibiotics. Such breakthroughs are extremely rare and the usual situation is that possible benefits of a new treatment appear evenly balanced by its possible (sometimes unanticipated) side effects.

The most scientific method of weighing up the advantages and disadvantages of alternative treatments is by conducting a 'randomized controlled trial'. All trials of drugs in hospitals are screened by ethical committees to make sure that no one is offered a treatment known to be less than the best currently available, and the treatments are allocated in a careful way to make sure that the doctors carrying out the trial do not choose the optimal patients to receive one treatment and others to receive an alternative. Suppose that, in the near future, a new drug called 'Antirheum' is developed which, as a consequence of a number of small trials, is thought to be effective in the treatment of rheumatism. A larger trial will then be set up, organized by experts in rheumatology and analyzed by statisticians. 'Antirheum' will be given to one half of the patients and aspirin might be given to the other half. In some cases the patients may take 'Antirheum' for a few months and then aspirin for an equal period of a few months. The doctors will be interested in the reports of the patients – which did they feel was best? – which gave them any problems or side-effects? And what objective changes can the doctor find on examining or testing the patients?

Sometimes in randomized controlled trials the actual nature of the treatment is kept secret from both the doctor and the subject – an active drug in a tablet form, for example, being compared with an inactive identical tablet. This overcomes the problem that enthusiasm for a particular treatment (rather than the treatment itself) may improve the illness.

Moving away from conventional medicine

Because there are still gaps in medical knowledge, and because patients do not always receive what they need in terms of cure, care or healing at the hands of doctors, there is a growing movement away from conventional modern medicine towards other methods of achieving health. Some of these methods use accumulated knowledge and have been tested against alternative treatments. Osteopathy is a good example: this form of treatment may succeed where rheumatology clinics have failed. Other methods use tradition as their hallmark, but may never have been tried in any careful way against

medical alternatives. Both homeopathy and acupuncture fall into this category – they may work but the proof from careful comparative studies is often lacking.

There is a third category of medicine which can only be described as 'fringe medicine', where individual practitioners stress one aspect of life as being at fault. It is difficult to know where fact and fiction merge here. We know, for instance, that our diet has much to do with the way we are, and that certain additives may possibly have harmful effects on our bodies. Milk allergy and hyperactivity in childhood are well-established examples. But on the fringe of this truth there are those who prescribe bizarre diets on the basis of bizarre tests and who may charge high fees for therapies that defy both sense and science.

There are also approaches to illness that are not conventional. Sitting at home counting out the pills may not be the best way to cope with disease. Meditation or Yoga may help. These are not alternatives to any medical approach, they are an adjunct. They try to reassess whether the 'You doctor – Me patient: You prescribe – I take' medical model is the best. The so-called holistic approach stresses that all aspects of life are related to health and wholeness. We may be ill because of a virus, but we may then go to the doctor or take to our bed because our life is unhappy and full of stress, or we may continue to work oblivious of the germ. Healing may come through what the doctor prescribes, but it is just as important to keep healthy spiritually and emotionally. Illness may strike us full of fear and resentment, anger and frustration, and these may be much more devastating to our health than any cancer or heart-attack. If we can learn to overcome these negative emotions, then we can remain healthy in the fullest sense of the word.

The limits of knowledge

Continuing advances in medical knowledge will help to reduce uncertainties but certainty is an illusion. There is a growing awareness of this both amongst those who prescribe treatments and amongst those who receive medical care: the result is a movement away from paternalism in medicine towards a more equal relationship. In this new atmosphere patients (and those who are close to them) have a right to know what they want to know about the illness, but also have a right *not* to be told what they do not want to hear. Understandably doctors find this distinction difficult to judge and we should give them guidance in whatever way seems appropriate so that they

can strike the right balance. One way to reconcile these uncertainties is through talking. Here the scope for help goes far beyond the hospital and the medical training that doctors are given; the more openly those who are ill can talk to their families and friends, the more effectively anxiety and frustration can be cured and tension alleviated.

*

The truly religious man does not claim to be endowed with any knowledge which he does not possess, and no teacher should attempt to impress his students with smatterings of dubious validity poured forth as though he were the confidant of the Almighty and not merely an observer of His mighty acts and mysterious ways.

M. H. Pappworth, *A Primer of Medicine*

3 · *Facing Illness in Hospital*

Doctors feel comfortable in hospital: it is, for many of them, their work environment, and they are familiar with most aspects of each department. Their training will have exposed them to all the different disciplines, and even though they may now be based in a specialist unit they understand the workings of wards, research departments, laboratories, X-ray departments and how all the different specialists and specialities inter-relate.

Patients, on the other hand, enter hospital with a fear of the unknown. They may not even know their way to the ward where they are expected, and do not know whom they will meet or how they will be treated. They may have only the vaguest idea of why they have been asked to come into hospital, or they may be admitted in a serious state of acute illness and find themselves literally being pushed about the hospital.

Visitors, too, will feel at a loss when faced with this unfamiliar environment. They are fearful of disturbing routines, of doing the wrong thing, of making fools of themselves. The patient's relatives, particularly, may be very sensitive when visiting: they want to know as much as possible but hesitate to ask questions – even if they know whom to ask.

This chapter aims to explain how the hospital structure works, who the people are that you, as a patient might meet, what their roles are, and how to make the most of meeting them. It then goes on to examine your role if you are a visitor to hospital – but the two sections are not mutually exclusive, for understanding what the patient goes through will help the visitor, and understanding the problems of visitors may help the patient!

The medical superstructure and talking to the doctors

(a) *House Officers:* Shortly after you first arrive in hospital, whether you are coming in as a 'booked' admission or arrive through an emergency department, you will be seen by a doctor. Let us assume that this is a young lady doctor. It is likely that she will introduce herself by name, and you should try and remember it (she will have a label on to help you). She will also try to remember *your* name. She might also say that she is the 'houseman' or 'house officer'. She is the most junior of the medical team, but she is also the most important to you. It is she who will organize everything that happens to you *medically* while you are on the ward, and will also prescribe the medicines that you may need. She is likely to come and sit by your bed for up to half an hour initially, and ask you a huge number of questions about yourself. Some answers can be organized in advance: a list of your current pills accurately set out in terms of type (copy the label carefully), strength (also written on the label) and how often you take them will help a great deal. Do not assemble one of each tablet, put them in a bottle and present them to the doctor! After all, how many thousands of small white tablets can there be? After talking, the doctor will examine you, write a lot of notes, prescribe any medicines that you need immediately, and finally explain to you what is likely to happen.

When seeing the house officer it is important to remember that she is trying to sort out in her own mind what is wrong with you, what further investigations should be done and what therapy you need. It is courteous, therefore, when she begins to ask the formal questions – 'How old are you? What is the main problem that you notice? When did it start? How often do you get the pain?' and so on – that you try and be brief but also accurate, without concealing relevant facts. The house officer knows that she has a limited time to get through the interview – she may therefore become much more curt and brusque in questioning if such questions as 'When did you first notice the problem?' are met with answers such as, 'Ah well, it was three days before Aunt Emily's cat first had kittens – I remember that clearly because one of them scratched me on the leg – and that must have been January . . . or was it April? . . .' It is obvious that you will then use up valuable time when she might be explaining things to you that you want to know, and it may sour your relationship a bit since she may pigeon-hole you mentally as 'over-talkative'!

Nor does she want to know about every itch and ache – we all itch and ache at times. At the end of her questioning and examination she is likely to tell you in outline what she thinks is wrong with you, and explain what needs to be done. It is at this point that you may be asked if there is anything that you want to know, and the doctor will mean this question. Ask. If you fear cancer and want to know whether it is a possibility ask, 'Do you think there is a possibility that this is cancer?' She may well say that no one can tell until after the tests, but at least she now knows that you want to know. If she says 'We are going to organise a CAT scan and a Barium meal' and you do not understand a word of it (Is that Aunt Emily's cat again?) then ask. Doctors are almost always very willing to explain things in any detail you want. The key to getting answers is to ask questions.

(b) *The other doctors:* The senior house officer has been in the business longer than the houseman. He or she may come and talk to you after the houseman, but is likely to concentrate on the main complaint. You may also be seen by a registrar or senior registrar – these are more senior doctors who are usually specializing in one particular branch of medicine. They will talk to you and confer with the houseman. The consultant is the medical boss of the group of doctors ('the firm'), and he or she is likely to see you in the company of the other doctors. The buck stops here. He or she will also be very open to questions from you about what is going on. The consultant may be a surgeon (Mister So-and-So), a physician (Doctor So-and-So) or a Professor (Professor So-and-So).

Medical students may hover in the background or may come and see you. They may even seem rather tiresome, but they do contribute to your medical care in many practical ways. They are the doctors of tomorrow (sometimes nearly literally), and are knowledgeable and conscientious – they have usually had some years of training before coming on the wards. In addition, if you allow yourself to be seen by medical students you will reap certain benefits – your medical details become a teaching 'case' and you may find that the consultant or senior registrar comes to your bed-side and looks at you in immense detail. This can only be beneficial in terms of your medical care and may even prove an enjoyable experience. You are, after all, in a position to learn along with the students. You can, however, opt not to be seen by medical students if you wish, and the doctors will certainly respect that decision.

The nursing and ward superstructure

When you arrive as an inpatient in a hospital ward you are likely to be asked for a great number of general details about yourself by a hospital clerk, some of which you may regard as impertinent – 'How many times have you been married?' – or irrelevant – 'Were you born in this country?' However, most of these questions are simply to enable the hospital authorities to compile accurate statistics about what is happening from day to day, who is being treated, whether they should be treated under the NHS, and who is the next of kin or person with whom the doctors should communicate if there is any crisis. You will usually be allocated a bed next, which may be in a large open 'Nightingale' style ward or, more usually these days, in a four-bedded room. You may get a single room, but remember that there are those whose medical needs make it essential for them to be alone in a side-ward. You may therefore be moved around after you have settled in.

Wards are run by sisters or male charge nurses, who both administer and nurse. Then there are staff nurses, who may be SRN ('State Registered Nurse', fully qualified after three years' training), or SEN ('State Enrolled Nurse', with a shorter training). In some hospitals there will be student nurses in their first, second or third year of training. In addition there are many people who have special functions: there are dietitians, physiotherapists, pharmacists, radiographers, pathologists, occupational therapists, social workers (who will help to sort out any problems arising at home as a result of the illness), ward auxiliaries, ward clerks (coping with ward paper-work), porters, and many others who may help with meals, newspapers, laundry, cleaning and so on.

The hospital thus runs as a huge organization of different people all fulfilling different roles. It is a great mistake to think that any are more important than any other – all of them have their function and all are people trying to do their job. They all deserve to be treated with respect and courtesy.

The chaplain

There are usually Anglican and Free Church chaplains attached to a hospital. Anglican chaplains may be appointed on a full-time basis in large hospitals; Free Church chaplains usually undertake the work part-time. Roman Catholic priests and other local clergy visit to see

their own parishioners. The chaplain or priest may come round and see the patient because of information given to the admitting clerk. If the patient particularly wants to see the chaplain, the Sister or one of the nurses should be informed and they will arrange for him to come. A chaplain can often be a useful confidant and may be a source of friendship and both spiritual and emotional strength.

If there is a chapel in the hospital it is always available for anyone, patient or visitor, to sit quietly to think and to pray. The chaplain may be on hand if needed. There may well be regular services, particularly on Sundays. It is always worth asking ward staff about these. If a Holy Communion Service is advertized either in the chapel or on the ward, it will be open to all.

Those in hospital are very vulnerable emotionally and spiritually. It is always wrong to take advantage of that. Equally, it is very important that vulnerability is acknowledged and help is offered when people wish it to be. That is the job of the chaplain, though many other staff may do it as well.

Coping with being in hospital

One major problem that you will face as an inpatient on a ward is that your personal freedom goes. You cannot go out, you cannot wake or go to sleep when you want to, your coffee may come at a time disagreeable to you (or it may turn out to be tea), you cannot watch your favourite television programmes (or you may have to put up with the background noise of other people's favourite television programmes when you long for quiet), you may not be allowed to smoke anywhere on the ward and your visitors may be limited in number and in the time they are allowed to see you. In addition, you may have a group of 'neighbours' in the ward who are not the company with whom you would normally choose to associate. If possible, the solution is nevertheless to strike up a friendship, or at least a sensible conversational relationship with your fellow patients. Many people visit friends that they have made in hospital long after the reason for their hospital stay has passed.

It is worth trying to regard the functioning of the hospital routine as being something interesting rather than restricting. Who are all these people, what roles do they play and what are their problems? The houseman may have been up all night, the ward sister may be short-staffed, the dietitian may be trying to give you a special diet (even if you don't like it), and the physiotherapist is not a bully –

she is trying to get you back to health as quickly as possible. Try and get to know who everyone is, preferably by name, as they come and see you. One lady recalls that when she was in hospital she kept a record in her diary of the names of those who saw her, what their position was, and (briefly) what they said or did. This not only made the stream of people coming through the ward more interesting, it also made it much more understandable.

The problems of visiting

When visiting someone in hospital it is important to establish beforehand the times allowed and any rules that the ward might have (limit to numbers, limit to time, restrictions on children) so that you are not disappointed or annoyed at the start. Telephone the ward in advance if you are in any doubt. Visitors to hospital often feel that they should take a small present for the patient and this may indeed be appropriate. But it can be simply an extravagance to spend a vast amount on flowers or on chocolates – the former will wilt rapidly in the hot hospital environment and the latter are generally unsuitable in any quantity. It is much more appropriate to take something of personal interest if you are a relative – for instance, the recent photographs of the grandchildren, or something to relieve the tedium of a restricted life-style. Back-copies of a favourite magazine; a knitting pattern and wool; a novel or book of crossword puzzles; a jig-saw and so on – even home-computers are welcomed in the wards these days!

On arrival many visitors find it hard to know what to talk about. Initially talk to the patient about his or her progress, and try to understand what you can of the technicalities conveyed to you. Do not try to avoid talking about illness. Some patients may want to talk at length about their fears of what may happen and, if you are a relative, this is especially important because you may want to discuss these apprehensions with the sister or doctor. Nearly all patients in hospital have a craving for news of family and home and you should think about all the trivial things that have happened which nevertheless take on large interest value – the new bicycle of a grandchild, the new hair-style of a neighbour, or the blackfly in the garden. If you are visiting as a friend, rather than as a member of the family, topics of conversation may be more difficult to find. Try and think in advance about subjects of common interest and whether there is any news to take – perhaps a church newsletter or the local paper will be all that is required.

Do not outstay your welcome: those sick in hospital can get very tired. If you visit as a friend, and the family are there, say 'Hello' briefly, exchange a few words and leave. The family takes precedence. If you feel that half an hour is enough (for you or the patient) aim to arrive half an hour before the end of visiting and you will then find that there is no embarrassment about leaving – you will be saved by the bell! It is also better to visit someone on a regular weekly basis rather than attempting visits every day when they first go into hospital, only to stop altogether when their stay is prolonged.

As family visitors, you may find yourselves asked to see the doctor about your relative. Such vague or indirect statements from the ward staff as 'Doctor So-and-So is quite willing to see you if you like' should be taken to mean 'Doctor So-and-So would definitely like to see you now and will not mind leaving supper; he will be disappointed if he is not contacted so please accept the invitation at once.' Information from doctors on wards is likely to be valuable, direct and honest – you will be able to assess something of the gravity of the situation or something of the expected outcome. You can also ask your own questions.

Special problems with intensive therapy units

You may, at some stage, visit someone in an Intensive Therapy Unit, Coronary Care Unit, Renal Unit or other highly sophisticated life-support unit. The overwhelming impression when you enter such a place is the quantity of electronic equipment that hangs from the walls or stands on the floor. There is the buzz of alarms and the bleep of drop-counters. There may be the mechanical hiss of ventilators or the flashing of warning lights. Try, as much as possible, to ignore all of this initially. You are visiting a person, not an Aladdin's cave. You may find the person that you are visiting is in a terrible state – barely conscious perhaps, with tubes running in and out of the bed, or perhaps even on a ventilator. What do you do? Pull up a chair in exactly the way that you would with a conscious friend, and take him or her by the hand if you can. Announce quietly who you are, even to an unconscious patient. Sit quietly, still holding the hand, and think your own thoughts. Stay for as long as you like – the staff will move you if they need to. Accept offers of tea and coffee from the staff and accept, *always*, offers to talk to the doctors. Remember that their decisions about this unconscious person will be helped by knowing from you what he or she would want, what their quality of life was

like and what the home circumstances are. Do not shun visiting unconscious patients – it can sometimes be easier than having to talk. In the case of the very weary in Coronary Care or Intensive Therapy Units, visit for a short time only, and go *immediately* if any of the medical staff imply you have been there long enough.

Coping with tears

Tears are common in hospitals – tears of frustration, of loneliness, of fear, of love and of boredom. But as well as being an entirely natural reaction, tears are often cleansing and healing emotionally – they do not need to be suppressed or regarded with embarrassment, and they will usually stop soon. Constructive use can be made of the situation by accepting what the tears mean. As a visitor, sit quietly through them – or even share them – rather than agitate for the patient to 'get a grip'. All you need do is to take the patient by the hand and simply hold on. Very often this can be the most helpful and rewarding of visits. Emotions expressed, accepted and understood bind us all together.

*

> Medicine is an art based on science, and is slowly moving away from art and towards science. The process is slow and can never be complete. . . . The future of medicine is bound to involve more and more technology, but it is to be hoped technology curbed by commonsense and tempered by humanity. Whatever technological empires are built, the most *important* person in the hospital will still be the patient.
>
> Weatherall, Ledingham and Warrell, *The Oxford Textbook of Medicine* (1983)

4 · Facing Illness at Home

Illness is, by its very nature, a nuisance. To a greater or lesser extent it intrudes on our lives, disrupting our plans, bringing anxiety and distress. Sometimes it creeps up insidiously, undermining independence and whittling away the quality of life – a slowly growing cancer, a progressive wasting disease or the inexorable advance of senility. At other times it can strike with a shocking abruptness and totally shatter our settled way of life. A moment of carelessness on a crowded road may result in a lifetime in a wheelchair. The successful business man running for his train may suffer a massive heart attack and never be fit for either running or business again. The sprightly grandmother may suffer a stroke and suddenly she cannot walk or talk or feed or dress herself.

Once the acute crisis is passed, all these illnesses will probably have to be coped with at home. They have to be faced not only by the sufferer, but by the family and friends as well. We are all aware that in a welfare society men and women need to learn that they are dependent upon one another. The welfare of the individual cannot be achieved in isolation from other people. This is never more true than when people are sick at home.

In fact all sorts of illness can be managed successfully at home, but the patient, the family and the visitor have all to be considered. They each have different needs which have to be recognized. Patients need care, the family needs practical support and reassurance and the visitor will need welcome and acceptance. In this context, of course, the doctor is a visitor, present only by the invitation of the patient or the family. He or she does not have the authority to insist on any plan of action and advises simply in the role of a trusted and knowledgeable friend.

1. *The patient*

We have all been ill for short periods of time at home. Home is the best place to be when we have a cold or 'flu or migraine or many other temporary ailments. We are lucky if there are others there to look after us, but we can rapidly become irritated with ourselves and aware of being a burden or nuisance if the illness drags on more than a few days. In chronic illness – illness which continues for a long time – frustration, introspection, pain, loneliness, separation, boredom, rejection and a sense of failure may all loom large. We need to be aware of all the practical problems that present themselves, all the questioning and all the fears that may beset the patient.

Practical problems

A major cause for concern for the invalid is suggested by the word 'dependence'. No one wants to be beholden to others for help all the time. St Paul's reminder that it is 'more blessed to give than to receive' (Acts 20.35) remains a very fixed idea. Sometimes it is harder to receive than to give: when we are ill we may find it difficult to accept help graciously. The male ego (bolstered sometimes by the term 'bread-winner') becomes very deflated when the wage packet becomes a welfare cheque. Pride in keeping the home running smoothly is badly dented when the housewife cannot get to the supermarket or even push the vacuum cleaner. Loss of a major sense such as sight or hearing can be a devastating blow to the mental state of a man or woman. For couples, failure to achieve satisfaction together sexually is a frequent and unwanted confirmation that independence has been undermined by illness. Individuals by their very nature are independent. Even comparatively minor disorders can be very major distractions when independence goes.

Questions

Any patient faced with more than a trivial illness may ask questions, wanting to know about the extent and the seriousness of the disease and the likely outcome and time course. But not everyone wants to know: some may be too fearful to ask, others may try to deny the seriousness of the problem and yet others may be too young or too sick to comprehend. Nevertheless, it has to be said that the 'healthiest way of being ill' is to come to terms with the truth, and it is better if

the family or those close to the patient can help to achieve this. One family called in a doctor late at night to see their mother. She was known by that family to have terminal cancer of the liver. She was comfortable but distressed by her yellowish colour. The family knew that nothing could be done about it, but had called the doctor to keep up the charade of puzzlement. How much better for all concerned if the truth could have been shared and cried about and faced together.

The future

A third area of concern for a sick person is the future. 'What will happen when . . . or if . . .?' can be a persistent and perplexing source of disquiet. In some chronic progressive diseases, like multiple sclerosis or cancer, the patient's mind stays clear. It becomes obvious to him or her that legs are weaker or body weight is going down. There are expressed or unexpressed fears: 'What will happen when I can't stand up, or walk, or even wipe my bottom?' Little imagination is needed to share the despair of these aspects of disease. And then there are worries about others: 'Will they cope? Will the family survive? What will happen to others who used to be dependent on me?'

Reactions to all these problems will obviously depend on the person concerned: some will be articulate while others find any consideration of the future numbs them with fear. There are two aspects of coping with this. First, it remains true that sharing fears will itself ease them; there may be no obvious answers to what might happen, but talking about it, even briefly, can help enormously. Secondly, fears for the future can multiply the horrific possibilities – in the words of Brutus from Shakespeare's 'Julius Caesar', we all tend to die many times before our death. Only one or two of the fears can come true: one cannot both die tomorrow and linger on for years as a burden to others, but many will be fearing both simultaneously. It is important to try and consider only a short time ahead in these circumstances and to trust that one will find the courage and resources to cope as and when needed – 'great your strength if great your need'.

Problems can often be solved when they arise: more help, new drugs, more visits, more shared care and so on. That is not to say that those caring or suffering do not need to think about the future, but that is different from being paralysed by fear. Illness needs to be faced together with others, and not suffered alone. Patients and helpers, family and visitors, can all help to enable this to happen.

2. *The family*

The basic family unit is one man and one woman living together in marriage – for better, for worse, in sickness and in health. That should mean a sharing of problems but it does not always follow quite that simply. Communication and love and companionship and mutual respect can all fall apart. Fortunately, though, for the most part couples do cope. Their relationship can even be strengthened by vicissitudes. The man and wife who have learned to share their life in all its diversities are indeed fortunate. And this understanding can be reflected in the children or parents or grandparents in the family and in the care they can all offer in times of need.

It needs to be remembered, of course, that these days there are an increasing number of single parent families – they will need extra support from friends and relations in times of illness. For them, both the practical problems and the sense of isolation may be more acute.

Practical problems

In two TV programmes entitled 'Simon's War' and 'Simon's Peace', a severely burned and wounded soldier from the Falklands War was shown recovering from his injuries. At first the mother was seen to be doing everything for him. Then one day when she returned home, Simon excitedly exclaimed, 'Mum, I made some tea and toast for myself!' He was so pleased that his relatives had to be told of his achievement by telephone. 'It was then', said Simon's mother, 'that I realized I shouldn't do everything but let him try – it's his independence that counts.'

In our concern for our loved ones, the natural instinct may well be to do everything for them, but this is rarely the kindest solution to the problems they face. The family can help most by being willing to make changes and by being able to anticipate the need for change: but the changes all need to be geared to helping the patient preserve or recover independence. Whenever possible, the changes need to be mutually agreed upon after discussion, not sprung on the patient as a *fait accompli*. The labour-saving gadgets, the reorganization of the kitchen, the moving of the bed downstairs – all these can be talked about and planned together. In Ritchie Russell House in Oxford, patients and their visitors are shown how rooms can be adapted, furniture and fittings modified, to let patients help themselves. Most

patients will be glad to discuss ways in which they can preserve a measure of independence and continue with activities they enjoy, like cooking or gardening, which also help them to maintain a sense of usefulness. The discussion and planning in themselves provide useful therapy – something interesting to think and talk about.

Previous plans may have to be changed – the new greenhouse may be re-thought and a sun-room substituted. Our dislike of pets can be put aside to allow a companiable cat or budgerigar. Illness can inspire a new sense of co-operation and forbearance in the family: what is necessary is willingness on everybody's part to adapt to meet the new circumstances.

The many practicalities of coping with increasing infirmity can often be discussed with health-care professionals. Health visitors are nurses with special training in home care for children and elderly people. Occupational therapists have studied rehabilitation and offer help in making a home easier to live in for invalids. Dietitians will give advice on how to eat sensibly and suitably. There are physiotherapists to ensure that muscles do not waste and psychotherapists to do the same thing for the mind. All these people constitute an impressive team and probably the general practitioner is the person best equipped to advise which discipline can be called in.

Certainly it is worth talking things through with some of these experts before rushing in a panic to make changes which may prove unnecessary or misguided. Moving the bed into the lounge may not be a good idea if there are no ground-floor lavatory facilities. Similarly, it may not be worth undertaking new building or structural alterations to a house if the outlook is only a few months of life. Some invalids will require a wheelchair, but many more just need a slightly modified ordinary chair with a convenient light or table or bookstand.

There will also be practical problems to do with sharing of care. Whether the patient is a much-loved partner racked by constant pain, or a difficult and confused elderly relative, the burden of constant attendance upon them should not have to be borne single-handed. It is important that care really is shared around among those willing to help. The self-inflicted martyrdom of some is fair neither to themselves nor to others in the family. An evening out, a family outing, a weekend break, or coffee with friends can often be arranged if there is someone who will 'sit in' for a time. The patient may object (and indeed some become tyrannical in affliction!), but remember

that everyone's health and sanity and good-humour are at stake. Better to allow a disgruntled patient an evening with someone else and feel happier yourself than to carry on coping, suppressing frustration and bitterness, in an attempt to agree to all demands made upon you.

Questions

Complete honesty among members of a family generally helps all concerned. The family should not feel that they need to 'absorb' the truth in order to protect the patient from it: rather they should see how to share it. Having faced the truth together, however bleak it seems, there is still room for hope and optimism, and even for dreams. Paul Tournier, a Swiss psychiatrist, describes how he suggested to a married couple where the wife had cancer that they discuss next year's holiday. Both knew that it was unlikely to happen, but they were able to enjoy studying the travel brochures together and laying plans – ideal therapy, based on a love of life rather than a pre-occupation with death.

Similarly family doctors need to develop honesty in their approach to illness in the home. Saying 'only an ulcer' to the patient and then telling of 'a severe cancer' to the family is an example of a most unhelpful practice in family care.

A GP relates how he was treating a man for terminal cancer. The wife forbade him to tell the patient the truth. This state continued for some weeks with the patient needing increasing amounts of sedation and painkillers. Finally the doctor did share the truth with his patient. The man accepted the inevitable. Funeral and financial arrangements were discussed with the family. From that moment sedation was not needed and painkillers were dramatically reduced. Caring by that family was being inhibited by a failure to share the truth, albeit from the best of motives. Sharing of the truth was a liberating experience.

The future

The family are all involved in the questions that begin 'What will happen when . . .?' We have already seen how an ability to anticipate tomorrow's problems and a willingness to make changes, both in the ordering of our home and the ordering of our priorities, can help in solving the practical difficulties. That still leaves many 'What if . . .? What when . . .?' questions unanswered and the family may dread

the possible answers as much as the patient. The future may appear grim, but we do need to remember that there are ways of alleviating the problems as they actually arise. As a social unit, the family shows a remarkable aptitude for rallying round and finding solutions. There is a huge body of professional help and advice available which can be tapped through the GP. And for the Christian, there is the assurance that whatever life throws at us we have God's constant companionship:

> Fear not . . . for thou art mine. When thou passest through the waters I will be with thee; and through the rivers, they shall not overflow thee: when thou walkest through the fire, thou shalt not be burned; neither shall the flame kindle upon thee (Isa. 43.1–2).

We may not be spared the flood or the fire, but even there God is with us.

3. *The visitor*

In the world of caring, how does somebody who is totally 'unqualified' fit in with all the trained professionals? There is a special place for the ordinary visitor. Doctor, nurse, parson or social worker need not deter us or keep us away. Indeed it is precisely the friend's visit that most sick people will prefer: the doctor comes because it is his job, and he discusses illness; the visitor comes because he or she wants to, and discusses life.

Practical aspects

The visitor can do much to help with small practical problems and to encourage continuing independence. You can collect books from the library, the paper or magazine from the shop, and so on. Another good idea is to have read the paper or article first so that you can point out things of mutual interest. Or you could, for example, discuss your last committee meeting with the invalid who used to be involved. It will all encourage the patient to maintain interests outside the sick-room and to feel that he or she is still involved in life.

The visitor can play a vital role in supporting the family as well as the patient. The occasional pie taken to the hard-pressed carers or the occasional pile of ironing taken to your own home can mean a great deal. It indicates that you are sympathetic to their plight as well as to that of the sufferer. They may be tired, anxious, distraught,

even angry – they will almost certainly be glad of a chance to pour out their side of the story to a sympathetic listener. Or you might consider that it would be possible to visit at a time that would allow the regular carers to get out of the house. A daytime visit might let the mother get to the shops, or an evening visit might allow a husband and wife to have a short night out. So routine visits that you might have been going to make anyway can become of much greater value to the family if you phone in advance and suggest that they use the time to get away from it all.

Questions

In the book of Job in the Bible, Job is portrayed as a rich farmer for whom everything went wrong. He lost his wealth and family. His friendly visitors were certain that Job's downfall was the result of God punishing his sins. That was no help to Job whose faith enabled him to say 'I know that my redeemer lives'. Job's God was loving: his visitors' God was intent on punishment. In the end Job triumphed in spite of bad visitors!

Conversation can sometimes be difficult for a visitor. Take the lead from the person concerned. Let them express their ideas and voice their thoughts. If they do not want to talk then of course learn the art of sitting quietly with them. A softly answered 'Yes' to the question 'Are you there?' is often therapeutically as potent as any medicine. The simple gesture of holding hands can convey, far more than words, the loving concern of one who does not know all the answers either.

Obviously discussion of disease will arise in our visits. We must not be ashamed to admit to an ignorance of the reasons for disease selectivity. In our limited way we are sharing the love that Jesus himself directed us to show. The discussion of her problems with the woman at the well of Sychar in Samaria (John 4.4–30) is an example of talking through a problem. We should not forget, however, that the love spoken of by Jesus was also straightforward, direct and practical. The example of the Good Samaritan (Luke 10.25–37), who helped the distressed traveller directly rather than discussing the whys and the wherefores of brigandry in Israel, can help us also. Like that ordinary Samaritan, we are trying to show love – our love and God's.

Visits need not be long. Like so much else in life, it is quality and not quantity that counts. Regular short visits when one just 'pops in' are more appreciated than one long and tiring encounter. It is

likely to be better for the visitor as well – conversation does not become exhausted and hours of time do not need to be set aside.

The future

When looking to the future, we need again to take our cue from the patient: to be prepared to talk about it or not to talk about it. We also need to be sensitive to the first signs of potential problems which may become more serious as time passes, and see if we can help to forestall them. A middle-aged lady was suffering from a progressively debilitating disease. She greatly disliked the idea of accepting help from others but rather expected her husband to do everything. One of her neighbours recognized this patient's problem. She dropped in often suggesting that as she did things for her own family there must be things she could do for the patient. Slowly the disease progressed. Equally slowly the patient accepted the offers of help – making life easier for all. The visitor never talked about long-term solutions or planning for the future but just got on with what needed doing. That is caring as it should be.

Finally, it is apparent that our Health Service is moving in the direction of community care. Surgical cases will be admitted to hospital for one day only. Small hostels in the community will replace large hospitals for the mentally sick and handicapped. Elderly people are being encouraged to stay in their own homes. Home care assistants will be trained by Social Services. All these straws in the wind seem to indicate that the importance of ordinary people caring for one another will not diminish. On the contrary such care will become the norm rather than the exception. In such a climate it will become our responsibility to share the love which we believe to be at the heart of God's purposes for us.

> Should it be ours to drain the cup of grieving
> Even to the dregs of pain, at Thy command,
> We will not falter, thankfully receiving
> All that is given by Thy loving hand.
>
> But, should it be Thy will once more to release us
> To life's enjoyment and its good sunshine,
> That which we've learned from sorrow shall increase us,
> And all our life be dedicate as Thine.

Dietrich Bonhoeffer, 'New Year', written in prison, 1945

5 · The Ill Child in Hospital

Organization of hospital care

The care of children in hospital has undergone a revolution in the last twenty or thirty years. Gone are the rows of beds with children sitting on them confined to that part of the ward, bored, anxious, waiting and hoping for a brief visit from their parents. Paediatric wards today are a kaleidoscope of toys and murals, of play areas and televisions, of books and Lego. The medical equipment stands incongruously among the paraphernalia of childhood. And parents are now expected to be in attendance rather than expected to stay away. All hospitals will make provision for parents to sleep in or near the ward, though the provision may be a little makeshift! The nurses are geared to the idea of a parent being nearby as an assurance to the child and as a help on the ward.

And in these days of increasing financial stringency in hospitals, it is gradually becoming necessary that a parent is present at times of crisis just to help with the nursing of the child. In a surgical ward there will not be enough staff to sit with everyone after an operation – what could be more reassuring than for a girl to come round from an anaesthetic to find that she is on the lap of her father or for a boy to wake in the night and find that his mother is on a camp-bed by his side?

Parental decisions

To have a child admitted to hospital presents an array of difficult problems and gnawing worries to any family. How will the child cope with hospital? How will the rest of the family manage if Mother is away? How long will the child be in hospital? Is the illness serious?

Can full recovery be expected? How soon? Will the child be lonely or frightened? Will the child be hurt in hospital? Additionally there are often immediate practical problems to be solved: getting the child to hospital, making sure that other members of the family know about the situation and, most importantly, ensuring that other children are not neglected.

The first decisions to be made when a child is taken ill and is admitted to hospital are those of sorting out who is to go with the child and who will stay at home. Two-parent families with other children will often divide the responsibilities of care between them, but sometimes parents cannot stop work, or the family has only one parent anyway. Then hasty arrangements need to be made: will neighbours look after the others while the parent goes to hospital with the child? Are there grandparents who can help? The doctor admitting the child to hospital from home may know about the possibility of temporary care from the social services, a health visitor or a district nurse.

When packing for the child, often in a rush, remember to take the favourite cuddly toy or blanket which could make all the difference between a good night and sleepnessness for him and you! Put in lots of changes of pyjamas or nighties and lots of tissues – the child may well be sick after an operation. Remember to take plenty of small change for telephone calls: the telephone may be the only line of communication between the parents in the next few days when they pass like ships in the night on their way to and from the hospital.

As a parent of a child in hospital, one becomes trapped in a sort of limbo. It may be unpleasant for the child, but at least it is the best place for him or her. For the parent it can be appalling. Initially there is likely to be endless waiting in a casualty or reception area. A nurse wanders in, takes some details and the child's temperature and then leaves. Time passes. A doctor comes in, introduces himself and examines the child, makes notes and leaves. Time crawls by. Another doctor comes in, often asks the same questions, spends a shorter time seeing the child and may outline the problem. He then leaves, and eventually the child is admitted to a ward. One solution to the problem of apparently endless time hanging on one's hands is to take in books to read oneself and to read to the child – an ideal time to read Roald Dahl's *Charlie and the Chocolate Factory* to a seven-year old or C. S. Lewis's *Tales of Narnia* to a ten-year old. Talking to the child is important too. Explain what you know of appendicitis to your son –

you may not know much but you will know more than he does: 'They put you to sleep for a short while, make a little cut here, take out the bit that hurts and sew you up again.' Don't say it won't hurt at all – it will not be true and your child will trust you less. Say that it will be uncomfortable for a little while, that medicines are to be had if it is painful and so on. At all times be honest with the child – one nurse reported that a child wandered about the ward when she arrived looking for the 'party' which had been promised by the parent. No good will come of such deceptions.

Once on a ward, the parent has to decide what he or she is going to do. If the plan is to sit with the child before an operation, and then stay afterwards as well, arrangements will need to be made with the staff on the ward about sleeping and toilet arrangements. Remember that the ward staff might (or might not!) give you some tea or coffee occasionally, but they almost certainly will not provide you with any food. The canteen or hospital shop may be shut as well. Time is likely to hang very heavily. Sleep will come with difficulty.

It is best to arrange a rota for short hospital stays. With two available parents, it is possible to stay with the child much of the time, but under many circumstances the child may have to be left for some period of time. It is best to try and avoid this with children between the ages of about one and three-and-a-half years. These are vulnerable years because the child understands only that it has been abandoned, but does not have the insight to see why. Older children can understand more of what is happening, but may become very lonely if left on their own for any length of time. Hospitals can be simultaneously frightening and boring.

If you are going to be on a ward with your child for some time, try and get to know the staff by name. If possible see in what way you can help them. Some children may not have parents staying in the ward, and they too might like to hear the story that you are going to read. Toys, as at home, get into a chaotic mess – tidying them up will leave the staff free to do other things.

Acute and chronic illness

Children may be admitted to hospital for only a day or two, or may be admitted for much longer periods of time. What parents do will depend very much on having some notion of this, and it is important to discuss it early on with the doctors concerned with the care of the child. It is only possible to keep a round-the-clock attendance with a

child for a few days at the most. After that some workable routine has to be found. The routine has to take into account all the needs of individual lives. What is the child's routine? Is schooling going to be provided? Are there times of day when television will keep the child occupied and parents can be away? What are the parents' routines? Can either get time off work easily? What are the commitments at home? Are there other children or ageing parents at home? Remember that proper care has to be taken of *everyone*, and that includes the frantic parent.

Once a child has settled in hospital, it is time for parents to review whether others are becoming neglected. Try and make sure that everyone has enough sleep – and that usually means getting home and into bed if possible. Sleeping in a bed provided on the ward is nice for the child, but often a problem for the parent in the long term. And other children in the family often feel badly left out. After all, they have missed out on all the excitement – the ambulance ride, and the cards and the presents that the ill child receives – and now they are missing out on their parents. What happened to the bedtime story? Daddy doesn't seem to know where the clothes are kept. Why are all the meals suddenly so awful?

All these problems need to be thought about in detail as time goes on. There are constant problems of the balance of care between individuals. It is no use wearing oneself out for the sake of one child and neglecting spouse and other children. It is from them, after all, that much enjoyment of life can still spring.

One should be especially careful in the situation where, all else having failed, there is the faintest possibility of cure elsewhere at enormous expense. Many families have ruined themselves financially and broken apart their relationship with their healthy children by fruitless searching for yet more therapeutic options. There is no easy answer, but to 'do the most' for a child may not necessarily be the right course. Remember that children too develop the capacity to cope in times of crisis.

Coming home

There is usually a sense of anticlimax when all is over and the child comes home. It will have been a huge strain, after all, for him or her as well as for the parents. Remember that this is likely to result in a time of bad behaviour, restlessness, hyper-excitability, tears and poor sleep: you need to be prepared since this emotional crisis may

persist for some days, or longer, depending on how long the child has been in hospital and what state of health he or she is in now. Patience will see it through.

*

The days of the omniscient doctor are on the decline. Most parents want a kind and conscientious human being to help their child rather than a mystical god: a mother brought her child with severe spina bifida and hydrocephalus to see the specialist. At the end of a long interview she was crying but happier –

'Last week I saw the other specialist; there he was in his white coat – he behaved as if he knew everything, yet he told me nothing. You tell me everything, yet you know nothing.'

S. R. Meadows and R. W. Smithells, *Lecture Notes on Paediatrics*

6 · *The Ill Child at Home*

When we talk of 'childhood illnesses', we normally mean the old faithfuls: mumps, measles, chicken pox and the seasonal round of coughs, colds and earache. It can seem endless to parents who are in the throes of sleepless nights and fretful days: they will have every sympathy with the sentiments of a sixteenth-century prayer: 'From winter, plague and pestilence, good lord, deliver us!' But parents can and do usually cope with these ordinary illnesses of childhood. Organizational problems of care may arise if both parents are working or if it is a one-parent family, but these difficulties are not insurmountable. Neighbours, employers, relatives, child-care groups or 'Universal Aunts' can be mobilized to give help for a short period of time. The illness probably lasts only a few days anyway, and children survive these hazards in their usual resilient way.

But there are childhood illnesses of a different, darker order. Some of the inherited diseases like muscular dystrophy and cystic fibrosis are potentially fatal. Others, like leukaemia and some of the cancers, will be harrowing for the child and the parents whatever the outcome, necessitating long and gruelling courses of treatment. Others again, like juvenile arthritis (Still's disease) may threaten a lifetime of discomfort. It is when faced with these tragedies of childhood, more perhaps than in any other sphere of illness, that we are filled with a sense of moral outrage and feel like shaking our fists at the heavens. Why do the young and innocent have to suffer? Why is life so unfair? When a seventy-year-old develops cancer we can say, 'Well, he's had a good innings' – but we cannot so easily rationalize a brain tumour in a seven-year-old who has not had any sort of innings at all.

There can be nothing harder for parents to bear than the suffering

and perhaps death of their children. Their apparent inability to do anything except stand by and watch oppresses them with feelings of helplessness and hopelessness, and it is not surprising if they often feel, too, a sense of bitterness. Childhood suffering used to be much commoner, of course: infant mortality took a terrible toll, as a walk round any churchyard bears out. We tend to think that 'in the old days' people were resigned to losing their children, that it was somehow easier for them. Perhaps their expectations of life were less: certainly they were more at home in the presence of death. But can it ever have been easy for parents to watch their children suffer and die? – especially in the days when there were none of our modern analgesics to relieve distress and dull pain. Can it have been easy for poor Queen Anne, bearing seventeen children of whom only one survived infancy and died before he reached his teens? Can it have been easy for the parents of the several little brothers and sisters buried together in an English country churchyard under a tombstone which reads:

They tasted of life's bitter cup,
Refused to drink the potion up,
But turned their little heads aside,
Disgusted with the taste, and died.

Grief was rationalized with the claim that life was not worth living anyway – just as centuries earlier the Greeks had rationalized their grief with the consolation that 'whom the gods love dies young'. But even if they really believed that life was too bad for their children or their children too good for life, parents must always have suffered with and for their children.

We are indeed lucky that in these days and in this country, serious childhood illness is relatively rare. We no longer have to worry about our children dying from diphtheria or cholera or typhus or scarlet fever or the plague – though it is salutary to remember that in many parts of the world they still do. We have innoculations to keep the killers at bay and an armoury of medicines to alleviate suffering in both major and minor illnesses. But the relative rarity of tragedy is, of course, no help to the unlucky few who still have to face it: in a sense, it only increases the sense of injustice. Some families have to undergo such appalling suffering that one feels only they have the right to speak about it.

A Methodist minister, Wilfred Bridge, gave a series of talks on

Radio Birmingham about his experiences when seriously ill in hospital. He entitled the series 'The Treasures of Darkness', a phrase borrowed from the Bible: 'I will give you the treasures of darkness' (Isa. 45.3). In context it refers to gold and silver found in the darkness of mines, but it contains too a promise from God about all the experiences of our life. Even the darkest days may yield strange and unexpected treasures.

First there are the children themselves, who so often show extraordinary courage and cheerfulness in the face of frightful illness. As so-called 'grown-ups', we may be shamed by the qualities which seriously ill children often seem to display so naturally – one reason perhaps why Jesus told us that true growing up involves in a sense growing down to 'become as little children'. So often they are free from resentment and self-pity, neither wallowing in regrets for the past nor obsessed with fears for the future. Then there is the treasure of families more closely bound together by the strong bonds of suffering love. And there is the treasure of paradox – the apparent contradiction whereby intensity of suffering may give a new intensity to all our other feelings, to our awareness of love and happiness and beauty. In this darkness, some may find rather than lose faith. A very young mother said when her daughter died, 'I do believe in God now and in heaven. She was so special and so beautiful and I loved her so much, death just can't be the end of her. There must be a God to love her and take care of her.'

A lively, happy toddler called Helen developed a brain tumour: it was removed by surgery but the operation left her totally incapacitated by irreversible brain damage. Now Helen is helpless, silent and immobile. In the period immediately following the operation, her parents met Mother Frances who is both the Superior General of the Anglican Society of All Saints and a Registered Sick Children's Nurse. They became close friends, and after Helen's return home from hospital Mother Frances periodically looked after her at the convent in order to give her parents a short break. From this tragedy and this friendship was born Helen House in Oxford – the first hospice in the world for children with chronic, life-threatening illnesses. Since it opened in 1982, it has proved a haven for seriously ill children and their families from all over the UK. Usually these are children who are being cared for at home and come to Helen House from time to time for short stays, either with or without other members of the family. 'Our aim', states the prospectus, 'is to provide a loving, sup-

portive environment for them and their families. The frequency of visits varies according to the individual needs of each family and we try, to the best of our ability, to meet those needs sensitively.'

Although Helen House exists to provide a break *from* home-care, it also provides a model *for* home-care, for it is, above all, homely – a small, informal establishment where the sick child, brothers, sisters, parents and grandparents (and even sometimes family pets!) can relax and enjoy themselves. It is recognized that, in order for this to be possible, the resources of modern medicine and the expertise of professionals should be mobilized to ensure that the sick child is as comfortable as possible – that 'pain and other unpleasant symptoms which can cause acute distress and anxiety are controlled or prevented'. That done, one day is taken at a time and simple, everyday pleasures relished without any sense of rush. At Helen House the jacuzzi is a great attraction, but it could just as well be a paddling pool in the garden. In the hospice or at home, the child can enjoy pets, gardens, games, books, videos and tapes, and, above all, the company of family and friends. There is no need for the ill child to be singled out for 'special treatment' (except in the medical sense, of course) to the exclusion of brothers and sisters, no need to count the days in a frenzied attempt to pack as many treats as possible into what time remains. What is important is for the child to be surrounded with love and to feel, so far as possible, a normal member of a normal family. This way the experience of illness becomes something which involves the whole family: all can benefit from the chance to stop rushing in different directions at numerous diverse activities, and enjoy simply being together.

> Ian was two and Jenny four when Ian developed leukaemia. When treatment in hospital didn't work, Ian came home. All the family contracted glandular fever, but the mother's response was 'at least we have an excuse to be at home together'. Ian's death was still two or three months away, but the family made the most of the chance to spend time together.

For the parents, there is at Helen House the support of a loving, caring staff who soon come to be regarded first and foremost as friends and who help to ease the terrible sense of isolation and helplessness. The achievement of the hospice is best summed up by the parents of a child who was a regular visitor there:

> To parents of a child with a serious, life-threatening illness, the idea of using a Hospice might imply a place of no-hope, signifying defeat in everyone's attempts to cure the child. It did so to us when we first took our son home from hospital, still suffering from a tumour despite surgery and radiotherapy. We refused to give up hope that he might live, and avoided visiting Helen House, though several people had suggested that we could be helped there. Eventually, when we were tired and desperate and Martin was too ill to stay at home any longer, we came to look.
>
> As soon as we saw the bright new building, the cheerful faces, the beautiful furnishings and tempting toys, we knew that here was a place where Martin would be well cared for, our elder son would have fun and we would have a rest. It soon felt as if the staff shared our problems, and it lightened our burden during the final weeks of Martin's life. If there is any hope for sick children it is here.

But this sort of supportive love and care does not need to come from a hospice. We quote the example of Helen House simply to show what can be done in this field. For a child at home, such support and care can come from friends and neighbours, as this case history from a GP bears out:

> During a medical examination, the doctor noticed that Thomas had to push his foot into his sock with his hand. When the doctor made further enquiries, it transpired that Thomas climbed stairs by putting his good leg up one step and then pulling his other leg up with his hands. Thomas' baby brother was not walking at all at the age of 18 months. Both children had the rare disease of muscular dystrophy. They are now in ordinary schools: their mother works hard to keep the family going. The school-master helps, other children help and neighbours help so that the mother can go out. This is very much a community situation, where casual neighbourly care keeps life more reasonable.

If all the family are involved in the living, they will also be involved in the dying, which is as it should be. 'If and when the time comes for a child to die', writes Mother Frances, 'we try to ensure that this happens with dignity, the child surrounded by the people he or she knows and loves best, whether at home or in Helen House. The friendship and support does not end there but continues for as

many months or years as the family wishes.' The pain and grief and desperate sense of loss which the death of a child brings to a family cannot be minimized and should not be trivialized with clichés of comfort. If we know a family in such distress, our hearts may fail at the prospect of having to face them and having to find something to say: we may back off, pretending to ourselves that they need privacy in sorrow or that such situations are best left to the experts. But they do not need privacy or professionals – they need friends, and it does not matter if one has no words other than 'I am so very sorry'. One can always listen; one can offer compassion – literally *suffering with* them; one can offer companionship – *sharing bread with* them; one can offer constancy – *standing firm with* them. From all this may come true comfort – *strength with and for* the sufferer. Remember that all the members of the family, in their different ways, have been bereaved. It is desperately hard for the parents but it is desperately hard too for the brothers and sisters. And remember how desperately hard it is for the grandparents, who in a sense carry a double burden – their own grief for a grandchild and the suffering which they undergo for their own children, the parents. Such wounds do not heal in a week, or a year, or maybe even in a lifetime.

Of course, not all serious illness is terminal. Many parents are coping at home with illnesses or chronic problems which do not always arouse the same immediate flood of compassion as terminal illness, but it is just as important for help and understanding to be forthcoming from the community.

> David had Down's Syndrome. Being an only child, at first his slow development didn't matter. But at three, when most children are starting to attend playgroup, he was hardly dry. David's mother talked to other mothers, and all agreed that he could be taken to the local play group. This first step of socialization was important as it allowed David to mix with other children and eventually attend ordinary school with his friends.

The special problems presented by mental handicap are considered in the next chapter. But there are lots of situations where, as a parent, you will need support and help. Your health visitor, GP or consultant may be able to supply names of specialist societies concerned with your child's illness or problem (some are mentioned in the appendix to this book). They, in turn, may be able to put you in touch with other parents nearby with whom you can liaise and share problems.

Do not be afraid, either, to ask for help from friends and neighbours so that you can get the occasional day off or evening out or even a weekend away with the rest of the family. This is not an admission of failure but rather a necessary refreshment for the one who takes the strain of caring. And if you are prepared to be on the giving end in this sort of situation, then you can be a tremendous asset in the local community. Perhaps your children are older, and you could cope with a child who, for example, has a dislocated hip, while the parents go away for a day or two. Social services are always on the look-out for foster parents for the children of parents in difficulties. One of the problems in this sphere of chronic childhood illness is a failure of communication. Both those who need help and those who would like to give help may have to take some initiative in order to make contact.

It is important to remember that there are less obvious cases than straightforward physical illness which need our active sympathy. Mental illnesses like schizophrenia may manifest themselves in teenage children, but, because of fear or lack of understanding, the attitude of the community is all too often one of avoidance. Yet in terms of heartache and worry, this strange, terrible disease takes a savage toll as parents helplessly watch the distortion of a personality and the wrecking of bright hopes for the future. The mother of a schizophrenic son wrote:

> Nearly always there was a lack of comprehension and perplexity followed by embarrassment, when I explained that he was mentally ill. Never once did anyone offer sympathy. In fact, we sensed a certain censure which extended not only to our son, but to the family as a whole. (Naomi Smith, *The Tangled Web*)

We must overcome our own ignorance and prejudices to be able to break through the cruel walls of isolation and suffering which can be built up around such a family.

Parents do not stop suffering with and for their children as they move into adulthood: but some parents may have to face the pain of suffering and loss before their child's life has even properly begun. A lot more understanding and sensitivity is needed – both from medical staff and the 'general public' – about still-birth and neonatal death. To go through the long months of pregnancy and then through the long hours of labour, only to end up with nothing, no one, leaves parents with an overwhelming sense of emptiness and loss that is

physical as well as emotional: 'My baby has been growing and moving inside me: now suddenly he is no longer there – where is he?'; 'We had a name ready, and a room and a cot and lots of little clothes: now they are all empty. What are we to do with them?' It is no help to say, 'Go away and get pregnant again as quickly as possible' or 'Never mind, you can always have another.' Such advice is as inappropriate as to tell a young widow within a day or two of her bereavement, 'Never mind, you can always find another husband.' The baby has been a real – if unknown – person to the parents for the best part of nine months, and they need to grieve for it. It is of the utmost importance that hospital staff do not feel that they need to dispose of the dead child in haste or secrecy: in almost all cases the parents will want to see it, to hold it and to be consulted about funeral and burial arrangements – above all, to know that it was real. Only then can they grieve properly for it; and only by grieving can they come through the desolation to new hope.

Equally devastating is the cruel 'cot death' syndrome, where an apparently healthy baby dies in its sleep for no very obvious reason, at any age from a few weeks to a year or so. In addition to the appalling shock and sense of nightmarish unreality, there may well be feelings of guilt. Because the causes of cot deaths still remain largely obscure, parents may start to ask themselves, 'Did we do something wrong? Could it have been avoided? Should we not have left him asleep in a room on his own? Was the bedroom too hot or too cold? Have we been feeding him wrongly?' – and, worst of all, 'Will people think we did it ourselves?' Questions do have to be asked, of course – and if they are not asked, no progress can be made in the search for the cause – but it is essential that doctors interviewing the parents should exercise the utmost tact, understanding and sympathy. They must acknowledge the full weight of such a crushing blow, allow the parents to express their bewilderment and bitterness, answer questions where they can, admit ignorance where they cannot, and do their utmost to allay feelings of guilt and blame. No one should try to dismiss the tragedy with comfort of the 'Well, never mind . . .' variety. In such situations comfort comes hard, and only through the sustained sympathy and understanding of doctors, family and friends over a long period.

In conclusion, it is important to remember that illness and even death are not the worst that can befall children. The man-made suffering which so many have to endure – lovelessness, neglect,

violence, abuse – is of a darker order altogether, cruelly destructive not only to the body but to the mind and spirit. What matters to children is a sense of safety. If the home is basically happy and loving, then they are safe in spite of suffering: in this atmosphere, love is not spoilt by sorrow but can be transfigured by it. For the ill child, as for the healthy one, such a home is the best place to be.

*

I'm not actually waiting for the day I go – I am too busy. I don't want to think about myself, about how poorly I am. I mean there's others even worse than me. I don't want sympatheticness; my brother and sister treat me like an 11-year-old brother and I don't know what I would do without them. At first when Mummy told me, I was, I can truly say, a bit frightened. But then, as I am getting older, I am beginning to understand and see through it . . .

Dying isn't really dying, it's just like coming from an old room into a new room . . . God has the answers, we have the questions, and only when we come to the end of our life will he tell us the answers. There's lots to look forward to – just meeting him, the sheer excitement of it – lots to look forward to whether you are living or dying . . .

An 11-year-old patient at Helen House, shortly before his death

7 · *Handicapped Children*

> When a woman is about to give birth she is sad because her hour of suffering is come: but when the baby is born, she forgets her suffering because she is happy that a baby has been born into the world (John 16.21).

For most parents, there is no moment more full of excitement, relief and pure joy than that when a new baby is laid in their arms – a perfect new human being, their own creation. But some parents are cheated of that magical moment. For them there is only the shock of realizing that something has gone badly wrong, that their child is congenitally deformed or damaged beyond repair by trauma at birth – or that something *may* be wrong which only months or years of anxious watching and waiting will be able to verify. For them, following the months of eager anticipation and the exhausting experience of childbirth, there is no triumph, no achievement, only the numbing realization, 'My child is handicapped – he will never be normal.' To see other mothers in the hospital nursing their perfect babies, even to hear normal babies crying in the next room, is a devastating experience.

And following the shock comes the humiliation. Although our rational minds tell us that there is no longer any stigma attached to handicap, emotionally the parents feel an overwhelming sense of failure. They have somehow 'botched the job', failed to achieve the result which everyone else seems to achieve so naturally. The baby may look odd so that you cannot show it off with pride. Indeed, you cannot show it at all without an explanation that may sound apologetic. And you know that this will get worse as the child gets older. A spastic toddler in a pushchair may not attract much attention, but a ten-year-old will, particularly if his limbs are twisted or constantly

jerking with involuntary movements. The mentally handicapped look odd too – there is no denying it – unattractive, even grotesque, childish but without childhood's charms, so that wherever you take them people will either stare as at a freak, or studiously avert their gaze.

So there comes upon the parents a terrible sense of isolation. Most young mothers naturally gravitate together, meeting at clinics and toddler groups and in their own homes to enjoy their children and to share both their normal day-to-day worries and their triumphs. But the parents of a handicapped child cannot enjoy hearing about the wondrous achievements of other people's children – how they can sit up unaided or pull themselves to stand or wave goodbye or recite nursery rhymes, or even how they have kept their parents up all night with teething troubles. The comparison with their own child, who cannot master any of these skills which others master so effortlessly, is too painful. Everywhere they look, normal healthy babies smile out at them – from the pages of catalogues, from television commercials, from other people's prams. The instinct is to shut oneself and one's child away from such painful reminders of the handicap.

And you know the trouble will not go away. It is not as though there is any hope of a cure. Nor, in these days of ubiquitous antibiotics and high-technology medicine, is there much likelihood of a kindly and timely death intervening; many of these children will live to a ripe old age. You know, too, that the problems will get worse rather than better as the years go by. As the child gets bigger and stronger it will become more difficult for parents whose own strength is decreasing to carry the sheer physical burden – to cope with lifting or with incontinence. Everyday, ordinary procedures will involve constant struggles. The skills a normal child masters almost by instinct – talking, dressing, eating, toilet training – have to be worked at every day for years and may still never be mastered. Everyday occurrences like putting on new clothes, having hair washed or nails cut, may trigger off panic reactions in the autistic child who cannot articulate his own irrational fears and cannot be comforted by reason or affection. The parent of the handicapped baby wonders if it will ever be possible to establish the proper two-way communication so essential to human relationships. Will the child ever be able to respond to affection? Or will the parents have to struggle on without even the reward of smiles and hugs and all the small signs of love which provide most parents with more than sufficient recompense for all the

trials of the early years of childhood?

And how will this handicapped child affect the marriage relationship? Can that be kept from breaking under the strain? It can indeed suffer if the burden is not properly shared: if the mother, for instance, throws herself into the caring of the handicapped child with such total dedication that the father feels himself excluded. And then it is necessary to ensure that if there are other children they do not feel resentful at the amount of time and attention which, of necessity, is devoted to the handicapped child. When a child who was both mentally and physically handicapped died suddenly, his older sister was delighted to see all his special equipment being taken out of the house and informed her grandmother, 'Now your little boy has gone.' She was implying that now they would have to take some notice of her. So somehow time and attention must be given to the normal children too. Parents must be sympathetically aware of the degree of frustration caused to siblings by the fact that they cannot do all the things which 'normal' families do, and aware too of the degree of embarrassment that they may suffer in front of their friends.

Outings and family holidays become major problems: the sort of holidays that the rest of the family needs and wants may be complicated by the presence of a handicapped child. Hotels may prove impossible. Even the seaside may present difficulties. One family whose two normal children relished the usual sand and sea in the summer found that their mentally handicapped child had a beach phobia: he would refuse to get out of the car when they arrived, presenting the parents with a dilemma. Should one parent take the other children down on to the beach while the second parent remained in the car with the handicapped child? – miserable for all concerned. Should they leave him in the car on his own and spend the morning down on the beach worrying whether he was all right, or in danger of hurting himself, or getting heat stroke, or being reported to the NSPCC? Or should they carry him fighting and screaming on to the beach, running the gauntlet of shocked and horrified onlookers and let him continue to fight and scream on the sand until his panic (as it eventually did) subsided? So all days, even holidays, are fraught with problems of which most parents – even those who claim that their children are 'difficult' – have no conception.

In all this it is the parents who are not only the carers but the sufferers – in almost all cases more resentful and bewildered by their terrible misfortune than the child itself. Those who have to look on

at the situation need to think imaginatively about how they would feel. Sympathy may not have to be expressed in words; theological speculation will not be called for unless the parents wish to discuss it in these terms. Indeed, what words or speculations can be remotely adequate to offer to distraught parents who are in the first throes of anguish and bewilderment? More important is your expression as you look at the child – and you need to look, not look away. You need to look and see him as a *person*, not a freak or a specimen, a person who through no fault of his own or his parents has had to embark on life with devastating disadvantages. And what counts is the constancy of your friendship to the parents over the years – to ease, by listening, the terrible load of problems and suffering, to be a bulwark against the overwhelming sense of isolation, and to share the triumphs.

For there are triumphs. Where life is so fraught with difficulty, every tiny achievement seems a major breakthrough and brings the most enormous satisfaction. One child who had been completely silent for his first four and a half years was playing at the kitchen sink when his grandmother tied one of her aprons round him to keep him dry. So incensed was he by this indignity that he burst out with 'Take it off'. That, indeed, seemed a miracle. The same boy, in his teens, finally mastered the tricky art of shoelace-tying. That, remarked his mother, was as great a triumph as all the GCE successes of her two other normal children.

There can be a positive side for those prepared to look, though it will emerge slowly and perhaps only in retrospect. The presence of a handicapped child in the family can bring out qualities in all the other members as they share the load together – grandparents, parents and children. The co-operation of all the generations calls for immense patience, fortitude, forbearance, understanding and good humour, such as might not otherwise be developed but from which all, not just the handicapped child, will benefit. A distinguished Oxford don had a mentally handicapped grandson – a crushing blow, you would think, for one who had moved all his life in circles where intellectual achievement counted for everything. Yet there grew up between the eminent scholar and the pathetic little boy a most rare and precious friendship: and the two of them would go off together hand in hand by bus or train to attend organ recitals and visit cathedrals. An oddly assorted pair, but both the richer for their companionship.

There are nowadays many agencies, both statutory and voluntary, to give the parents of handicapped children support from the cradle to the grave. The child is not left on the parents' hands all the time, and no longer are children shut up at home for years on end (although this does still occasionally, and appallingly, occur). Even the most severely handicapped will be transported from home to places of education and care so that parents have some break during the day, and longer breaks may be possible. Every effort will be made to help physically handicapped children to develop and express their full potential intellectually: modern technological gadgets can be a miracle in giving these children the powers of communication or mobility. When the mentally handicapped become too old for school, some occupation for them can be found in training centres and sheltered workshops where simple manual tasks help to give a sense of purpose and usefulness. They can also be encouraged to pursue their own special interests: many of these children do have limited areas of special interest in which they may grow very knowledgeable, whether it be church architecture, football teams or domestic plumbing.

It may be disputed whether all handicapped children are at present enabled to achieve their full potential. There has been considerable publicity recently for new forms of treatment for children with a certain form of brain-damage. The treatment is based on intensive and prolonged stimulation, both mental and physical, to try to re-educate the brain – encouraging the healthy part to take over the functions of the damaged part. Some British children have benefitted enormously from treatment available in the USA and in Hungary, and one can only admire the superhuman efforts made by their parents on their behalf. But only a few are in a position domestically or financially to take advantage of such chances. It would seem clear that the medical establishment in this country needs to look more closely at the work that has been done in this field, and perhaps be less ready to advise parents to abandon hope of improvement. But even if such forms of treatment do become more widely available, they put a gruelling strain on the rest of the family, and on the child – the regime may literally occupy every waking moment. Parents will have to consider carefully before committing themselves to a life-style which may prove too costly to the family as a whole. So unless or until a lot of the weight of such intensive treatment can be borne by professional carers – and financed by the state – many parents

may feel that it is incompatible with the needs of the whole family. They will decide that it is more important to surround the handicapped child with an atmosphere of love and happiness, to involve him in normal family life as much as possible, and, within the limits of that normal family life, to encourage him as far as possible along the road to achievement and independence.

There may come a time when even with help at home the struggle becomes too great. Because of age or illness or the death of the partner, the parent may no longer be physically or psychologically able to cope. Handing your child over to the care of some sort of institution will at any stage of life be a terrible wrench: there are bound to be feelings of guilt at 'giving up'. Perhaps we should learn to regard our limitations as in themselves a form of guidance. 'I no longer have the strength to cope: the time has come to entrust my child to those who do.' And there are bound to be abiding worries about the child's welfare: how can strangers, even if they claim to be experts, possibly understand the child with all his needs and idiosyncracies as well as the parent who has cared for him since birth? Will they remember to brush his teeth, wash his hair, cut his toenails? Will they fill him up with medication to 'keep him quiet'? Will he still be able to have some of his own possessions, pursue his own interests, go to church? Will they notice when he is unwell or in pain if he is unable to tell them? These worries will not go away, but they can, to some extent, be allayed by frequent visits, or by having the child home periodically. Above all, it will help to foster a friendly relationship with the institution staff, who will welcome information and advice about the patient if it is offered tactfully, without criticism, and accompanied by appreciation for all their efforts.

In all this the church can play a vital role – a place where both child and parents can feel accepted. Not just accepted in spite of the handicap, but accepted *and* valued. For the handicapped have much to teach us. The children who struggle against disabilities to achieve what other chidren can do with ease, or remain cheerful through innumerable operations and courses of painful treatment – they are the truly valiant. And the mentally handicapped may show some of the qualities highlighted in the beatitudes, the true poverty and simplicity of spirit which remains uncluttered and uncorrupted by success or greed or anxiety.

A party of mentally handicapped patients from a Birmingham hospital, with staff and parents, were given a week's holiday out of

season at an East-coast holiday camp. Seeing some of the patients milling around the little camp shop, uncertain what to buy, uncertain how to ask for what they wanted, uncertain how to pay for it, one mother remarked to the girl behind the counter, 'You must find this very trying.' 'Not at all', replied the girl. 'It is a pleasure to help these people – they are so gentle and polite. Our normal customers come in here and are rude, quarrelsome, complaining, abusive. They are the ones who are trying.' And another member of the camp staff, watching the patients eagerly helping the waitresses to clear away one of the meals, commented, 'These are the ones who will get the front seats in the Kingdom of Heaven.' It makes one wonder: who, in the eyes of God, really are the handicapped?

*

God is love: and He enfoldeth
All the world in one embrace:
With unfailing grasp He holdeth
Every child of every race.
And when human hearts are breaking
Under sorrow's iron rod,
Then they find that self-same aching
Deep within the heart of God.

Timothy Rees

8 · *Miracles*

Introduction

One of the most mystifying things about illness is why some people get better and some people do not. Even when all the physical signs and symptoms are well understood, the mystery remains and, for those involved in caring for people who do not recover, it is a very awesome and disturbing one. The mystery is apparently deepened for the religious mind when the sick person is surrounded by the prayers of faith for his or her recovery, prayers which do not seem to work. There is, after all, something in religion which leads us to expect miracles. Is God not in control? Can he not do what he likes? Did not Jesus work miracles? Were his disciples not taught to ask for whatever they wished, believing they would receive it?

The questions tumble out one after the other, especially when someone close to us is involved, one for whom we and others have prayed in great faith. Can we expect miracles? It is perhaps worth sparing a few moments to consider how we use the word 'miracle' in our everyday speech.

Some years ago a stricken aircraft landed on a West German autobahn amidst all the traffic. Its wings were ripped off as it went under one of the bridges and it was brought to a shuddering halt. 'Only' a few people were killed in the crash; the majority survived. 'It's a miracle!' proclaimed all the newspapers the following day.

Here is a young couple speeding through the night to the maternity hospital for the birth of their first child. They will stay together through the birth as they planned. And in the cold light of the dawn a new father emerges, shell-shocked and exhilarated all at the same time; 'It's a miracle' he says to himself over and over again, 'It's a miracle!'

It is almost twenty years ago that man went to the moon, the result of a sustained concentration of vision, planning and scientific and engineering brilliance. We have almost forgotten Neil Armstrong's crackling 'One small step for mankind' and the fuzzy television pictures of men playing golf in a lunar bunker. But at the time we all said, 'It's miraculous!'

And then there is that feat of brain surgery where the surgeon, using all his skill and the latest techniques of microsurgery, is able to remove the offending tumour and the patient recovers to full health again. 'It's a miracle!' all say in great admiration and not a little thankfulness.

Common to our use of 'miracle' to describe these four separate occurrences, there is a sense of wonder at something we have really no right to expect. We are being taken beyond our normal experience into unknown territory and even if we know, deep-down, that it is the most natural thing in the world, like the birth of a child, we still have no second thoughts about calling it a miracle. It is miraculous to us we say, if to no one else!

It is worth bearing this in mind when we narrow down the word 'miracle' to refer to a very specific set of circumstances in which the usual 'laws of nature' as they are called are transcended. When someone close to us is desperately ill and apparently there is no hope, our final thought may well be 'We need a miracle now'. By that we mean that despite all that the medical people say, another hand will be seen in the situation and, against all the odds, he or she will get better.

This is often our last hope and why should we be robbed of it? After all, the doctors are the first to admit that they do not know everything. As we saw in a previous chapter, there are limits to our knowledge. But even where medical knowledge is reasonably complete, unexpected things can and do happen. Moreover, the Christian faith encourages us to believe in miracles. After all, the gospel picture of Jesus is of someone who went about doing good and healing the sick. Perhaps, then, the miracles of Jesus are as good a place as any to start.

The miracles of Jesus

Towards the end of the sixth chapter of Mark's Gospel there is a description of the excitement that followed Jesus everywhere he went in Galilee. He had already established his reputation as a healer

and now the merest rumour that he was in the area was enough to encourage families and friends to bring out the sick and lay them by the roadside in the hope that Jesus would pass that way. At one point the gospel writer seems to indicate that a personal encounter with Jesus is unnecessary: simply to touch the fringe of his garment is enough (Mark 6.53–6). We are left with an exciting image of Jesus striding about the countryside, freely dispensing the healing strength of God to all in need.

The individual descriptions of Jesus healing the sick tell a different story, however. Such a series of incidents is recorded by Mark in the previous chapter in which three people are healed, Legion the madman, the unnamed woman with a haemorrhage and Jairus' daughter (Mark 5).

First of all, Jesus encounters a madman living amongst the rocks and tombs of the cliffs on the east side of the Sea of Galilee. According to the beliefs of the time, he was possessed by unclean spirits, hence his name 'Legion'. Jesus, always a man of his times, accepts that Legion is possessed (although we might want to call his illness by a more modern term), and transfers the spirits to a nearby herd of swine. When Legion wishes to accompany Jesus back across the lake, Jesus forbids him: 'Go home to your own folk and tell them what the Lord in his mercy has done for you' (v. 19). In other words, this was a victory for the power of God allied to faith, just as the storm on the lake had been (Mark 4.35–41), and therefore was a proclamation of the good news.

Jesus returns to the west side of the lake and is immediately besought by Jairus to come and heal his daughter who is 'at death's door' (v. 23). On the way to Jairus' home, a woman with a severe haemorrhage edges through the crowd and touches his cloak in the belief that this will cure her. Immediately, with that great sensitivity that he possessed, Jesus knew what had happened. 'Power had gone out of him' (v. 30). Perhaps, after all, the picture of Jesus striding through the countryside, healing all who were put in his path, is not the only one. Healing took its toll, wearied him in the intensity of it all, both physically and mentally. Perhaps the health of others was only won at enormous cost to himself. Nevertheless, when he confronts the woman and sees her helplessness and just a little faith, he pronounces her well. His compassion for those who cannot help themselves is boundless.

When finally he arrives at Jairus' house, he discovers that the little

girl is dead. Perhaps the woman with the haemorrhage has delayed Jesus over long? But Jesus encourages Jairus to keep up his faith and eventually the little girl is restored. The situation is so remarkable that the precise words of Jesus in their original language are remembered, 'Talitha cum' – 'Get up, my child'. What is even more remarkable is Jesus' insistence that Jairus should say nothing about the whole incident. What better publicity could there have been for Jesus and yet he orders everyone to keep quiet. It is a situation repeated more than once in the healing miracles of Jesus (Mark 1.43 and 7.36).

Such a brief survey of only three of Jesus' miracles cannot possibly do justice to a subject which is so intricate, so varied and ultimately so mystifying. But already certain things begin to emerge. A personal encounter is at the heart of healing. On the part of the sick person or a near relative, that encounter required a degree of faith that was not always found amongst those who heard Jesus. Such a faith meant that people were willing 'to take a risk on Jesus', to trust him with their lives. And on Jesus' part, it seems that healing was not 'on tap' and indiscriminate. It took time to build up a degree of trust, it made great demands upon his physical, emotional and spiritual energy. And always there seems to have been the dilemma between public and private, in which the natural tendency for self-display is always rejected. One sometimes has the feeling as one re-reads the miracle stories that, although many of them took place in public and therefore could not be kept quiet, Jesus disliked any kind of publicity because it would lead to a quite unworthy appreciation of who he was.

Interestingly, John says on one occasion that this is precisely what happened after the feeding of the five thousand. The people surrounded him to make him their king, the wrong sort of king for the wrong sort of reason: 'In very truth, I know that you have not come looking for me because you saw signs, but because you ate the bread and your hunger was satisfied' (John 6.26). Jesus knew only too well that miracles could and would produce the wrong sort of reactions in people. That is why he refused the first and second temptations to turn stones into bread and to throw himself from the pinnacle of the temple (Matthew 4.1–7). That is why he steadfastly declined to give a sign from heaven to those who asked (Matthew 16.1–4). And he did so to the bitter end, even when they ridiculed him on the Cross: ' "He saved others," they said, "but he cannot save himself. Let the

Messiah, the King of Israel, come down now from the cross. If we see that we shall believe" ' (Mark 15.29–32).

Why did Jesus perform miracles? So far as we are able to tell they were not simply done out of compassion. They were certainly not done to prove who he really was, or he would have responded to the call for signs. No, the miracles of healing, and many of the nature miracles too, are best understood if they are seen as pointers to Jesus' central message, that of the Kingdom of God breaking into peoples' lives if only they would open their eyes and ears to perceive it. Incidentally, that is why the gospel writers seem to prefer to record those stories in which the blind recover their sight, the dead hear and the dumb are made to speak. Those were exactly the sort of things to look out for when the Messiah was about to come, said Isaiah, and Jesus quoted his very words in the synagogue at Nazareth (Luke 4.18–19).

Did the miracles of Jesus really happen?

There have been two responses to that question. One says that we have to believe in miracles because even to question them, let alone disbelieve them, means that we are rejecting the whole gospel picture of Jesus. The second response says that we cannot possibly believe that the miracles happened because that sort of thing just does not happen – it is 'unscientific'.

There is, however, a third possible response, because you can say, if you wish, a very reverent 'I don't know. Miracles are not part of my understanding of the way life goes and yet, for the four gospel writers, they were evidently very important. The feeding of the five thousand, and the healing stories, spoke volumes to them about who Jesus was. It would be arrogant to set their record aside and yet I find miracles very difficult and – I just don't know.'

Why is it that such reverent agnosticism in religious matters is usually regarded as rather less than right? After all, in the world of scientific enquiry, for example, it is quite in order to confess one's ignorance in the face of the vast complexity of a particular subject. That shows a proper humility in the face of truth but at the same time is a spur to keep on thinking. So it may also be in religion. There is no commandment which says we must be certain about everything or that 'faith' makes everything easy. The touchstone of faith in the gospels is not whether or not you believe in miracles. Even the greatest miracle of all, the resurrection, only 'produced' faith in one

or two disciples. The relationship of faith to the miracles of Jesus is this: faith makes the gospel picture of Jesus as the worker of miracles *understandable*, it does not necessarily make the miracles *credible*. We may maintain a deep faith in Jesus and still say of his miracles, 'I don't know. That is not my understanding of how things happen.'

Do miracles happen today?

Reverent agnosticism – 'Lord, I just don't know' – may also be a very good place from which to begin to answer the question of whether or not miracles happen today. When we speak of 'miracle' in relation to illness, we generally mean 'God intervening to heal, suspending the usual laws of nature to put things right.' Of course, no one would be foolish enough to say that the 'laws of nature' are unbreakable. One of the things one learns in dealing with disease is that unusual and unexpected things can and do happen. The so-called 'laws of nature' are really descriptions of what normally happens in most cases. But there is always room for surprise in observing and understanding what does and can happen. In the last century, all of the progress in chemistry was based on the understanding of atoms – those 'indivisible' particles of matter. And atoms *are* indivisible under most circumstances, but one would be living in great ignorance if one still believed that they could never be divided. Our present society, with all the ambiguities of nuclear power for both peace and war, has that fact at its core. But you may still do chemistry experiments and be sure that the atoms will not divide! There is this everyday consistency in what happens which enables us to talk about the natural order. We do not know everything, but we do know a little more than we did. And what little we know leads us to expect that there is far more that we *do not* know than we ever thought possible. There are more things in heaven and earth than are dreamt of in our philosophy.

It may be that God in his great wisdom and kindness respects our little bit of knowledge. He who in some way, by some gigantic original miracle, set the whole created universe in motion and formulated the laws which preserve and maintain it – he surely has the power to transcend his own laws if he will for his own special reasons, as he did at the resurrection. But if God were constantly butting in, constantly disrupting the rhythm and regularity of the natural order, how totally disconcerting that would be! The more we understand of nature's laws, and the workings of the universe, the more we depend on those laws for our sense of security and stability. We

understand the law of gravity: how unnerving it would be if the occasional apple fell upwards instead of downwards. We understand the concept of orbiting planets: how unnerving if one morning the sun rose in the west and galloped across the sky in a couple of hours. Similarly, the more we understand of the workings of our own bodies, the more unnerving it would be if they started to behave in totally unpredictable ways. And the more difficult it would be to formulate new theories, to push forward with new research, to find new cures. In our rational, 'scientific' age, we depend on what we already know to advance in knowledge: and it may be that God chooses to work his miracles these days through that knowledge, through the questing and the patience and the dedication and the cleverness of man, rather than by waiving the rules and intervening himself to set things right. Even in those cases out of the blue, where healing seems quite literally to be 'miraculous', it may be that with a more perfect understanding we would see that the 'rules' were not in fact being broken but rather enhanced and made incredibly more complex and coherent than we already see them to be.

The fact remains that when we are at the limits of our physical and spiritual strength we still hope for miracles. It is worth thinking further, then, about ways in which they do happen today. This will involve enlarging our understanding of what a 'miracle' is. If we are prepared to do that, we will see that miracles do happen today, but not always in the way we expect. If we want a miracle as a piece of instantaneous magic, then we are expecting something that is neither present today nor described in the New Testament. If, however, we regard a miracle as the breaking in of God's power to us, then we see that both then and now miracles are a reality.

(a) *The miracle of the body itself* Perhaps the greatest miracle is the extra-ordinary healing power of the body itself, enabling recovery to take place without any conscious effort on our part. Doctors seek to remove what may be interfering with that power. They may give it a boost so that it can work unaided, but it is the healing inside us all that completes the cure. A surgeon may take out an inflamed appendix, but it is our own body that heals up the scar and tidies up the sewing inside! We move towards health naturally: it is the God-given norm that we are created in such a way that we have a built-in repair system. Considering how complicated the body is, it is remarkable that 'breakdowns' are so rare.

(b) *The miracle of modern medicine* The understanding that the healing grace of God may reach us in a multitude of ways leads us on to a positive view of modern medicine. For can we not say that one way God has chosen to heal in our day is through the skill, the devotion, the caring of the medical professions? Is it not a miracle that these days the blind can be made to see by removal of a cataract? And that the lame man walks with his artificial hip? Is it not a miracle that childless couples can conceive with fertilization having taken place outside the body? Should we not be thankful for hearing aids and bifocal glasses and ointments for dry skin and lotions to kill head lice? Why do we regard all these things as ours and not given by God? Why is it that because we understand part of the processes of disease that we have the arrogance to exclude God altogether?

Take, for example, the case of penicillin. In 1928 Alexander Fleming noticed the effect of a mould on a culture of bacteria which he had prepared before his summer holidays. The mould had got on to the bacteria by sheer chance but Fleming saw its significance and penicillin was discovered. But it was left to Howard Florey and E. B. Chain to develop penicillin for clinical use, growing the mould in some old bed-pans, and making the first trials on human beings in Oxford's Radcliffe Infirmary in the early months of 1942. Like so many stories, that of penicillin is a mixture of chance, intuition and brilliance, but its results in the treatment of infection have been miraculous. We have antibiotics that have now conquered the scourge of most bacterial diseases. Diphtheria and meningitis are still with us, but do not invoke the horror they did fifty years ago. And what about tuberculosis? It has become a rare and curable disease.

And there are even more remarkable stories of miracles which we never think about at all. Smallpox used to be a terrible plague. Those who contracted it would either die or recover with terrible and permanent scars. But because of careful and world-wide co-operation under the auspices of the World Health Organization, smallpox has been *totally* eradicated! In the 1970s, medical students were taught how to distinguish chicken pox from small pox – now that would be an irrelevance! Is that not a miracle? The fact that it has taken a lot of hard work by us makes it more like, rather than less like, the miracles of Jesus.

Much religious talk of miracles implies that God might take over

when human healing skill is at an end. Is it not more constructive, more true to the God of creation, to affirm that God is at work not as some supernatural backstop, who in any case only seems to catch the ball of faith some of the time, but as the patient inspirer of all discovery, who works out his healing purposes through the hand and brain of those prepared to use their talents for the good of all men and women?

(c) *Miracles of sudden healing* Sudden healing is probably what we all mean by a miracle: this moment I have an arthritic leg and hip, and the next moment I do not. Perhaps it is worth stating here a scientific principle which is all-pervasive through every aspect of our mental, emotional, physical and spiritual lives. This principle is that '*nothing comes without a cost*'. There was a cost to Jesus for his miracles: it is described in the New Testament. For the Christian, there was a cost for the resurrection and our salvation – theologians have argued about why and how, but we can all understand the fact and the agony of the crucifixion. There has been a cost to the miracles of modern science – it is counted in time and human lives.

There are no doubt those who can effectively channel power in the right direction by the very nature of who or what they are, and healing can be found from them at a cost of their strength, our faith and God's power. But notice that this is not some sort of magic trick. Some have undoubtedly believed it is. They look for the sort of sudden miracles which produce healing when all the doctors have failed. To meet our need, there are not a few clergymen and others who claim to heal by faith and who advertise their services as ones at which miracles will take place. The ban on publicity which so often Jesus enjoined on those he healed does not seem to affect them. To be present at their healing services is to be confronted by the tragic sight of so many of the chronic sick who present themselves in a desperate but understandable desire to be well. Let it be said that there is a world of difference between such healing services and the quiet, dignified laying on of hands that takes place within the pastoral ministry of a local priest or minister. Here there are no quick results offered, no dramatic gestures or prayers. Simply there is the recognition that our health and our ill-health have spiritual dimensions as well as physical ones and that the grace of God is available to us in many ways if we are ready to receive it.

We should never underestimate God's healing power. Doctors are

confronted day by day with aspects of health that they do not understand. Some patients get better and some do not, but there is not always a rational explanation of why that should be so. One cannot avoid noticing that there are those alive today whom the doctors had predicted would be dead, and that there are those who had 'incurable' disease who are well. To call such things 'miracles' simply avoids the issue if that is just another way of saying that we do not understand it! On the other hand, it *is* possible to accept it as a manifestation of God's grace to us, not earned by our faith or demanded by our prayers. Something for which we can simply give thanks to God.

(d) *The miracle of growing spiritually and emotionally* When something goes wrong we ask, with our own usual self-centred bias, 'Why me?' A more rewarding question may be, 'Why not me?' The people we most love and admire are usually those who have had experience of suffering and have made something worthwhile out of it. Why should not we be a camp-follower in the noble army of martyrs? What can we learn from this strange and painful experience?

We experience dependence on others and this is important, particularly perhaps if we have always been able to cope well on our own. For once we have to be on the receiving end of help and learn to appreciate the good-will and sympathy and practical kindness which pain and weakness call forth. Spiritually too, we who have always been able to pray for ourselves and for others are likely to find that in our own illness we cannot pray for ourselves at all. Others do the job for us. Eventually something will be asked of us in the way of courage. Why not?

We also have a chance to achieve a new kind of personal relationship with those nearest to us. We find that our marriage partner manages to cope with the running of our home in our absence and our children rise to the occasion. They all make time to visit, looking on us with anxious, loving eyes. This is our chance to respond by expressing gratitude. We are bound to find ourselves saying, 'I had a frightful night but a young doctor/nurse/Sister sat with me and made me a cup of tea . . .' or, 'They made me get up and I walked a few steps but felt awful and was glad to get back to bed. But tomorrow I'm going to walk a bit more and feel a bit better.' This will be the reward for anxious watchers. The patient becomes attractive as well as pitiful.

Often, when the body defences are all down, some feeble little

thing called our spirit starts to stir and stretch. We may be more receptive to the influence of those elements in Christianity which we have ignored before because we did not seem to need them. We become 'as little children' and therefore capable of 'entering the kingdom'. The silent handclasp of a loved or loving visitor is symbolic of the handclasp of God. It expresses complete understanding of our weakness. It asks nothing of us except that our hand is to lie in theirs with trustful abandon. This may in itself release power into us or it may enable normal healing processes to work better than they can do when we are in a state of agitation and fretfulness. It also establishes a contact which we know can last whatever happens to our physical condition.

These are all miracles of growth in stature and wholeness, and they may continue to flourish even when our bodily strength declines away. Sometimes there is no cure, no miraculous answer to the faithful prayer for life. But there is healing, a healing that goes far beyond physical well-being. In 1983, Bishop John Robinson learned that he had cancer, and he preached a sermon about it in his parish church in North Yorkshire. He spoke of the God who can be found in cancer as in everything else, of his initial shock and then the realization that he must round off his account, as he called it. This included preparing for heaven but not in some sentimental Victorian way.

> Rather, for the Christian it is preparing for eternal life, which means real living, more abundant life, which is begun, continued but not ended now. And this means it is about a quality of life not quantity. How long it goes on here is purely secondary. So preparing for eternity means learning really to live, becoming more concerned with contributing to and enjoying what matters most – giving the most to life and getting the most from it, while it is on offer. That is why, amongst other things, we are shortly off to Florence and Venice, where we have never been before . . . (*The Guardian*, 7.11.83).

Is that not a miracle of healing in a very special way, a triumph of God's grace?

We look for signs and wonders, miraculous happenings and cures. We get frustrated with God when they do not happen and we overlook the fact that miracles of a totally different and far more important dimension are happening in our lives and in those near to us. We cannot escape the randomness of human nature, for we are bound

in the bundle of life, subject to all its ills – and yet, St Paul believed, 'Our citizenship is in heaven'. As he says,

> I am convinced that neither death nor life, nor angels nor principalities, nor things present nor things to come, nor powers, nor height, nor depth nor anything else in all creation will be able to separate us from the love of God (Rom. 8.38–9).

We are a part of nature and yet have the capacity to transcend it. God has set within us an essential dignity which seeks the truth and which has the courage to rise above the most debilitating kind of disease. That is a very special miracle.

*

> There is nothing that God hath established in a constant course of nature, and which therefore is done every day, but would seem a Miracle, and exercise our admiration, if it were done but once.
>
> John Donne, Easter Day Sermon, 1627

9 · *Praying about Illness*

Whether we normally pray a lot, a little, or not at all, when life comes to the crunch most of us will find ourselves saying over and over again inside our heads, 'Please don't let the worst happen . . . please don't let it be cancer . . . please don't let my child die . . . please don't let it hurt too much . . .' We may feel that we are being shamefully naive and that this is not a legitimate form of prayer. Certainly it is a form of prayer that can easily degenerate into a sort of superstitious mutter if we resort to it in every minor and totally secular crisis: 'Please let me find that lost library book . . . please don't let the dentist discover any holes in my teeth . . . please let me pass my driving test . . .' This is wishing, not praying, and we would be foolish to expect it to 'work'. But when life is dark and desperate, when we are distraught or appalled, then a naked wish may become the most urgent and earnest prayer that we have ever prayed. And we need not be ashamed. The first thing that Jesus told his disciples when they asked for a lesson on prayer was that we should address God as 'Father'. We are not pleading with some temperamental, power-glutted potentate to notice us and have mercy, but pouring out our troubles to an attentive and sympathetic father. What could be more natural than to tell him, 'The one thing I want more than anything in the world at this moment is . . . for my baby to survive . . . my wife to get better . . . the X-ray to be clear . . .'? This is how Jesus himself prayed when things came to the last awful crunch in Gethsemane: 'The one thing I want more than anything else in the world is for this ordeal to be removed' (Mark 14.36).

When we pray like this, we are not – or should not be – trying to twist God's arm, or thinking that we can prevail on him to change his mind. It is a bad mistake to try and lay down conditions to God:

'This is what I want, and if you don't let me have it I shan't believe in you any more' – like the child who threatens 'I won't be your friend any more.' God will not be tested like this. But it is a mistake also to imagine that God is in some way testing us, and that if he does not answer our basic 'gut prayers' in the way we want, it is because we are not good enough or our faith is not strong enough. This would seem to be a highly dangerous assumption, but one which is unfortunately too prevalent in some popular 'healing' movements. What a devastating effect it must produce on good, sincere, suffering people to feel that they or their loved ones are not to be healed because they have not believed hard enough. Their problems, far from being helped, are compounded by a sense of total inadequacy. We do not believe that this is how God, or prayer, works at all: there is no exclusive club where, once we have earned membership, we have unlimited access to some magical power at and for our own convenience. After all, Jesus' prayer in Gethsemane did not 'work' for him in that limited sense.

But, of course, he did not stop at the point of telling God what he most wanted and most feared. He went on to add, 'Yet not my will but Thine be done.' Surely all our praying, for ourselves in illness or for others, needs to be accompanied by that rider. It does not have to be a statement of resignation, of passively bowing one's head to the bludgeonings of chance and resolving meanwhile to keep a stiff upper lip; it can be, as it was for Jesus, an act of acceptance, creative and forward-looking.

The whole problem of suffering and pain is a mystery far too deep and dark for our comprehension: we cannot understand why the innocent should be struck down or why some should recover from serious illness and others not. We do not believe that God *wants* bad things to happen to us. But we do believe that *if* the bad things happen, we will be given the strength and grace to see them through in his way: that *whatever* happens we can, with his help, turn it into a positive experience from which we can gain new insights and may receive new, unexpected mercies. Neville Ward, in his book *The Use of Praying*, suggests that our prayer should be: 'In this situation that has come to me I want to know and do God's will as fully as I can.' He continues, 'The result of adopting this attitude is not that the struggle ceases, but that what it is all about changes completely. For the Christian believer, in suffering, the struggle is not 'about' *enduring* the suffering, but *serving God in it*.' If we pray in this spirit, then there

are things which we can ask for ourselves or others and trust that we will receive – strength and grace, patience and self-control, and the assurance that we, or they, are in God's hands whatever happens, whether there is physical recovery or not. So we can tell God in all honesty what we want, and then trust in him for the rest.

Now we believe that God knows what we want and what we need before we ask and maybe before we even know ourselves, that he understands and loves each one of us more fully and deeply than we can ever understand or love. So what is the point of praying? What, specifically, is the point of praying for others when they are ill? By doing so, we are offering up our love and concern to God which we believe is pleasing to him. And we believe that somehow prayer puts a positive charge into what otherwise might be a negative situation. When we pray for sick people, we surround them with an atmosphere of love and compassion which in some way combines with God's love and compassion to promote the cause of health. Prayer is not an attempt to persuade God to change his mind (as though the illness were his will), but it may change the prevailing spiritual climate and thus provide an atmosphere in which God can work more freely.

Doctors are the first to agree that a positive attitude on the part of the patient is a major step towards health, and that nothing hinders healing more than resentment or anger or self-pity. Prayer is a way of trying to co-operate with God to create an atmosphere where health – and that is something far more than physical well-being – can prevail. It is a partnership which may also involve the skill of doctors and the care of nurses and the products of modern technology.

The sick person cannot necessarily do this for himself. Angela Ashwin, in her book *Heaven in Ordinary*, recalls how, after a serious illness, her baby son had to have several X-rays of his heart. 'As he was only a baby, I had to stand behind him in the X-ray room, supporting him under his arms and holding him still in the beam of radiation. This is a parable of intercession. We stand still, facing the rays of God's love, and hold someone in that beam of light, as I held Andrew. It is a partnership with God for the sake of someone else.'

The same idea underlies the story in Luke's Gospel (Luke 5.18) of the four friends who brought a paralysed man to Jesus and let him down through the roof. Luke comments that it was 'when Jesus saw their faith' that he was able to heal. They were – both literally and metaphorically – carrying their friend with the strength of their love and concern, doing for him what he could not do for himself. We are

so closely bound to one another in complex mutual interdependency, and at no time more closely – physically, emotionally, and spiritually – than when illness strikes. Trapped in a cage of pain or despair, those at the centre may feel unable to pray at all, but then the prayers of their friends may bear them up on strong arms of love.

One lady who had passed through a long period of stress and felt at an all-time low ebb of health and spirits, confided to a fellow church member that she felt at rock-bottom. 'That's it', came the reply, 'at the bottom there is rock.' When crisis or tragedy threaten to overwhelm us, it may be all we can do to cling to the knowledge that there is no depth of suffering or pain or darkness which Jesus himself has not plumbed: that he is with us there even when we cannot see him. What may seem at first a grim hanging-on to a shred of faith becomes in itself a prayer and a life-line. If we go willingly into the darkness, it may be that we shall find it full of his presence: and he will not leave us comfortless.

*

When experience is lived through without regrets and reservations . . . it is found that what looked unendurable, as it appeared on the horizon of possibility, proves itself quite a different thing, as though someone shares the load when the moment comes for taking it on . . . What looked, as it was approached, as the place of sacrifice, turns out to be the place where it is found that the Lord provides, the truth about God being that He is not a taker but a giver.

Neville Ward, *The Use of Praying*

10 · *Death and Bereavement*

One often feels most helpless in circumstances of death and bereavement. Death has such an air of finality about it. There are no second chances, no putting right of things said or done imperfectly the previous day. There is often a feeling of failure. 'Did I do all I could?' we ask ourselves.

> A young house officer recalls confidently assuring a thirty-year old patient in the coronary-care unit that he was not dying. Almost immediately the man had a cardiac arrest and died forty minutes later despite intensive resuscitation attempts. The doctor sat for a while with the patient's wife, drinking the ward sister's tea. There was little that he could say by way of consolation. There had been no warning. But that did not prevent him getting out his records on his return to the unit. Had he missed anything? What could he have done differently? He left feeling wretched. The coroner's report later confirmed a large clot in the lung.

Nothing more could have been done, but that did not ease the young doctor's feeling of helplessness.

There will be many times like this, when death comes as a sickening blow, especially to the young and those for whom the agenda of life is still full. But that is not the whole story, for people may actually be content to die.

> For five months Hilda had been fighting a losing battle with cancer. Then one day, there was a smile, a squeeze of her husband's hand and a faint, 'Thank you, doctor.' Five minutes later forty-two-year-old Hilda was dead.

And then there was Paddy.

'But I haven't even been baptized doctor! Heaven means nothing to me.' A week later the local vicar baptized Paddy in the house where he had been a lodger for a long time. He was sixty-eight with no relatives, only a caring landlady. Three weeks passed and the Bishop arrived to confirm Paddy a member of the Church of England. In Paddy's eyes, that was the passport to the heaven he had ignored all his life.

Just two examples of people who died successfully, one might say. Their carers – a husband, a landlady, a vicar, a GP – all played their parts until death intervened in a perfectly natural way.

It is this possibility, the possibility of death coming almost as a friend, that gives hope to the carer. With sudden death, an accident, a suicide, a massive heart-attack, one can only try to pick up the pieces in the lives of the bereaved and this is in itself a work of grace and hope. Caring in those circumstances has another purpose, one of giving a new sense of direction in an emotional desert, and we shall return to this later. But caring for the sick who will die of their illness has to be viewed differently. At its highest, it is not standing hopelessly by, administering first-aid only; it is a full participation in the greatest of all mysteries – like Paddy's landlady, who was not a bit-player in a scene of little importance, but a major character in the biggest scene of Paddy's life.

Of course, we do not often see ourselves in this role. We are simply doing what we can, drawn into a situation far more deeply than we first intended. We like to see ourselves – the friend, the neighbour, the church visitor – as 'outsiders', peripheral to the main scene being played out in the sick room. But there is little doubt that if we are prepared to give the time, the patience, the energy, the sheer determination to keep going, then we shall see that we are playing a much more positive role, one which can make a real contribution to the quality of life of the dying and perhaps even to their understanding of what is happening.

The biggest single factor preventing us from becoming involved with the dying is fear. We worry lest we do or say the wrong thing. We fear that our concern may be misinterpreted, that we shall be taken for interfering busy-bodies by the family. Perhaps we fear that we may have an exaggerated perception of what is going on. What if things are not as serious as they appear? We do not wish to seem foolish. In any case, people have a right to privacy, a right to do

things in their own way. Who are we to offer help? What do we know?

There is also the very real fear of the process of dying. Most of us, fortunately, face death so infrequently that we are not sure we can cope with it. We are concerned that more and more demands will be made of us. We are anxious lest something should actually *happen* at the moment of death.

What we need to understand is that the close family of a desperately sick person have many fears of their own, and of a very similar kind to ours. They too are anxious about whether or not they will be able to cope. They worry, perhaps, about money and its availability at the right time. Families will be concerned about the shopping, about meeting the children from school, about keeping the sheets clean. As time goes by, they may get frantic for some rest and at the back of their mind is the nagging question 'What will *happen* and what will life be like afterwards?'

And let us never underestimate the fears of the person at the centre of it all. There is nothing in our education and very little in our experience of life that can adequately still the natural fears of dying. These anxieties centre around what will happen to the family afterwards; whether there is a heaven or hell and what they are like; what will happen in the transition from life to death. Will I suffer? 'I want to wake up dead, Doctor', is how more than one patient has succinctly expressed that fear. There are also feelings of loss, of being separated from a life partner, of not attaining particular goals in life. There is the feeling of being alone, of no one caring.

Fear surrounds dying at all points. If we as carers are afraid of becoming involved, we need to realize that those fears are more than matched by those for whom dying is becoming a reality. But it is precisely the 'becoming involved' that is the beginning of a coming to terms with our fears, and this leads to self-understanding and a sharing of courage and deeply hidden resources. This experience is frequently expressed in the words, 'I never thought I could do it, but I received strength from somewhere.'

The fact is that we can overcome our natural fears although we will never quite be rid of them or of the sense of inadequacy to meet such difficult situations. Even the professional carers, the doctors, nurses, clergymen, will often confess their feeling of helplessness and the poverty of their response to what is asked of them. This very sense of inadequacy may in itself be a link with the dying person. Dame Cicely Saunders, who founded the hospice movement, said in a

radio interview, 'Your helplessness is what you have to offer. You have that in common with the ill person. So you are together with them in that experience. That is what they need.'

And despite our sense of helplessness, there are things to be learned from experience, pointers to the help that we may give the dying, whether we are a member of the family or simply a friend who is standing by. For instance, conversation with a dying person should be no different from conversation with anyone else. There are no special conversation pieces for such occasions. Of course, it is likely that we shall have known the person for some time before things get to the critical stage and therefore we shall have plenty to talk about. But there are always clues for conversation if we look for them – family photographs, books by the bedside, a pet dog or cat, a picture on the wall, the television set in the corner. Questions that require more than a simple answer of 'Yes' or 'No' are always best, except where the person is only capable of the merest nod of the head. Generally, questions beginning with 'What' or 'How' are better than 'Why' questions. We may perhaps share ideas about the new project we have in hand, the new committee we are forming, the car, or whatever else interests the person. Silent companionship, especially between old friends, has a special place. Gradually, we come not to fear the times of silence and we may learn when it is more appropriate to take a person's hand or gently to smooth their brow with our hand and simply smile. Remember to smile. Indeed, laughter is not always out of place; neither, on the other hand, is our own willingness to display sadness.

But perhaps the greatest gift is to look directly into a person's eyes, something which always requires great courage, but never more so than in circumstances of dire illness. For it is our eyes and the attention of our gaze which will show the honesty of our concern and it is the other person's eyes which will show their pain, their fear, or their serenity. It is in the corner of an eye that a tear will quietly form when a tender spot has been touched in the conversation.

Encouragement to go on doing things is vital. Short walks, where possible, short drives in the car, even moving from one room to the other, can all mean much to an ill person. So can seemingly humdrum things like knitting squares, making toys, or writing Christmas cards.

What it all adds up to is this. Being a carer is hard work and demands thought and effort. The immediate family know this better than anyone. But the visitor to the home or hospital also learns it if

the job is taken seriously. We need to think beforehand what our opening conversation might be, what the topics are that will keep the talk going beyond the initial pleasantries. But we also need the determination to keep going, week by week, especially through the bad times when what we have to offer does not seem to amount to very much. In addition, it takes a degree of sensitivity to respond to what the situation requires. Are there some occasions, for example, when to stay over-long and to talk too much means only that a person is left tired out by our visit?

Caring for the dying, however, is not just giving. There is a profound way in which we also receive. Who could not marvel at the supreme courage shown by some in the most adverse circumstances?

Martha was fifty when a severe stroke left her paralysed from the neck downwards. She was kept alive by a respirator which worked through a tracheostomy tube in her neck. She was awake, however, and could communicate by screwing up her eyes; a quick blink meant 'Yes' and a slow blink meant 'No'.

'Are you comfortable Martha?' Quick blink – 'Yes'.

'Is there anything you want?' Slow blink – 'No'.

The ritual was much the same day after day. But how much did she understand? One day it was put to the test.

'Is the Prime Minister Winston Churchill?'

'No!' (emphatic).

'Harold Wilson?'

'No!'.

'Mrs Thatcher?'

'Yes!'

The enquiring doctor worked his way through the Cabinet. She knew many of the ministers, even those who had changed since her stroke. She could, of course, hear the radio which was on constantly in the unit but that was still good going. Other questions were tried until finally a senior registrar asked about the exchange rate.

'Could I get three dollars for a pound?'

'No!'

'Between one and two?'

'Yes'.

And so on through the decimal places. The senior registrar thought that she was a couple of points out. But if she was that alert inside, the staff reasoned, a switch board operated by the

muscles of her face should allow her to communicate. An appeal was launched and the machinery was bought. By moving her face she could select a letter on a display unit and the letter was then transferred to an electric typewriter. At last Martha could tell us what she wanted.

There was excitement the first day that Martha had her machine. She produced the names of her family, two of her grandchildren and one or two other words, then painstakingly she typed out the words,

'The Lord is my shepherd, I shall not want.'

Despite being almost totally locked in her body, Martha communicated hope, faith and contentment. She died very quietly about a year later.

There is perhaps another factor in caring for the dying that only gradually emerges as we reflect upon our experience. It has to do with our sense of time. The sick person is coping with two time zones. There is the time zone that encompasses the hospital ward or the sick room, with its inevitable routines and long periods of potential boredom and inactivity, sometimes emphasized by the phrase 'being laid aside'. This is intersected by the time zone of 'the world outside' when visitors arrive laden with fruit and 'foreign' duties and schedules: 'Good Gracious, is that the time! I must fly!' – fly where? Why, back to the real world, to real time, of course.

Viewed from the visitor's angle, the difference in time zones also seems acute. As you enter the ward or sick room you enter a different world, where time seems suspended. How achingly slowly the clock struggles through the hour. But as you leave to rejoin a familiar world you may also pause to remember that while you are going home, cooking the tea, meeting the family or a friend, doing your work or going to the cinema, that sick person is still back there, still being nursed, still struggling with the pain or anxiety that inactivity will not let him forget.

The problem of time becomes even more acute when caring for a dying person because another aspect of time becomes apparent, one which is inescapable. Time is running out. Things are being done for the last time: a Christmas party, a birthday celebration, an anniversary, the first daffodils of spring, the last autumn leaf. Time is running out, but equally, each moment has a *timeless* quality about it, to be enjoyed, made the most of. This is most gloriously true when the

dying person knows fully what is happening and can share the intensity of each experience with a friend, a husband or wife. A Methodist minister in hospital with an apparently incurable disease described how he 'experienced a fierce passion for day-to-day living – a tremendous sense of gratitude for the richness of life up to that point – for wife, children, friends, neighbours, home, garden – the ordinary run of life, that sometimes seems humdrum' (Wilfred Bridge).

The way in which time is changed is seen in the story of Mr Farmer:

> Mr Farmer had only three months to live, possibly less. It was too short a time to arrange long-term plans for sheltered care or a hospice. He had no relatives to care for him and it was impossible for him to look after himself. He just needed to stay in hospital, fully aware of what was happening. It was arranged with the ward sister that he should be allowed to come and go as he liked. He was encouraged to take walks around the grounds, go to the hospital library, to the League of Friends shop, even the cafe over the road. Five days later an angry ward sister confronted the doctors on their round. 'I cannot stand Mr Farmer's behaviour. I never know where he is – he's late for meals, always wandering off and sometimes he isn't back until nine or ten o'clock.'
>
> The doctors replied, 'Yes, that's the idea. Nothing can be done medically!' To which the sister retorted, 'Well, he disrupts the ward routine!'
>
> The following day Mr Farmer was moved to another ward where a Mauritian charge nurse understood how to temper efficiency with caring, perhaps because he had a different sense of time and of priorities. Mr Farmer died very quietly in the night about three weeks later.

As time goes by in our care of the dying it will occur to us that there is another task waiting to be done. That task is the care for the bereaved, a task that may well begin within the lifetime of the dying person. There will come the moment when we have to make a decision which, if we take it seriously, will have long-term repercussions. Are we prepared for a task that may run into years, for it is now evident that the grief process, as it is called, does not end three weeks after the funeral. It has scarcely begun.

Initially, at least, there may be several people caring for the bereaved. The young policeman who has to tell the next-of-kin about

a fatal accident; the relatives who feel they are floundering and not doing very well; the doctor who tries to explain what has happened; the hospital chaplain or bereavement officer who tries to comfort or indicate what to do next; the minister who will take the funeral. All of these carers may have some contact with the bereaved.

Some will have received training for just such occasions as these, but the training has not always fitted them to cope very well and often it is a case of 'playing by ear' – a shake of the hand, a word of sympathy, a silent or a spoken prayer, a sharing of tears, a cup of tea, a glass of whisky. All of these may help or perhaps none of them will. Death is too personal to be put off by practised effort. And yet those awkward moments of truth have to be gone through and a direct and sympathetic concern is nearly always helpful.

Dr Colin Murray Parkes and others have shown us what a complicated thing grief is and how often guilt, anger and a questioning 'Why?' are mixed together. 'Why has this thing happened to X? He was the kindest man imaginable!' 'If only I had been with her, things might have been different!' 'Why did the ambulance take so long?' 'If only the doctor had seen her five minutes earlier.'

Unexpectedly, anger may show itself, fixing itself on the one who has gone, upon God, upon other people who are still healthy and happy. It is an anger that, undealt with, leads to bitterness, resentment and ultimately to isolation.

If we take upon ourselves the care of the bereaved, we must be prepared for a long wait in which the actions and the mood of the bereaved seem inexplicable. Grief seems to change some people's personalities for a time, making them incapable of seeing 'the bright side' or realizing that they still have the rest of the family, or a job, or their own health. If our caring amounts to telling people to pull themselves together, or blandly assuring them that time heals, we shall almost certainly fail because these represent shortcuts through pain which do not really exist. Rather, the tools for the job are patience, understanding and sometimes a willingness to take harsh words and angry looks without shrugging our shoulders and getting out as fast as we can.

The word 'sympathy' is often used in relation to the dying and the bereaved. It literally means 'to suffer with', as does its sister word 'compassion'. We cannot, of course, completely enter into another's experience, knowing and feeling everything that he or she does. But as human beings we nevertheless have the capacity to sympathize,

to stand alongside, at least to help take the weight of suffering. There are even some instances in which the pain of the carer may actually be harder to bear than that of the dying person; for instance in cases of unconsciousness. But always a certain distance is needed if one is not to be overwhelmed by the enormity of another's suffering. This distance acts as a buffer zone. In fact, the surprising thing about true sympathy is that it gives space for the sufferer to have room to be himself. True sympathy asks questions like: 'How can I help without taking over or making all the decisions?' 'How can I care without imposing my personality or my own wishes on that sick person, that widowed person?' How can I avoid jumping to quick and easy conclusions when I haven't been bothered to listen?'

The very asking of these questions, of being aware of the other as a person, leads to the setting up of that space between us which is so essential to healing. At the point where we recognize the space between us in true sympathy, we pass beyond fellow feeling into an understanding of what it means to be human beings in relationships.

Finally, there is one way of showing our care, our sympathy, which underlines this idea of space – by writing a letter. Avoid offers of help which can never be realized. These are futile. So is jargon and triteness. A simple message is enough to allow real love and concern to come through. A short comment on what the dead person has meant to you is always supportive. We may wish to emphasise our message by sending flowers *after* the funeral.

It is in caring for the dying and the bereaved that we become most aware of our own mortality. Perhaps this is what ultimately lies behind the fears which prevent us from getting involved in the first place. The dying and the bereaved are on the frontiers of human experiences. As Christopher Hughes Smith, the 1985 Methodist President, has put it, 'They are pioneers and they are there for us.'

Contact with such people, who are testing the outer edges of things, confronts us with the possibility of our own dying. If we have any sort of life-perspective, religious or not, it is now that we really need it. And we need it to work for us. Christian people believe in the strong love of God demonstrated in Jesus. That love does not answer all questions, neither does it protect us from the bad times. But from experience, ours and others, we perhaps begin to learn that it *is* strong and that it will see us through. 'Though I walk through the valley of the shadow of death, I will fear no evil – for Thou art with me' (Psalm 23).

The promise of God's companionship in all the walks of our life, in our pain and in our dying, is something we can cling on to even when total darkness seems to cover the face of the earth and hide him from our sight. But there is more to it than that. Not only does God come, in Jesus, to be our companion, but he calls us to be his companions: not only does he walk with us in our world, but calls us to walk with him in his. The spirit of our generation is against the old-fashioned promises of rest, reward and a better life. But we do believe that there is something called Eternal Life, which begins in the here and now: that the quality of life and the quality of love which Jesus makes possible are the kind that death cannot touch. We believe that nothing is wasted in the presence of that love, that every circumstance of life, no matter how apparently futile, will in the end be seen to be part of a greater whole. And we have by no means relinquished the Christian hope of our weakness made strong by God's love, of our imperfections made whole by the power of Christ's resurrection.

*

Death is nothing at all . . . I have only slipped away into the next room . . . I am I and you are you . . . whatever we were to each other, that we are still. Call me by my old familiar name, speak to me in the easy way which you always used. Put no difference into your tone; wear no forced air of solemnity or sorrow. Laugh as we always laughed at the little jokes we enjoyed together. Play, smile, think of me, pray for me. Let my name be ever the household word that it always was. Let it be spoken without an effort, without the ghost of a shadow on it. Life means all that it ever meant. It is the same as it ever was; there is absolutely unbroken continuity. What is this death but a negligible accident? Why should I be out of mind because I am out of sight? I am but waiting for you, for an interval, somewhere very near just around the corner. All is well.

Canon Henry Scott Holland

11 · *Finding a Way Through*

Illness is important. Its impact upon the sick person, the family or the carer should never be minimized. There are degrees of illness of course. Everyone is below par for some of the time. We are usually able to shrug off minor ailments, but sometimes even they can seem worse than they really are. When, for example, we are under pressure at work or coping with other problems at home, even minor illnesses can take their toll. In fact, it is not always easy to see which is cause and which is effect, such is the complexity of human nature. Do colds and headaches and the like make it more difficult to deal with pressure at work or at home, or does that pressure make us more susceptible to such minor illnesses? In other words, are they symptoms of a deeper problem? This inter-relationship between the various aspects of our lives indicates the seriousness with which we should heed the whole question of health. It is not merely a question of physical well-being.

However, we have been dealing in this book mainly with serious illness. When this strikes, there appear to be two possibilities. Such illness will either be an opportunity for personal growth or it will be a cause of stultification – an expansion or a contraction of our personal awareness and of the world of our personal relationships.

Serious questions are raised for us, perhaps for the first time: Can we cope? What will happen to the family? How will my career be affected? How much will it hurt? People with treatable disorders, such as superficial cancers, are reminded of their own mortality, even though they have a high chance of being cured. And those who get drawn in, either because they already belong to the family circle or because they are caring enough to visit, to stop, to bake or to wash are brought face-to-face with difficult and occasionally unpleasant realities.

It is as the questions are raised in the mind of the sick person or in the mind of those who are doing the caring that the opportunities for growth occur. We have all met people who radiate warmth and joy in the most terrible circumstances. We are drawn naturally to them. They actually give us something which we need, particularly the assurance that things may not go so badly with us when it is our turn. Equally, we have met those who are full of resentment. It is easy enough to blame them, to shun them, to put off the visit, to get angry with them. We almost say to them 'Why aren't you more appreciative of what I am doing for you?' Typically, we have put ourselves centre stage, ignoring the more important question of why the person is reacting bitterly. In their shoes, we might be exactly the same.

A large element of caring, then, is about enabling all concerned to find a way through suffering without allowing one's spiritual fibre to fall apart. Suffering can produce a confusion of negative and positive feelings which often cluster around a spoken or assumed 'Why me?' There is no general answer to the question. Sometimes, we have to acknowledge painfully that we have brought a certain illness upon ourselves. Smoking, lack of exercise, bad diet are now known to be linked with certain forms of cancer, heart disease, diabetes and so on. Accordingly, there must be times when we do indeed take our life in our own hands. We have a certain amount of responsibility for our own health. So, in some circumstances, to ask 'Why me?' is a dodging of the real issue.

But what of the leukaemic child, the lung cancer victim who is not a smoker, the man who jogged every day and still had a heart attack? It would be unjust to suggest that they were in any way at fault. Chance has taken a hand.

No matter how far back we press the responsibility for illness, and some would go as far as God himself, we are still left with a mystery in most cases. Indeed, much serious disease is perceived by doctors to be largely random in its occurrence. We do not know why this person should suffer, that person apparently escape scot-free. On the theological front, it is important to be honest with ourselves. We do not understand, even from afar, the intricate relationship between our pain and a God of love. There is no answer in these terms as to why an Ethiopian famine should occur or why a severely deformed child should be born. But what we do know is that people do not have to admit defeat and it is a most glorious fact of life that many do not. As Mother Julian of Norwich pointed out six centuries ago, 'He

said not, "Thou shalt not be troubled, thou shalt not be travailed, thou shalt not be distressed": but he said, "Thou shalt not be overcome".'

True enough, some people do give up the struggle. But they are not always to be chided or blamed. What in their upbringing prepared them for this moment? Some people become tyrants in illness, enslaving a spouse, a child, an unsuspecting but loving friend or neighbour. How often must illness have been cursed by one in the prime of health who has been trapped by another's helplessness or self-centredness.

But happily there are the stories to be told of new awakenings, of unlikely humour, of indescribable courage, yes, of resurrection even. We should not allow the darker side of things to overshadow the sheer human dignity that is also likely to be present.

Sometimes illness brings unlooked for consequences. For instance, it can produce healing of a quite unexpected kind. Here is a man who has not seen his son for twenty years. They did not quarrel and fall out, they just drifted apart and somehow for the son it did not matter too much that he had not spoken with his father for so long. But the news of his father's serious illness and imminent operation awakened an old affection, overcoming the carelessness of the years, and he hastened to his father's bedside. A new kind of healing was in the process of taking place.

The name of Anthony Nolan is known to millions. A little boy's courageous but unsuccessful struggle against bone marrow disease determined his parents to organize themselves and others to provide funding and resources to help other sufferers from the disease. Not only money is involved. Donors are also coming forward to see if they have the right kind of bone marrow which can be used to help people like Anthony Nolan. Similarly, the new science of transplant surgery means that the tragic death of one child can bring new life and health for another suffering from an otherwise incurable disease. It will not ease the desperate pain of the bereaved parents – but the knowledge that someone, somewhere will be eternally grateful to their child for the gift of life, may touch their grief with gentleness.

On 5 October 1959, an organization called Cruse was founded by a Quaker, Mrs Margaret Torrie. Although not a widow herself, she called together a small group of widows to learn from them about the needs and the problems which bereavement and society's attitudes towards bereavement create. A vast reservoir of unmet need was then

discovered; there were after all three million widows in society at large. Although it has its consultant and experts, Cruse is essentially a 'self-help' organization that is now country-wide, still growing and, of course, including both widows and widowers. Like so many of its kind, it began with a particular need and that unfathomable human capacity for responding positively to a bad experience.

Life is not, of course, a romantic fiction where 'the good end happily': not everyone can manage to triumph over adversity. Some people do collapse under the strain of suffering, but equally many find a way through and it is to help perhaps a few more to do just this that this book is written.

The role of the neighbour, of the visitor and, of course, of the relative, can be crucial in finding a way through. They cannot themselves enter into another's experience of suffering completely. There are some journeys that we must undertake alone. But the carer can absorb some of the shock and the pain and thus make it easier to bear. And indeed the pain which, for instance, a parent will feel at her child's illness will be of a keener nature than the child's because it belongs to a different order of pain, one intimately linked with love.

The question that confronts the carer is this: 'What is true sympathy?' As we have seen on several previous occasions, an essential ingredient in true sympathy is imagination, the imagination to place ourselves in another's shoes. It is only as we develop this capacity that we begin to order our caring, without losing its spontaneity, so as best to help.

Imagination will prevent us seeking to take over completely, doing everything, taking all the decisions. As we recognize that the sick person is nevertheless a person, limited and hedged about as she or he may be, we stop ourselves from imposing our views and our personality on them. Because we understand that things may not only look different from his point of view, but may in fact be different just because he is involved and not us, we resist jumping to quick but perhaps inappropriate solutions.

The more we release our imagination, the more we understand that true sympathy involves the granting of enough space, in which we can give to one another the dignity which belongs to us all. A large part of that dignity is preserved if one is allowed to make decisions, involved in treatment options and after-care, helped to face family worries and encouraged to face personal anxiety with confidence.

According to the evidence of the gospels, the sympathy with which

Jesus approached sick people seems to have had two sides to it. His warmth and support for them shines through. He touched the leper without hesitation. He was grieved by the hard-heartedness of those who would have forbidden him restore a withered hand just because it was the Sabbath. He approached the madman Legion without a moment's fear. But he also seems to have left space for people to move towards him, space in which they could identify for themselves exactly what they wished from him: 'Do you really want to be made well?' Ultimately, he respected people's freedom to make their own decisions, to the extent that he allowed someone like the rich young man to reject his offer of help. In the same way, his relationship with the disciples left room for their individuality to express itself, even though that meant misunderstanding, and in his hour of need betrayal and desertion.

Jesus offers a significant clue to all our relationships, particularly the caring ones. Few of us like to be taken over, no matter how much we long for someone who is truly sympathetic to our needs. We may make mistakes, take longer than we should doing something relatively easy, even hurt ourselves a little. But those things belong to us as persons in our own right. Of course we need people to be there, sometimes at great cost, to encourage, support, do the 'impossible' things. But let there be spaces. The spaces between us will not remain empty. Like the child's clothes which are two sizes too big, they allow room for growth.

However, just as it would be a mistake to try to take over or dominate, so it is also a mistake to under-estimate the essential dignity that belongs to the 'patient'. W. H. Vanstone, in his book, *The Stature of Waiting*, has described the change that takes place in the life of someone admitted to hospital. From being an active person who does lots of things, he suddenly becomes someone to whom things are done, not only carried along by unfamiliar routines, but quite possibly unable physically to do the things which once were easy. The change to the status of 'patient' can be dramatically sudden, from doing to being done to. The patient has been 'handed over' to others and becomes the recipient of care. It is natural enough to resent this new position, easy to dismiss it as inferior, especially as we value activity and independence so much.

But Vanstone draws our attention to Jesus who was betrayed, literally 'handed over', by Judas. From that moment, Jesus too changed from doing to being done to, from action to passion. And

yet it was in his new status as 'patient', one who waits for whatever will be done to him, that he most truly revealed God. Through his passion God wrought our salvation. May it not be that through the dependence of those for whom we care, through their very helplessness, if that be the case, we and they become exposed to possibilities and resources which otherwise would pass unnoticed? We have seen in more than one instance, how the special dignity that belongs to a patient does precisely this, making possible as it were small acts of salvation.

It may be asked, 'Why have we not encouraged people to get beyond their suffering to the discovery of God, rather than talking rather lamely of just finding a way through?' Since all of us think and live within the Christian context, the question is a fair one. Indeed, the title for this final chapter was originally, 'Through Pain to God'. The more we thought about our work, however, the more we realized that many people do not get that far, so that what they discover in the end cannot be described as 'God' in any formal sense. Many indeed do not get through at all. Their illness is too great for them, not just physically but mentally and spiritually. But that does not mean that God has deserted them, or that because their response has not been up to it they are denied the final break-through to God. Others win through to a serenity, a trust, a sense of something whole, a stability that can only be God-given and they joyfully acknowledge it.

The fact is that the picture is varied in the extreme and it would be unjust to impose upon it the template of Christian triumph. The caring professions and the ranks of the dedicated but unpaid army of carers are filled by those of every faith or of no faith, in just the same way that those for whom they care may be atheist, agnostic or believer. Most would be happy enough simply to find a way through and to express it in their own way.

But of course we hold fast to Christ's promise that he is the resurrection and the life (John 11.25). We maintain our Christian hope that at the last we shall see God, face to face, for only that can be a worthwhile completion of the human experience. That hope, however, is not just a future hope beyond our imagining. For just occasionally we catch the fleeting impression that the secret of the universe is not darkness and tragedy but rather victory and joy.

It is easy enough to concentrate on the darker side of things, to believe that all is brought to nothing by pain and disease and death.

But that is not the total picture, for we have seen how many men and women there are who will declare that the real secret of life, for all its shadows, is good and trustworthy and belongs to God. They teach us that resurrection is always at hand; the ability to make a fresh start or a new relationship, that is resurrection. The ability to rise above injury, pain and debilitating disease, that most certainly is resurrection. And when our earthly time is over, we journey on into whatever new life is prepared for us – resurrection – where Christ is all in all.

*

This, this is the God we adore,
Our faithful, unchangeable friend,
Whose love is as great as his power,
And neither knows measure nor end:

'Tis Jesus, the first and the last,
Whose Spirit shall guide us safe home;
We'll praise him for all that is past,
And trust him for all that's to come.

Joseph Hart (1712–68)

HELPING AGENCIES

We have listed here some of the helping agencies associated with specific illnesses. The list is not intended to be comprehensive – that would have meant over 2000 addresses altogether – but is a brief guide to what is available.

Alcoholics Anonymous
11 Redcliffe Gardens
London
SW10 9BG Tel: 01 352 9779/9669

National Ankylosing Spondylitis Society
The Royal National Hospital for Rheumatic Diseases
Upper Borough Walls
Bath
Avon
BA1 1RL Tel: 0225 65941

Anorexic Aid
Gravel House
Copthall Corner
Chalfont St Peter
Buckinghamshire Tel: Gerrards Cross 84844

British Rheumatism and Arthritis Association
6 Grosvenor Crescent
London
SW1X 7E9 Tel: 01 235 0902

The National Society for Autistic Children
1a Golders Green Road
London
NW11 8EA Tel: 01 458 4375/6

The Royal National Institute for the Blind
224–228 Great Portland Street
London
W1N 6AA Tel: 01 388 1266

Marie Curie Memorial Foundation (Cancer)
124 Sloane Street
London
SW1X 9BP Tel: 01 730 9157

The Association of Carers
Medway Homes
Balfour Road
Rochester
Kent.

National Association for the Welfare of Children in Hospital
Exton House
7 Exton Street
London
SE1 8UE Tel: 01 261 1738

The National Childbirth Trust
9 Queensborough Terrace
London
W2 3TB Tel: 01 221 3833

The Cystic Fibrosis Research Trust
5 Blyth Road
Bromley
Kent
BR1 3RS Tel: 01 464 7211

The Royal National Institute for the Deaf
105 Gower Street
London
WC1E 6AH Tel: 01 387 8033

British Diabetic Association
10 Queen Anne Street
London
W1M 0BD Tel: 01 323 1531

The Royal Association for Disability and Rehabilitation
25 Mortimer Street
London
W1N 8AB Tel: 01 637 5400

The British Dyslexia Association
4 Hobart Place
London
SW1 Tel: 01 235 8111

The British Epilepsy Association
Crowthorne House
Bigshotte
New Wokingham Road
Wokingham
Berkshire
RG11 3AY Tel: Crowthorne 3122

The Haemophilia Society
PO Box 9
16 Trinity Street
London
SE1 1DE Tel: 01 407 1010

The Chest, Heart and Stroke Association
Tavistock House North
Tavistock Square
London
WC1H 9JE Tel: 01 387 3012

Helen House (Children's Hospice)
37 Leopold Street
Oxford
OX4 1QT Tel: 0865 728251

The Leukaemia Society
45 Craigmoor Avenue
Bournemouth
Dorset Tel: Bournemouth 3749

MIND (National Association for Mental Health)
22 Harley Street
London
W1N 2ED Tel: 01 637 0741

The Multiple Sclerosis Society
286 Munster Road
London
SW6 6AAP Tel: 01 381 4022

The Muscular Dystrophy Group of Great Britain
Nattrass House
35 Macaulay Road
London
SW4 0QP Tel: 01 720 8055

Parkinson's Disease Society of the United Kingdom
81 Queen's Road
London
SW19 8NR Tel: 01 946 2500

The Spastics Society
12 Park Crescent
London
W1N 4EQ Tel: 01 636 5020

ACKNOWLEDGMENTS

We gratefully acknowledge the following sources, and would like to thank those who have given us permission to use their copyright material.

Angela Ashwin, *Heaven in Ordinary*, Mayhew McCrimmon, Great Wakering, Essex

Dietrich Bonhoeffer, *Letters and Papers from Prison*, The Enlarged Edition, SCM Press 1971

Howard Booth, *In Search of Health and Wholeness*, Methodist Division of Social Responsibility, 1 Central Buildings, Westminster, London SW1H 9NR

Wilfred Bridge, 'The Treasures of Darkness', a series of talks broadcast on BBC Radio Birmingham. Copies available from 5 St John's Close, Stratford-on-Avon, CV37 9AB

Dame Cicely Saunders, in an extract from a BBC Radio 4 'Midweek' interview; St Christopher's Hospice, 51–59 Lawrie Park Road, Sydenham SE26 6DZ

Helen House, 37 Leopold Street, Oxford OX4 1QT

Timothy Rees, 'God is love: let heaven adore him' A. R. Mowbray & Co. Ltd

Naomi Smith, *The Tangled Web*, Johnson Publications Ltd, London

D. J. Weatherall, J. G. G. Ledingham and D. A. Warrell, *The Oxford Textbook of Medicine*, OUP 1983

J. Neville Ward, *The Use of Praying*, Epworth Press, 1 Central Buildings, Westminster, London SW1H 9NR

Bible quotations are from The New English Bible, Second Edition 1970, used by permission of Oxford and Cambridge University Presses and Good News Bible 1976 used by permission of The British and Foreign Bible Society

Lightning Source UK Ltd.
Milton Keynes UK
UKOW051432290413

209938UK00011B/246/P

CS0041304 6TRP

CW01677071

FACING ILLNESS

Despedirse a la francesa

EN: To take French leave
FR: Dire au revoir à la française

Marcharse sin avisar, sin despedirse. *Había mucha gente en esa fiesta y de repente no los vimos más,* ***se habían despedido a la francesa.*** Entre la nobleza francesa del siglo XVIII, se consideraba una muestra de educación, una deferencia que se tenía para no interrumpir una reunión. Hoy en día esta expresión es de uso común en España, Gran Bretaña o Alemania, mientras que en Francia o en Italia se dice: "despedirse a la inglesa".

To leave without warning, without saying goodbye. *Había mucha gente en esa fiesta y de repente no los vimos más,* ***se habían despedido a la francesa*** (There were loads of people at the party and then suddenly they'd gone – **they'd taken French leave**). Among 18th Century French nobility, it was considered a sign of politeness or deference not to interrupt a gathering. Nowadays this expression is used in Spain, Great Britain and Germany, while in France and Italy the phrase "to take English leave" is used.

Partir sans prévenir, sans saluer. *Había mucha gente en esa fiesta y de repente no los vimos más,* ***se habían despedido a la francesa*** (« Il y avait beaucoup de gens à cette fête et tout à coup, on ne les a plus vus, **ils avaient filé à l'anglaise** »). Dans la noblesse française du XVIIIe siècle, cette pratique était considérée comme une preuve d'éducation, une marque de respect qui consistait à ne pas interrompre une réunion. De nos jours, cette expression est utilisée en Espagne, en Grande-Bretagne et en Allemagne, alors qu'on dit en France et en Italie « filer à l'anglaise ».

Mojar el churro

EN: To wet the churro
FR: Tremper son churro

Voz malsonante que implica, desde una perspectiva androcéntrica, mantener relaciones sexuales. *Esta noche se ha puesto muy guapo, ¡a ver si* ***moja el churro****!* Una práctica muy española es tomar churros con chocolate, tradición culinaria consistente en sumergir una fritura cilíndrica en chocolate fundido caliente. Se acostumbra a usar de esta metáfora poco elegante para aludir al coito desde una óptica masculina.

A rude phrase that refers, from an androcentric perspective, to having sexual intercourse. *Esta noche se ha puesto muy guapo, ¡a ver si* ***moja el churro****!* (He's all dressed up tonight, maybe he'll get to **dip his wick!**) Eating churros with chocolate is a very Spanish custom, a culinary tradition that consists of submerging a deep fried cylinder of dough into hot melted chocolate. This rather coarse metaphor tends to be used to refer to coitus from a male point of view.

Expression grossière signifiant, du point de vue d'un homme, avoir des relations sexuelles. *Esta noche se ha puesto muy guapo, ¡a ver si* ***moja el churro****!* (« Ce soir il s'est fait très beau, il va peut-être **tremper son biscuit !** »). Prendre des churros avec du chocolat chaud est une coutume très espagnole, une tradition culinaire qui consiste à plonger ces beignets cylindriques dans du chocolat fondu. On a coutume d'utiliser cette métaphore peu élégante pour désigner le coït dans une perspective exclusivement masculine.

A buenas horas, mangas verdes

EN: Green sleeves in good time
FR: À la bonne heure, les manches vertes

Frase que se aplica a quien llega tarde, cuando su ayuda ya no resulta útil. *Llegas ahora que hemos terminado de recoger toda la casa.* ***¡A buenas horas, mangas verdes!*** El origen de esta expresión hace referencia a la fama que precedía a los cuadrilleros de la Santa Hermandad, soldados que lucían un uniforme de mangas verdes y que, por lo visto, siempre llegaban tarde a la escena del delito para prestar socorro.

A phrase applied to someone who arrives late, when their help is no longer needed. *Llegas ahora que hemos terminado de recoger toda la casa.* ***¡A buenas horas, mangas verdes!*** (Now you get here, when we've finished tidying up the house. It's **a bit late in the day!**) The origin of this phrase refers to the members of the Holy Brotherhood, soldiers who wore a uniform with green sleeves and who seemingly always arrived too late at the scene of the crime to provide assistance.

Phrase qui s'applique lorsque quelqu'un arrive trop tard, alors que son aide ne sert plus à rien. *Llegas ahora que hemos terminado de recoger toda la casa.* ***¡A buenas horas, mangas verdes!*** (« Tu débarques maintenant qu'on a fini de ranger toute la maison. **Pas trop tôt, tu arrives après la bataille** »). L'origine de cette expression fait référence à la réputation des chevaliers de la Sainte-Hermandad, lesquels arboraient un uniforme aux manches vertes et, à ce que l'on dit, arrivaient toujours trop tard sur les lieux du crime pour porter secours.

Cuando las ranas críen pelo

EN: When frogs grow hair
FR: Quand les grenouilles auront du poil

Expresa las remotas posibilidades de que algo ocurra. *Sigo enfadada con él, le volveré a dirigir la palabra* ***cuando las ranas críen pelo.*** Dicho que resalta el surrealismo de una situación o un hecho, y por consecuencia su clara imposibilidad de suceder. *Cuando las vacas vuelen* o *cuando las gallinas meen* son otras frases de mismo significado.

Expresses the remote possibility of something occurring. *Sigo enfadada con él, le volveré a dirigir la palabra* ***cuando las ranas críen pelo*** (I'm still annoyed with him. **Pigs will fly** before I talk to him again). A saying that emphasises the surreal nature of a situation or event, and thus the impossibility of it ever taking place. Other phrases with the same meaning include *cuando las vacas vuelen* (when cows fly) or *cuando las gallinas meen* (when chickens pee).

Exprime les probabilités minimes que quelque chose se produise. *Sigo enfadada con él, le volveré a dirigir la palabra* ***cuando las ranas críen pelo*** (« Je suis toujours fâchée avec lui, je lui réadresserai la parole **quand les poules auront des dents** »). Expression qui fait ressortir le caractère irréaliste d'une situation ou d'un fait, et par conséquent la claire impossibilité que ceux-ci adviennent. *Cuando las vacas vuelen* (« quand les vaches voleront ») ou *cuando las gallinas meen* (« quand les poules pisseront ») sont d'autres expressions ayant la même signification.

Estar a dos velas

EN: To be down to two candles
FR: Être à deux chandelles

Estar sin dinero. *A ver si me pueden adelantar el pago de este trabajo porque este mes* ***estoy a dos velas.*** De dudosa procedencia, la hipótesis más verosímil explica que en las iglesias, una vez finalizada la misa, quedan sólo dos velas encendidas que alumbran únicamente el sagrario y dejan el resto del recinto en la penumbra.

To have no money. *A ver si me pueden adelantar el pago de este trabajo porque este mes* ***estoy a dos velas*** (I wonder if I can get an advance on this job because **I'm poor as a church mouse** this month). Of doubtful origin, the most likely hypothesis is that in churches, once Mass is over there are only two candles left alight illuminating the side chapel, leaving the rest of the building in shadow.

Être sans le sou. *A ver si me pueden adelantar el pago de este trabajo porque este mes* ***estoy a dos velas*** (« J'espère qu'on pourra m'avancer la paie de ce travail parce que ce mois-ci, **je suis fauché** »). L'origine de cette expression n'est pas claire, l'hypothèse la plus vraisemblable est la suivante : dans les églises, une fois la messe terminée, il ne reste que deux bougies allumées qui éclairent uniquement l'autel et laissent le reste de l'édifice dans la pénombre.

Tener el culo pelado

EN: To have a bald arse
FR: Avoir le cul pelé

Estar experimentado, curtido en algo. *Llevo mucho tiempo en este negocio, he pasado por todas las situaciones y* ***tengo ya el culo pelado.*** Se suelen asociar la experiencia y la costumbre con la imagen de una piel curtida y encallecida; en este caso, un trasero pelado de tanto desgaste.

To be experienced or a veteran at something. *Llevo mucho tiempo en este negocio, he pasado por todas las situaciones y* ***tengo ya el culo pelado*** (I've been in this business a long time and I've experienced every kind of situation; **I'm an old hand** by now). Experience and practice are usually associated with an image of leathery, calloused skin; in this case, a bald arse through so much wear and tear.

Être expérimenté, chevronné dans un domaine. *Llevo mucho tiempo en este negocio, he pasado por todas las situaciones y* ***tengo ya el culo pelado*** (« Cela fait longtemps que je travaille dans ce domaine, j'ai vécu un tas de choses et **je connais par cœur** »). On associe d'ordinaire l'expérience et l'habitude à l'image d'une peau tannée et calleuse ; dans notre cas, un derrière pelé par l'usure.

Pisando huevos

EN: Stepping on eggs
FR: Marcher sur des œufs

Con excesiva lentitud. *¿No puedes ir un poco más rápido? Parece que vas* ***pisando huevos.*** El vocablo *huevo* es muy recurrente en la lengua coloquial como sinónimo de "testículo" (véase p. 30). Aquí, sin embargo, se alude al huevo de la gallina y a la extrema cautela que exigía andar en los gallineros de antaño, donde los huevos se escondían entre la paja.

Excessively slowly. ¿No puedes ir un poco más rápido? *Parece que vas* ***pisando huevos*** (Can't you go a bit faster? You're going **at snail's pace**). The word *huevo* (egg) recurs often in colloquial language as a synonym for "testicle" (see pg. 30). Here, however, it alludes to the egg of the chicken and to the extreme caution required when walking around in hen houses in the past, where the eggs where hidden under the straw.

Avec une lenteur excessive. ¿No puedes ir un poco más rápido? *Parece que vas* ***pisando huevos*** (« Tu ne peux pas aller un peu plus vite ? Tu avances **comme un escargot** »). Le terme *huevo* (« œuf ») est souvent employé dans la langue parlée comme synonyme de « testicule » (voir p. 30). Toutefois, ici, il s'agit d'une allusion à l'œuf de la poule et à l'extrême prudence qu'il fallait pour pénétrer dans les poulaillers d'autrefois, où les œufs étaient cachés dans la paille.

Crecerle a alguien los enanos

EN: To have one's dwarfs grow on one
FR: Avoir les nains qui grandissent

Tener mala suerte de forma reiterada. *Por si fuera poco, después del accidente pillé la gripe.* ***Me están creciendo los enanos.*** Derivada del enunciado *Pongo un circo y me crecen los enanos,* la frase escenifica de manera cínica y surrealista el colmo del infortunio: que los enanos de un recién inaugurado circo se pusieran a crecer repentinamente y arruinaran el espectáculo.

To repeatedly have bad luck. *Por si fuera poco, después del accidente pillé la gripe.* ***Me están creciendo los enanos*** (As if that wasn't enough, after the accident I got the flu. **It's going from bad to worse!**) Derived from the saying *Pongo un circo y me crecen los enanos* (I set up a circus and the dwarfs grew on me), this cynical, surreal phrase exemplifies the height of misfortune: when the dwarfs in a newly established circus start to grow all of a sudden, ruining the show.

Être dans une période de malchance. *Por si fuera poco, después del accidente pillé la gripe.* ***Me están creciendo los enanos*** (« Comme si ça ne suffisait pas, après l'accident, j'ai attrapé la grippe. **J'ai vraiment la poisse** »). Dérivée de l'énoncé *Pongo un circo y me crecen los enanos* (« Je monte un cirque et mes nains grandissent »), cette phrase montre de manière cynique et surréaliste le comble de l'infortune : les nains d'un cirque venant d'être inauguré qui se mettent soudain à grandir, gâchant ainsi le spectacle.

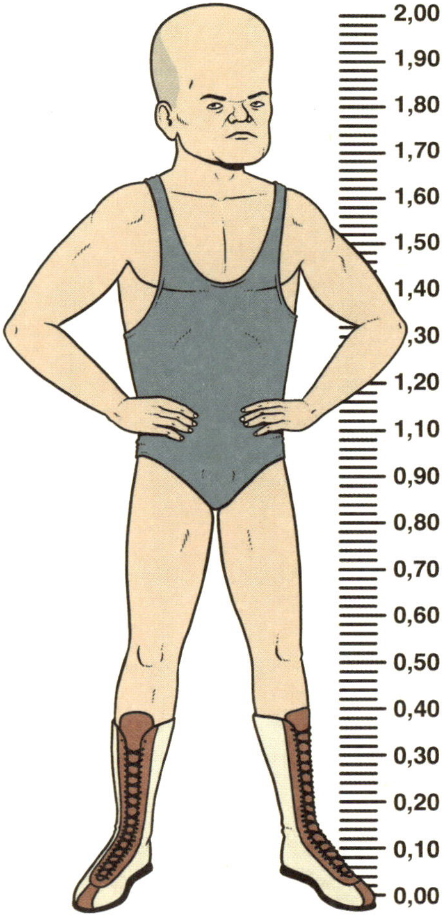
2,00
1,90
1,80
1,70
1,60
1,50
1,40
,30
1,20
1,10
0,90
0,80
0,70
0,60
0,50
0,40
0,30
0,20
0,10
0,00

Salir del armario

EN: To come out of the closet
FR: Sortir du placard

Dar a conocer abiertamente las creencias o ideas, y en especial la orientación homosexual. *Él no asumía para nada su sexualidad, pero al mudarse de ciudad por fin* ***salió del armario.*** En la tradición literaria, el armario suele ser un lugar que encierra secretos inconfesables, como un amante o un cadáver. Cuando el armario se abre, sale a la luz lo que estaba oculto.

To openly reveal one's beliefs or ideas, especially with regards to homosexual orientation. *Él no asumía para nada su sexualidad, pero al mudarse de ciudad por fin* ***salió del armario*** (He hadn't come to terms with his sexuality at all, but when he moved to another city he finally **came out of the closet**). In literary tradition, the closet or cupboard tends to be a place that conceals shameful secrets, such as a lover or a body. When the closet opens, whatever was hidden comes to light.

Faire connaître ouvertement ses croyances ou ses idées, et en particulier son orientation homosexuelle. *Él no asumía para nada su sexualidad, pero al mudarse de ciudad por fin* ***salió del armario*** (« Il n'assumait pas du tout sa sexualité, lorsqu'il s'est installé dans une autre ville, il a enfin **fait son coming out** »). Dans la tradition littéraire, le placard est traditionnellement un lieu qui renferme des secrets inavouables, un amant ou un cadavre, par exemple. Quand il s'ouvre, ce qui y était caché jaillit à la lumière.

Tener narices

EN: To have noses
FR: Avoir des nez

Tener valentía, atrevimiento. *El presidente, tras aprobar la ley de reforma laboral,* ***no ha tenido narices*** *para hablar con la prensa.* Antiguamente, una nariz prominente era considerada un rasgo de nobleza y un indicativo de firmeza y determinación. Sin embargo, la misma fórmula también puede tener un cariz negativo y señalar asombro o rechazo: ***¡Tiene narices*** *que el niño esté llorando en su fiesta de cumpleaños!*

To be brave or daring. *El presidente, tras aprobar la ley de reforma laboral,* ***no ha tenido narices*** *para hablar con la prensa* (After passing the labour reform law, the president **didn't have the guts** to talk to the press). In the past, a prominent nose was considered a noble trait and a sign of determination and resolve. The same saying can, however, have a negative sense and indicate astonishment or disapproval: ***¡Tiene narices*** *que el niño esté llorando en su fiesta de cumpleaños!* (That child's **got a nerve** to cry at his own birthday party!)

Avoir du courage, de l'audace. *El presidente, tras aprobar la ley de reforma laboral,* ***no ha tenido narices*** *para hablar con la prensa* (« Le président, après avoir approuvé la loi de réforme du travail, **n'a pas eu le cran** de s'adresser à la presse »). Autrefois, un nez proéminent était considéré comme un trait de noblesse et un signe de détermination et de fermeté. Cependant, la même formule peut aussi avoir un sens négatif et marquer la stupéfaction ou le rejet : ***¡Tiene narices*** *que el niño esté llorando en su fiesta de cumpleaños!* (« **Ça, c'est fort,** cet enfant qui pleure le jour de son anniversaire ! »).

Los cojones de corbata

EN: [To have one's] balls at one's tie
FR: Les couilles de cravate

Expresión malsonante que indica miedo. *Se enteró de los despidos masivos en su empresa y se le pusieron* ***los cojones de corbata.*** Se suele decir que el miedo y la angustia provocan que se forme un nudo en la garganta. Cuando a alguien se le ponen "los huevos" o "los cojones" de corbata, se da a entender de forma muy gráfica que la ansiedad es tal que los testículos se le suben a la garganta, a modo de corbata anudada al cuello.

Vulgar expression indicating fear. *Se enteró de los despidos masivos en su empresa y se le pusieron* ***los cojones de corbata*** (He found out about the mass redundancies at his firm and **it scared the shit out of him**). It is said that fear and anxiety give one a lump in one's throat. When someone's *huevos* ("eggs", slang for testicles) or *cojones* (balls) go up to one's tie, it's a very graphic way of saying that someone is so anxious his testicles have gone up into his throat, like a tie knotted at the neck.

Expression grossière qui désigne la peur. *Se enteró de los despidos masivos en su empresa y se le pusieron* ***los cojones de corbata*** (« Il s'est rendu compte des licenciements massifs dans son entreprise, et il a eu **les boules de sa vie** »). On a coutume de dire que la peur et l'angoisse déclenchent la formation d'un nœud dans la gorge. Quand il vient à quelqu'un des *huevos* ou *cojones* (des « œufs » ou des « couilles ») de cravate, la forme très graphique qui est évoquée donne à comprendre que son anxiété est telle que ses testicules lui remontent dans la gorge, à la manière d'une cravate nouée autour du cou.

No ser moco de pavo

EN: To not be a turkey's bogey
FR: Ne pas être de la morve de dindon

Tener importancia, no ser una nimiedad. *Lo que nos va a costar la reforma* **no es moco de pavo,** *tendremos que ahorrar.* El *moco de pavo* poco tiene de mucosidad: designa la membrana que esta galliforme tiene sobre el pico y que no representa gran utilidad. En germanía, podría haberse denominado *moco* a la cadena de los relojes de bolsillo; cuando se "desplumaba" al *pavo* –el incauto–, se le dejaba sin reloj y con la cadena colgando.

To be important, to be no small thing. *Lo que nos va a costar la reforma de la casa* **no es moco de pavo,** *tendremos que ahorrar* (The cost of doing the house up **is no trifle,** we'll have to save up). The *moco de pavo* (turkey's mucus or bogie) has little to do with mucus: it refers to the membrane on this Galliforme's beak, which is largely useless. In underworld slang it may have described a pocket watch chain; when the *pavo* (dupe) was pick-pocketed, he was left without a watch and just the chain dangling.

Avoir de l'importance, ne pas être une bagatelle. *Lo que nos va a costar la reforma* **no es moco de pavo,** *tendremos que ahorrar* (« Ce que va nous coûter la rénovation, **ce n'est pas une mince affaire,** il va falloir qu'on fasse des économies »). Le *moco de pavo* n'a pas grand-chose à voir avec la mucosité : il désigne la membrane que ce gallinacé a sous le bec et qui ne présente pas grande utilité. En argot, *moco* a pu désigner les chaînes des montres à gousset : quand on « plumait » le dindon – l'imprudent –, celui-ci se retrouvait sans sa montre, avec la seule chaînette.

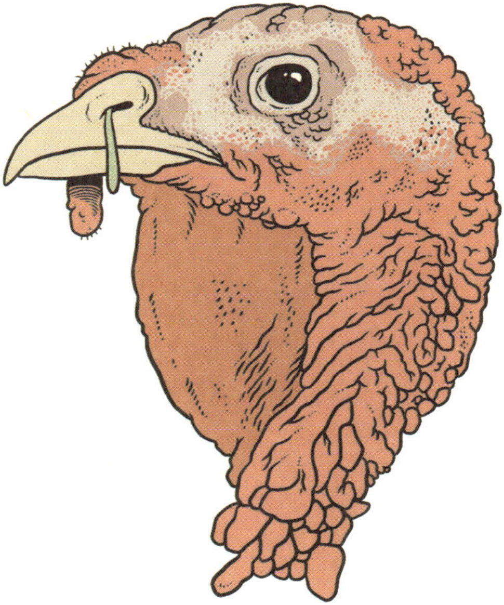

A tumba abierta

EN: Into an open grave
FR: À tombeau ouvert

Con velocidad, de manera temeraria. *Temía hacer el ridículo delante de los demás esquiadores, así que se lanzó* ***a tumba abierta*** *sobre la pista negra.* Este modismo indica que son tales la temeridad y el riesgo asumido por el imprudente que la tumba parece abrirse ante él, presta para acogerle.

Quickly, recklessly. *Temía hacer el ridículo delante de los demás esquiadores, así que se lanzó* ***a tumba abierta*** *sobre la pista negra* (He was afraid of looking like an idiot in front of the other skiers so he launched himself **at breakneck speed** down the black run). This expression indicates that someone is behaving in such a reckless, risky fashion that a grave seems to be opening up at his feet, ready to receive him.

À toute vitesse, de manière téméraire. *Temía hacer el ridículo delante de los demás esquiadores, así que se lanzó* ***a tumba abierta*** *sobre la pista negra* (« Il craignait d'être ridicule devant les autres skieurs, aussi se lança-t-il **à tombeau ouvert** sur la piste noire »). Cette expression indique que la témérité et le risque encouru par l'imprudent sont tels que la tombe semble s'ouvrir devant lui, prête à l'accueillir.

Estar en Babia

EN: To be in Babia
FR: Être en Babia

Estar distraído, despistado. *La profesora estaba explicando el ejercicio y él no hacía ni caso,* ***estaba en Babia.*** En la Edad Media, los reyes de León pasaban temporadas de descanso, alejados del mundanal ruido, en Babia, comarca montañosa de la provincia. Por extensión, afirmar que los reyes estaban en Babia daba a entender que no se enteraban de nada, alcance actual de la locución.

To be distracted, to be inattentive. *La profesora estaba explicando el ejercicio y él no hacía ni caso,* ***estaba en Babia*** (The teacher was explaining the exercise and the guy wasn't paying any attention, **he was miles away**). In the Middle Ages, the kings of León used to holiday far from the bustle and noise of the city, in Babia, a mountainous region of the province. To say that the kings were in Babia came to mean that they were ignorant of everything, the current meaning of the phrase.

Être distrait, être ailleurs. *La profesora estaba explicando el ejercicio y él no hacía ni caso,* ***estaba en Babia*** (« La maîtresse était en train d'expliquer l'exercice, mais il n'y faisait pas attention : **il était dans la lune** »). Au Moyen Âge, les rois de León passaient la belle saison loin de la rumeur mondaine, en Babia, une contrée montagneuse de la province. Par extension, dire que les rois étaient en Babia revenait à expliquer qu'ils n'étaient au fait de rien, ce qui est la signification actuelle de cette locution.

BABIA

Dorar la píldora

EN: To guild the pill
FR: Dorer la pilule

Suavizar la mala noticia que se le da a alguien para hacerla menos desagradable. *En la entrevista no le dijo nada de los horarios horrorosos de este trabajo, más bien le* ***doró la píldora.*** Antaño, las píldoras se referían a un purgante en forma de bolita de sabor muy amargo. Para disimularlo y facilitar su ingestión, los boticarios solían recubrirlas de un tinte dorado.

To tone down bad news given to somebody so as to make it less disagreeable. *En la entrevista no le dijo nada de los horarios horrorosos de este trabajo, más bien le* ***doró la píldora*** (In the interview she didn't tell him anything about the job's awful hours; **she sweetened the pill** instead). In the past, a pill was a small round purgative with a highly bitter taste. To disguise this and make taking them easier, apothecaries would coat them in gold dye.

Adoucir une mauvaise nouvelle que l'on donne à quelqu'un pour la rendre moins désagréable. *En la entrevista no le dijo nada de los horarios horrorosos de este trabajo, más bien le* ***doró la píldora*** (« Durant l'entretien, elle ne lui a rien dit des horaires atroces de ce travail. Au contraire, elle lui a bien **doré la pilule** »). Autrefois, le terme pilule désignait un purgatif en forme de bille au goût très amer. Pour le dissimuler et faciliter son ingestion, les apothicaires avaient coutume de le recouvrir d'une teinture dorée.

Buscar tres pies al gato

EN: To look for three legs on a cat
FR: Chercher trois pattes au chat

Tratar de justificar lo injustificable, de buscar excusas imposibles. *Sabían perfectamente que se trataba de un caso de corrupción, que* ***no busquen ahora tres pies al gato*** *para hacernos creer lo contrario.* La expresión original, recogida en el *Tesoro de la lengua castellana* de Covarrubias (1611), era "buscar cinco pies al gato", es decir, buscar algo que no existe, por mucho empeño que se le ponga.

To attempt to justify the unjustifiable, to look for impossible excuses. *Sabían perfectamente que se trataba de un caso de corrupción, que* ***no busquen ahora tres pies al gato*** *para hacernos creer lo contrario* (They knew perfectly well it was a case of corruption, they'd better not start **splitting hairs** now to persuade us otherwise). The original expression, recorded in Covarrubias' *Tesoro de la lengua castellana* (1611), was *buscar cinco pies al gato* (to look for five legs on a cat), that is, to look for something that does not exist, no matter how hard one tries.

Tenter de justifier l'injustifiable, de trouver des excuses impossibles. *Sabían perfectamente que se trataba de un caso de corrupción, que* ***no busquen ahora tres pies al gato*** *para hacernos creer lo contrario* (« Ils savaient parfaitement qu'il s'agissait d'un cas de corruption, qu'ils n'aillent pas **chercher midi à quatorze heures** pour nous faire croire le contraire »). L'expression originale, répertoriée dans le *Tesoro de la lengua castellana* de Covarrubias (1611), était *buscar cinco pies al gato* (« chercher cinq pattes au chat »), c'est-à-dire chercher quelque chose qui, quoi qu'on fasse, n'existe pas.

Dar calabazas

EN: To give someone pumpkins
FR: Donner des courges

Negar a alguien algo que pretende, en particular un requerimiento amoroso. *Estaba enamorada de Luis desde su infancia, pero **él le dio calabazas.*** En la época de la antigua Grecia y a lo largo de la Edad Media, se solían atribuir propiedades anafrodísiacas a la calabaza, cuyas pepitas eran recomendadas para reprimir la libido, al enfriar ardores o alejar pensamientos lujuriosos.

To refuse someone a thing they want, particularly in matters of the heart. *Estaba enamorada de Luis desde su infancia, pero **él le dio calabazas*** (She'd been in love with Luis since they were children, but **he gave her the brush off**). In Ancient Greece and throughout the Middle Ages, pumpkins were believed to have anti-aphrodisiacal properties, and their seeds were recommended for treating the libido, cooling ardours or banishing lecherous thoughts.

Refuser à quelqu'un ce qu'il souhaite, en particulier une attente amoureuse. *Estaba enamorada de Luis desde su infancia, pero **él le dio calabazas*** (« Elle était amoureuse de Luis depuis son enfance, mais **il l'a envoyée sur les roses** »). À l'époque de la Grèce antique et au cours du Moyen-Âge, on avait coutume d'attribuer des propriétés anaphrodisiaques aux courges, dont les graines étaient recommandées pour réprimer la libido, refroidir les ardeurs ou éloigner les pensées luxurieuses.

Hacer el indio

EN: To do the Indian
FR: Faire l'Indien

Hacer el tonto. *Deja de* ***hacer el indio*** *y actúa de forma adulta de una vez*. En su origen, la frase hace referencia a la extrañeza de los primeros conquistadores de América por la indumentaria y el comportamiento de los amerindios. Algunas fuentes sostienen que se acuñó tras la conmemoración en 1892 del descubrimiento de América en Madrid, donde se organizó una cabalgata con numerosos figurantes disfrazados de indios, "haciendo el tonto".

To act like a fool. *Deja de* ***hacer el indio*** *y actúa de forma adulta de una vez* (Stop **monkeying around** and act like an adult for once). The phrase has its origins in the astonishment felt by the first conquistadors of America at the attire and behaviour of the Amerindians. Some sources claim it was coined after the 1892 commemoration of the discovery of America in Madrid, where a procession was organised with various actors dressed as Indians, "playing the fool."

Faire l'idiot. *Deja de* ***hacer el indio*** *y actúa de forma adulta de una vez* (« Cesse de **faire l'idiot** et comporte-toi en adulte pour une fois »). À l'origine, cette expression fait référence à l'étonnement des premiers conquistadors devant les costumes et les mœurs des Amérindiens. Certaines sources soutiennent qu'elle est née à Madrid, en 1892, à la suite de la commémoration de la découverte de l'Amérique, lors de laquelle fut organisé un défilé avec de nombreux figurants déguisés en Indiens, qui « faisaient les idiots ».

Cagarse en la mar

EN: To shit in the sea
FR: Chier dans la mer

Expresión malsonante de enojo, rabia o despecho. *No encuentro mi pasaporte por ninguna parte,* ***¡me cago en la mar!*** En el registro informal, muchos eufemismos coexisten con las expresiones blasfemas a las que sustituyen: en el que nos ocupa, *la mar* no alude al océano, sino a la Virgen María, de la misma manera que "cagarse en diez" se emplea como equivalente de "cagarse en Dios", o "cagarse en la leche" elide el más prosaico "cagarse en la leche que mamaste".

Vulgar saying expressing annoyance, anger or hatred. *No encuentro mi pasaporte por ninguna parte,* ***¡me cago en la mar!*** (I can't find my passport anywhere, **damn it!**) Many euphemisms co-exist with the blasphemous expressions they substitute in the informal register: in this particular one, *la mar* (the sea) refers not to the ocean, but to the Virgin Mary, in the same way that *cagarse en diez* (to shit on the number ten) is used as an equivalent to *cagarse en Dios* (to shit on God), or *cagarse en la leche* (to shit on the milk) condenses the more prosaic *cagarse en la leche que mamaste* (to shit on the milk you suckled).

Expression grossière désignant la colère, l'énervement ou l'irritation. *No encuentro mi pasaporte por ninguna parte,* ***¡me cago en la mar!*** (« Je ne retrouve mon passeport nulle part, **ça me fait chier !** »). Dans le registre familier, de nombreux euphémismes coexistent avec les jurons qu'ils remplacent : dans celui-ci, *la mar* ne désigne pas la mer, mais la Vierge Marie, de la même manière que *cagarse en diez* (« chier sur dix ») s'emploie comme équivalent de *cagarse en Dios* (« chier sur Dieu »), ou *cagarse en la leche* est une élision du plus prosaïque « chier dans le lait qu'on a tété ».

Cortar el bacalao

EN: To cut the cod
FR: Découper la morue

Mandar, decidir. *En este equipo de trabajo se nota que es Enrique* ***quien corta el bacalao.*** *Los demás se dejan llevar.* El bacalao salado formaba parte de la dieta básica de las clases populares en el siglo XIX. Quien lo cortaba y distribuía solía ser el padre, es decir, el que mandaba dentro del núcleo familiar.

To be in charge, to decide. *En este equipo de trabajo se nota que es Enrique* ***quien corta el bacalao.*** *Los demás se dejan llevar* (In this team it's clear that it's Enrique **who wears the trousers.** Everyone else just follows his lead). Salted cod formed part of basic diet of the working classes in 19th Century Spain. It tended to be the man of the house who cut it and served it, that is, the one who was in charge in the family unit.

Commander, décider. *En este equipo de trabajo se nota que es Enrique* ***quien corta el bacalao.*** *Los demás se dejan llevar* (« Dans cette équipe de travail, on remarque que c'est Enrique **qui mène la barque.** Les autres se laissent porter »). La morue salée faisait partie de l'alimentation basique des classes populaires au XIXe siècle. Celui qui la découpait et la distribuait était généralement le père de famille, c'est-à-dire celui qui commandait au sein du foyer.

Ser un chorizo

EN: To be a chorizo
FR: Être un chorizo

Ser un ladronzuelo. *Siempre intentan timarnos con los contratos de telefonía,* ***son todos unos chorizos.*** El *chorizo* entendido como "ratero" no tiene nada que ver con el conocido embutido de carne adobada de cerdo: mientras este último encuentra su raíz semántica en el latín SALSICIUM, el primero proviene del caló *chori,* que significa "ladrón".

To be a petty thief. *Siempre intentan timarnos con los contratos de telefonía,* ***son todos unos chorizos*** (People are always trying to con us with phone contracts, **they're a load of crooks**). The word *chorizo* as meaning "pickpocket" has nothing to do with the well known sausage made of marinated pork: while this word has its semantic root in the Latin SALSICIUM, the first comes from the Spanish Gypsy word *chori,* which means "thief."

Être un voleur. *Siempre intentan timarnos con los contratos de telefonía,* ***son todos unos chorizos*** (« Ils essaient constamment de nous escroquer avec leurs contrats de téléphonie, **ce sont tous des voleurs** »). Le terme *chorizo* au sens de « chapardeur » n'a rien à voir avec la célèbre spécialité charcutière : tandis que cette dernière trouve sa racine sémantique dans le mot latin SALSICIUM, le premier provient du terme gitan *chori,* qui signifie « voleur ».

Hacerse una paja mental

EN: To make oneself a mental straw
FR: Se faire une paille mentale

Hacerse un lío, especular con ideas sin fundamento. *Deberían dejar de* ***hacerse pajas mentales*** *y proponer planes concretos y realistas.* Esta expresión malsonante sitúa en un plano intelectual la acción de masturbarse, para ilustrar un estado de confusión y desatino, alejado de toda lógica o racionalidad.

To get oneself into a mess, to dwell on ideas with no basis. *Deberían dejar de* ***hacerse pajas mentales*** *y proponer planes concretos y realistas* (They ought to stop **building castles in the air** and put forward some realistic, specific plans). This vulgar expression places the action of masturbating (in slang, *paja*) on an intellectual level, in order to emphasise a state of confusion and misguidedness, far removed from logic or rationality.

Se monter un cinéma, faire des plans sur la comète avec des idées sans fondement. *Deberían dejar de* ***hacerse pajas mentales*** *y proponer planes concretos y realistas* (« Il faut qu'ils arrêtent leur **masturbation intellectuelle** et qu'ils proposent des plans concrets et réalistes »). Cette expression grossière déplace l'action de se masturber (*paja,* en argot) sur le plan intellectuel, dépeignant ainsi un état de confusion irraisonnée, éloigné de toute logique ou rationalité.

Estar hecho un adán

EN: To look like an Adam
FR: Avoir l'air d'un Adam

Dicho del hombre descuidado en su arreglo personal. *Siempre va al trabajo sin peinar y sin afeitar,* ***hecho un adán.*** Su origen alude a la desnudez del primer hombre y se refiere, por extensión, al varón dejado, desaliñado. Sebastián de Covarrubias cita este proverbio: "Todos somos hijos de Adán y Eva, sino que nos diferencia la seda".

Said of a man who doesn't take much care with his appearance. *Siempre va al trabajo sin peinar y sin afeitar,* ***hecho un adán*** (He always goes to work unshaven and without brushing his hair, **a real scruff bag**). This saying alludes to the first man's nakedness and, by extension, refers to any unkempt, disheveled male. Sebastián de Covarrubias quotes this proverb: "We are all children of Adam and Eve, and only silk distinguishes us."

Se dit d'un homme qui néglige son apparence. *Siempre va al trabajo sin peinar y sin afeitar,* ***hecho un adán*** (« Il ne se peigne et ne se rase jamais pour aller au travail, **il n'a l'air de rien** »). Son origine se rapporte à la nudité du premier homme et fait allusion, par extension, aux hommes négligés, débraillés. Sebastián de Covarrubias cite le proverbe suivant : « Nous sommes tous des enfants d'Adam et Ève, seule la soie nous différencie ».

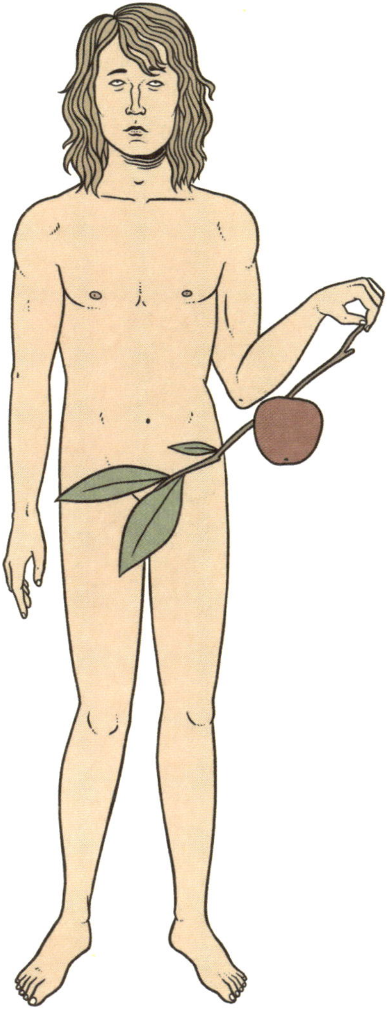

Matar el gusanillo

EN: To kill the little worm
FR: Tuer le vermisseau

Aliviar el hambre momentáneamente. *Tengo hambre y todavía es pronto, voy a tomarme un piscolabis para* ***matar el gusanillo.*** Según la creencia popular, el rugido estomacal característico del hambre era producido por parásitos que habitaban nuestras entrañas, por lo que se recomendaba ingerir un trago de aguardiente para eliminarlos. En nuestros días, se estila *matar el gusanillo* con un refrigerio entre horas.

To temporarily relieve one's hunger. *Tengo hambre y todavía es pronto, voy a tomarme un piscolabis para* ***matar el gusanillo*** (I'm hungry and it's still early – I'm going to have a snack to **take the edge off**). According to popular belief, the characteristic rumbling noises the stomach makes when hungry was produced by parasites living in our gut, and taking a sip of strong liquor was recommended to get rid of them. Nowadays, it is customary to "kill the little worm" with a snack between meals.

Calmer sa faim pour quelque temps. *Tengo hambre y todavía es pronto, voy a tomarme un piscolabis para* ***matar el gusanillo*** (« J'ai faim, mais comme c'est bientôt l'heure de dîner, je vais juste prendre un en-cas pour **me caler** »). Selon la croyance populaire, les bruits d'estomac caractérisant la faim étaient produits par les parasites habitant nos entrailles. C'est pourquoi on recommandait de boire une gorgée d'eau-de-vie pour les éliminer. De nos jours, on a coutume de « tuer le vermisseau » en prenant un casse-croûte entre les repas.

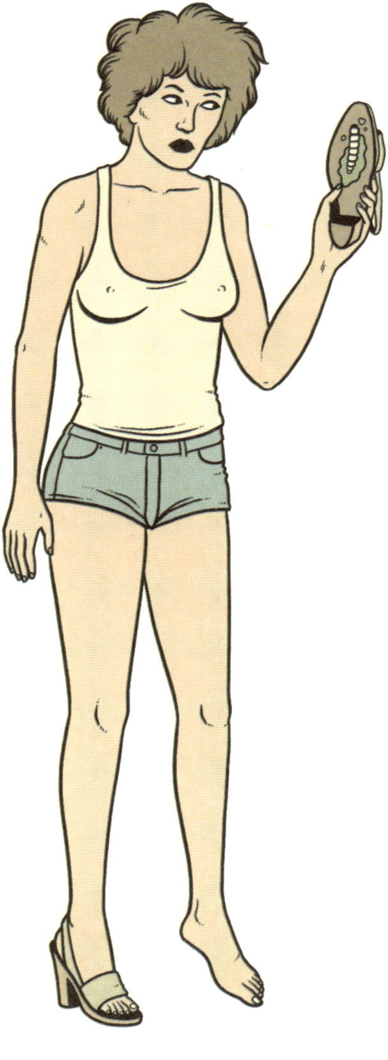

Naranjas de la China

EN: Oranges from China
FR: Oranges de Chine

Exclamación indicativa de incredulidad o rechazo. *Todos los políticos dicen que la crisis ha acabado.* ***¡Naranjas de la China!*** En el siglo XVI los portugueses introdujeron en la península el cítrico oriundo de China, y en aquella época parecía inconcebible que las naranjas procedieran de tan remoto lugar.

An exclamation indicating astonishment or an unwillingness to accept something. *Todos los políticos dicen que la crisis ha acabado.* ***¡Naranjas de la China!*** (All the politicians say the crisis is over. **Pull the other one!**) In the 16th Century, the Portuguese introduced this citrus fruit native to China to the Iberian peninsula, and at the time it seemed inconceivable that oranges could come from such a remote place.

Exclamation indiquant l'incrédulité ou le refus. *Todos los políticos dicen que la crisis ha acabado.* ***¡Naranjas de la China!*** (« Tous les politiques disent que la crise est finie. **Tu parles !** »). Au XVIe siècle, les Portugais introduisirent dans la péninsule ibérique cet agrume chinois, et il semblait inconcevable à l'époque que les oranges viennent d'un lieu si éloigné.

Bajarse los pantalones

EN: To drop one's trousers
FR: Baisser son pantalon

Ceder de manera humillante. *Insistió, pero al ver que no había manera de reducir el precio, no tuvo más remedio que* ***bajarse los pantalones*** *y aceptar la oferta.* Los pantalones se han considerado durante mucho tiempo símbolos de lo masculino y, por ende, de la autoridad, tal y como recalca el giro "llevar los pantalones". Consiguientemente, bajárselos y quedarse sin ellos equivale a perder el honor.

To give in in a demeaning way. *Insistió, pero al ver que no había manera de reducir el precio, no tuvo más remedio que* ***bajarse los pantalones*** *y aceptar la oferta* (He insisted, but when he realised there was no way they were going to reduce the price all he could do was **swallow his pride** and accept their offer). Trousers have long been considered a symbol of masculinity and, as such, of authority, as the saying *llevar los pantalones* (to wear the trousers) clearly demonstrates. To drop them and be left without them is therefore equivalent to losing one's honour.

Céder de manière humiliante. *Insistió, pero al ver que no había manera de reducir el precio, no tuvo más remedio que* ***bajarse los pantalones*** *y aceptar la oferta* (« Il a insisté, mais comme il n'y avait pas moyen de baisser le prix, il n'a pas pu faire autrement que **baisser son froc** et accepter l'offre »). Le pantalon a longtemps été considéré comme un symbole de virilité et, de ce fait, d'autorité, comme dans la tournure *llevar los pantalones* (« porter la culotte »). Par conséquent, baisser son pantalon, se retrouver sans lui, équivaut à perdre l'honneur.

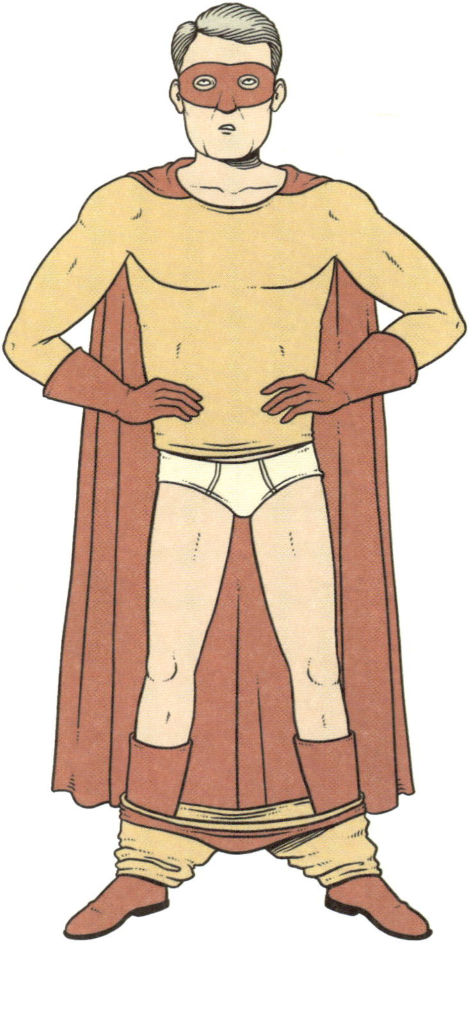

Quitarse el muerto de encima

EN: To get the dead man off one
FR: Se débarrasser du mort

Desprenderse de un lastre o de una responsabilidad. *Esta tarea es muy complicada y requiere mucho tiempo, a ver si puede encargarse Eva y* ***me quito el muerto de encima.*** En el habla coloquial, puede interpretarse *muerto* como un asunto fastidioso o una carga penosa, cual cadáver que pesara sobre nuestra conciencia. Así se entiende en los ejemplos "cargar con el muerto" o "echarle el muerto a alguien".

To cast off a burden or responsibility. *Esta tarea es muy complicada y requiere mucho tiempo, a ver si puede encargarse Eva y* ***me quito el muerto de encima*** (This task is really complicated and requires a lot of time; maybe Eva can take it on and I can **get that monkey off my back**). In colloquial language, *muerto* (dead person) can be understood as a tiresome business or weighty load, like a corpse that weighs on our conscience. This is how it is understood in the phrases *cargar con el muerto* and *echarle el muerto a alguien* (to pin the blame on someone else).

Se débarrasser d'un fardeau ou d'une responsabilité. *Esta tarea es muy complicada y requiere mucho tiempo, a ver si puede encargarse Eva y* ***me quito el muerto de encima*** (« Ce boulot est très compliqué et demande beaucoup de temps, peut-être qu'Eva pourra s'en charger et **je serai débarrassé de ce boulet** »). Dans la langue parlée, on peut comprendre ce « mort » comme une tâche assommante ou une obligation pénible, tel un cadavre qui pèserait sur notre conscience. C'est ainsi qu'il faut l'entendre dans les exemples *cargar con el muerto* ou *echarle el muerto a alguien* (« refiler la patate chaude à quelqu'un »).

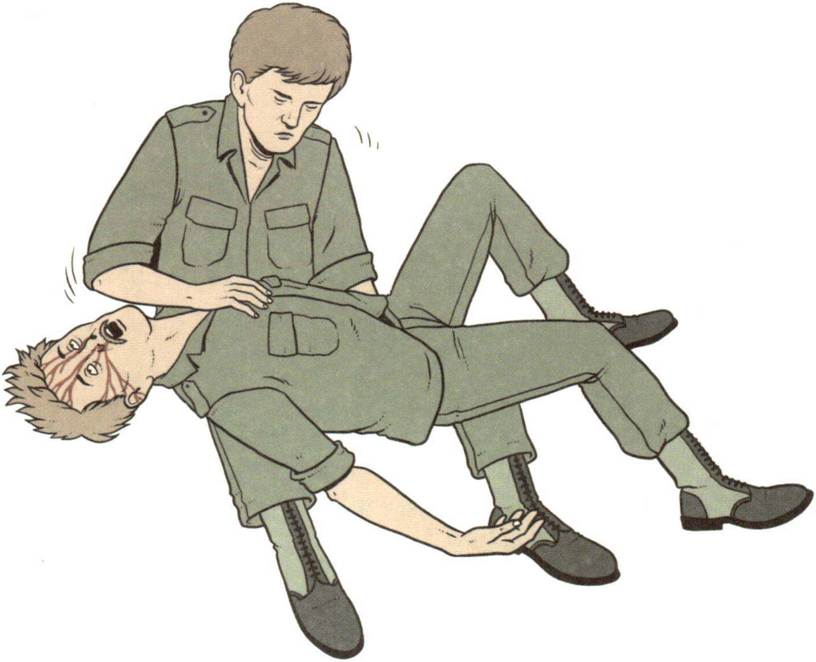

Comerle a alguien la oreja

EN: To eat someone's ear
FR: Manger l'oreille à quelqu'un

Intentar convencer a alguien con halagos. *Mi hijo lleva toda la tarde* ***comiéndome la oreja*** *para que le compre ese puzzle.* Cuando se le come a alguien el coco, se intenta influir solapadamente sobre su voluntad. Cuando se le come a alguien la oreja se persigue el mismo objetivo, pero la cercanía al pabellón auditivo permite que se haga de manera más melosa y lisonjera.

To try to persuade someone through flattery. *Mi hijo lleva toda la tarde* ***comiéndome la oreja*** *para que le compre ese puzzle* (My son has been **buttering me up** all afternoon to get me to buy his that jigsaw puzzle). When someone eats another's *coco* or head, they are trying slyly to influence the other person's intentions. When someone eats someone's ear, meanwhile, the same objective is being pursued but the proximity to the auditory apparatus means this can be done in a sweeter, more enjoyable manner.

Tenter de convaincre quelqu'un par la flatterie. *Mi hijo lleva toda la tarde* ***comiéndome la oreja*** *para que le compre ese puzzle* (« Mon fils **ne m'a pas lâchée** de la soirée pour que je lui achète ce puzzle »). Quand on mange la tête *(el coco)* à quelqu'un, c'est-à-dire qu'on lui prend la tête, on essaie de manipuler sournoisement sa volonté. Quand on lui mange l'oreille, on poursuit le même objectif, mais la proximité du pavillon auditif permet de le faire de manière plus mielleuse et agréable.

Ser un as

EN: To be an ace
FR: Être un as

Persona que sobresale sobre las demás en su profesión o en sus habilidades. *No hay quien lo gane,* ***es un as*** *jugando al póker.* El as suele ser la carta de máximo valor en una baraja de naipes, es la que lleva el número uno. Sin embargo, en el siglo de oro, la expresión era de índole injuriosa, entendiéndose el *as* como el diminutivo de "asno", y se empleaba de manera eufemística para llamar a alguien "burro".

A person who excels in his profession or skills. *No hay quien lo gane,* ***es un as*** *jugando al póker* (No one can beat him, **he's an ace** at poker). The ace tends to be the card with the highest value in the deck, and bears the number one. In the Golden Age, however, the expression was offensive and *as* was understood as a diminutive of *asno* (ass), and was used euphemistically to refer to someone as a donkey.

Personne qui se distingue des autres dans sa profession ou par ses talents. *No hay quien lo gane,* ***es un as*** *jugando al póker* (« Il est imbattable, **c'est un as** du poker »). D'ordinaire, l'as est la carte qui possède la valeur maximale dans un jeu de cartes, celle qui porte le numéro un. Pourtant, au Siècle d'Or, cette expression était bien plus injurieuse, car il fallait entendre *as* comme diminutif du terme *asno* (« âne »). On l'employait alors de manière euphémique pour traiter quelqu'un d'imbécile.

A

Echar sapos y culebras por la boca

EN: To emit toads and snakes from one's mouth
FR: Cracher des crapauds et des couleuvres par la bouche

Proferir blasfemias, jurar, maldecir. *Ya no pudo contener su ira y empezó a* ***echar sapos y culebras por la boca.*** Este modismo hace referencia a la manera de representar antiguamente al individuo a quien se le practicaba un exorcismo, y de cuya boca brotaban demonios.

To blaspheme, curse or swear. *Ya no pudo contener su ira y empezó a* ***echar sapos y culebras por la boca*** (He could no longer contain his rage and started **spitting feathers**). This idiom refers to an old way of representing people who were subjected to exorcisms, out of whose mouths demons would pour.

Proférer des blasphèmes, jurer, maudire. *Ya no pudo contener su ira y empezó a* ***echar sapos y culebras por la boca*** (« Il n'a pas pu contenir sa colère et s'est mis à **jurer comme un charretier** »). Cette expression fait référence à la manière dont on représentait autrefois les gens sur lesquels on pratiquait l'exorcisme, et par la bouche desquels sortaient des démons.

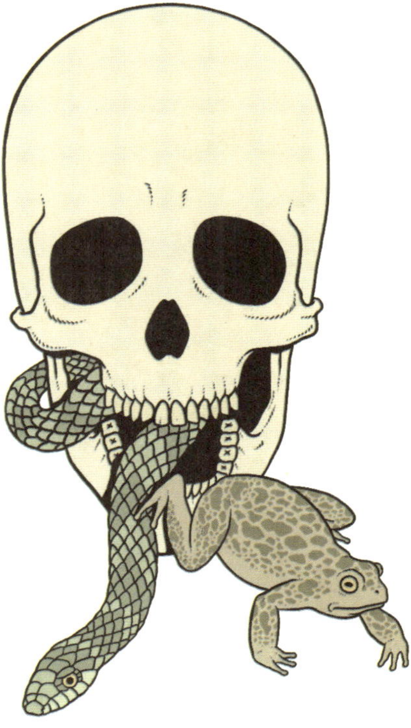

Tela marinera

EN: Naval fabric
FR: Toile marinière

De raigambre andaluza, hace referencia a la magnitud o la gran dificultad de algo. *Me ha costado **tela marinera** educar a este perro, ladraba todo el rato y se lo comía todo.* El sentido hiperbólico de este modismo tiene su explicación en la gran cantidad de tela que requería la confección del velamen de una embarcación.

Andalusian in origin, this phrase is used when talking about something of great scale or difficulty. *Me ha costado **tela marinera** educar a este perro, ladraba todo el rato y se lo comía todo* (It's been **a Herculean task** training this dog: he used to bark all the time and eat everything in sight). The large quantity of fabric needed to make sails for a ship explains the hyperbolic meaning of this idiom.

D'origine andalouse, cette expression fait référence à l'importance ou la grande difficulté de quelque chose. *Me ha costado **tela marinera** educar a este perro, ladraba todo el rato y se lo comía todo* (« J'ai eu **un mal fou** à éduquer ce chien, il aboyait tout le temps et il mangeait tout »). La grande quantité de toile que nécessitait la confection des voiles d'une embarcation donne tout le sens hyperbolique de cette expression.

Quemarse las pestañas

EN: To burn one's eyelashes
FR: Se brûler les cils

Estudiar con empeño. *Tengo el examen de matemáticas dentro de un mes y me paso los fines de semana* ***quemándome las pestañas.*** Esta locución verbal describe, no sin exageración, las largas horas de estudio, normalmente de noche y a la luz de velas que, de tanto inclinarse sobre los libros el estudioso, podían acabar quemándole las pestañas. Se documenta también la variante "quemarse las cejas".

To study hard. *Tengo el examen de matemáticas dentro de un mes y me paso los fines de semana* ***quemándome las pestañas*** (My maths exam is in a month and I'm spending all my weekends **burning the candle at both ends**). This somewhat exaggerated phrase paints a picture of long hours of study, usually at night and by the light of a candle, which might well end up burning the student's eyelashes because he spends too much time bent over his books. The variant *quemarse las cejas* (to burn one's eyebrows) has also been recorded.

Étudier de manière acharnée. *Tengo el examen de matemáticas dentro de un mes y me paso los fines de semana* ***quemándome las pestañas*** (« J'ai mon examen de mathématiques dans un mois et je passe mes week-ends à **bûcher** »). Cette locution verbale décrit, non sans exagération, les nombreuses heures de révision, comme il se doit de nuit et à la lumière des bougies où, à force de se pencher sur les livres, on peut finir par se brûler les cils. On rencontre également la variante *quemarse las cejas* (« se brûler les sourcils »).

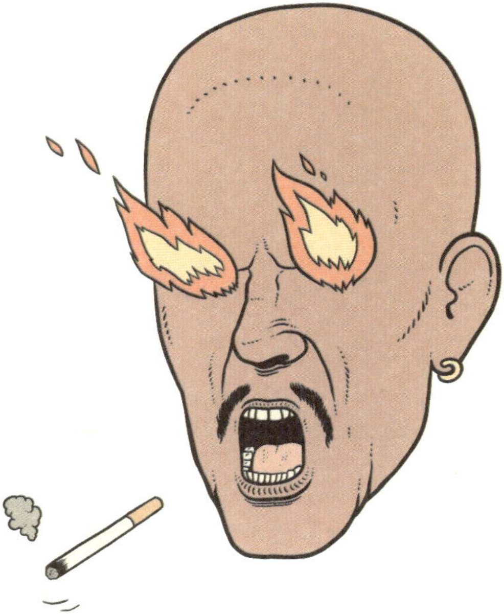

Tirar la casa por la ventana

EN: To throw the house out of the window
FR: Jeter la maison par la fenêtre

Derrochar, despilfarrar. *Me aumentaron el sueldo el mes pasado, me fui de compras y **tiré la casa por la ventana.*** Dicho vinculado, al parecer, con la instauración en España de la lotería, que llegó de la mano de Carlos III en 1763, y que extendió la costumbre entre los premiados de arrojar los enseres viejos por la ventana, como señal de cambio de vida.

To splurge, overspend, squander. *Me aumentaron el sueldo el mes pasado, me fui de compras y **tiré la casa por la ventana*** (My salary went up last month so I went shopping and **blew it all**). A saying apparently linked to the establishment of the lottery in Spain, which came in under Charles III in 1763, and which saw winners throwing their old belongings out of the window, as a sign their lives had changed.

Gaspiller, dissiper. *Me aumentaron el sueldo el mes pasado, me fui de compras y **tiré la casa por la ventana*** (« On a augmenté mon salaire le mois dernier : **j'ai claqué tout mon argent** en faisant plein d'achats »). Expression liée, semble-t-il, à l'instauration en Espagne de la loterie, qui fut mise en place par Charles III en 1763, et dont les gagnants prirent l'habitude de jeter leurs vieilles affaires par la fenêtre, pour montrer qu'ils changeaient de vie.

Diálogo de besugos

EN: Dialogue of breams
FR: Dialogue de daurades

Conversación carente de lógica y que resulta absurda. *Creo que no nos estamos entendiendo, mejor si lo hablamos mañana y dejamos ya este* ***diálogo de besugos***. La voz *besugo* comprende dos acepciones: pez o, por extensión, persona necia. Así, es recurrente en el coloquio el uso metafórico de *pez* –vertebrado acuático de poco seso– para personificar la majadería. Es el caso de "ser un merluzo" o "estar pez".

A conversation lacking in logic and is which thus nonsensical. *Creo que no nos estamos entendiendo, mejor si lo hablamos mañana y dejamos ya este* ***diálogo de besugos*** (I think we're both misunderstanding each other, we'd be better off leaving it till tomorrow because we're just **talking at cross purposes**). The word *besugo* has two meanings: fish or, by extension, stubborn person. The metaphorical use of the word "fish" – aquatic vertebrate with little brains – is therefore commonly used in conversation to describe someone's stupidity. This is the case with *ser un merluzo* (to be stupid) or *estar pez* (to not have a clue).

Conversation qui manque de logique et qui est donc absurde. *Creo que no nos estamos entendiendo, mejor si lo hablamos mañana y dejamos ya este* ***diálogo de besugos*** (« Je crois que nous ne nous comprenons pas. Mieux vaut qu'on en reparle demain, parce que là, nous menons un **dialogue de sourds** »). Le terme *besugo* a deux sens : poisson ou, par extension, imbécile. Ainsi, on emploie souvent dans la langue parlée l'usage métaphorique de *pez* – vertébré aquatique de peu d'intelligence – pour personnifier la bêtise. C'est aussi le cas dans l'expression *ser un merluzo* (« être un idiot ») ou *estar pez* (« nager complètement »).

Cagarse en los muertos de alguien

EN: To shit on someone's dead
FR: Chier sur les morts de quelqu'un

Fórmula vulgar de enfado y de desprecio. *Han intentado estafarme,* ***¡me cago en sus muertos!*** Muchas blasfemias recurren al verbo *cagar*: "cagarse en Dios", "en la leche", "en la mar" (véase p. 46) para manifestar rabia. En este caso, la ofensa es mayúscula, ya que la maniobra se perpetra sobre los difuntos de la persona en cuestión.

Vulgar expression of annoyance and contempt. *Han intentado estafarme,* ***¡me cago en sus muertos!*** (They tried to rip me off, **damn their eyes!**) Many blasphemous sayings resort to coarse language and the verb *cagar,* or "to shit:" *cagarse en Dios* (to shit on God), *en la leche* (on the milk), *en la mar* (in the sea – see pg. 46), to express anger. In this case, it's a serious insult, since the action is being inflicted upon the dead relatives of the person in question.

Formule vulgaire de colère et de mépris. *Han intentado estafarme,* ***¡me cago en sus muertos!*** (« Ils ont essayé de m'arnaquer. **Les cons !** »). Beaucoup de jurons font appel au verbe *cagar* : *cagarse en Dios* (« chier sur Dieu »), *en la leche* (« dans le lait »), *en la mar* (« dans la mer », voir p. 46) pour manifester sa colère. Dans le cas qui nous occupe, la suprême offense consiste à accomplir cet acte sur les défunts de la personne en question.

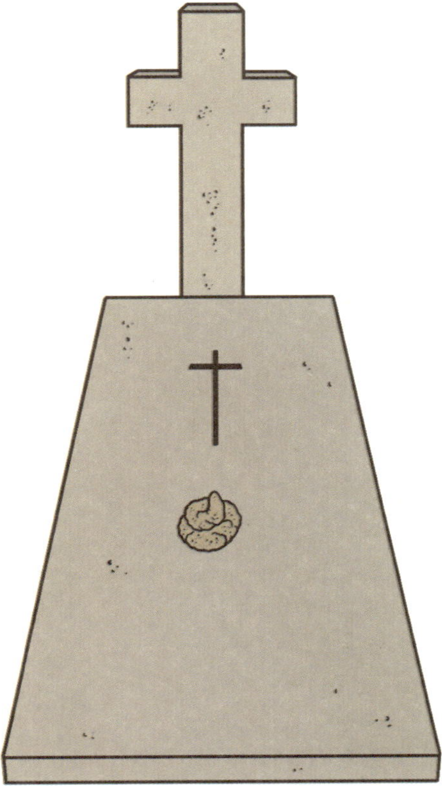

Tener una torrija encima

EN: To have a piece of French toast on top of one
FR: Avoir du pain perdu sur la tête

Estar despistado o borracho. *Ricardo me tuvo que explicar dos veces el camino a su casa porque yo* ***tenía una torrija encima*** *y no me enteraba de nada.* La torrija es una rebanada de pan empapada en leche o vino, rebozada con huevo, frita y condimentada con azúcar. Parece que la expresión compara este pan embebido con el estado mental adormilado propio de quien ha absorbido mucho alcohol.

To be distracted or drunk. *Ricardo me tuvo que explicar dos veces el camino para llegar a su casa porque yo* ***tenía una torrija encima*** *y no me enteraba de nada* (Ricardo had to explain how to get to his house twice because I was completely **out of it** and didn't have a clue what was going on). A *torrija* is a slice of bread soaked in milk or wine, coated in egg and then fried and dusted with sugar. It seems that the expression compares the wine-soaked bread of the *torrija* to the dozy mental state of someone who has consumed too much alcohol.

Être distrait ou soûl. *Ricardo me tuvo que explicar dos veces el camino para llegar a su casa porque yo* ***tenía una torrija encima*** *y no me enteraba de nada* (« Ricardo a dû m'expliquer deux fois le chemin pour aller chez lui parce que **je tenais une bonne cuite** et que je ne comprenais rien »). La *torrija* est une tranche de pain trempée dans du lait ou du vin, puis mouillée dans de l'œuf, frite et sucrée. Il semble que cette expression compare le pain imprégné de vin de la *torrija* à l'état mental d'abrutissement de quelqu'un qui a bu beaucoup d'alcool.

Perder hasta las orejas

EN: To lose even one's ears
FR: Perdre jusque ses oreilles

Perderlo todo. *Si seguimos yendo al casino para jugar a la ruleta, vamos a acabar* ***perdiendo hasta las orejas.*** Antiguamente, perder las orejas era el castigo que se les reservaba a los ladrones: al primer hurto, recibían una zurra de azotes. Si reincidían, se les amputaban las orejas, para que se les reconociera enseguida como malhechores. A la tercera fechoría, eran condenados a la horca.

To lose everything. *Si seguimos yendo al casino para jugar a la ruleta, vamos a acabar* ***perdiendo hasta las orejas*** (If we keep on going to the casino to play Russian roulette, they're going to end up **taking the shirts off our backs**). In the olden days, losing one's ears was a punishment reserved for thieves: after the first theft, a thief would be whipped. If he reoffended his ears would be amputated, so he would be instantly identified as a criminal. A third misdemeanour would earn him a hanging.

Tout perdre. *Si seguimos yendo al casino para jugar a la ruleta, vamos a acabar* ***perdiendo hasta las orejas*** (« Si nous continuons d'aller au casino pour jouer à la roulette, nous allons **y laisser notre chemise** »). Autrefois, perdre les oreilles était le châtiment que l'on réservait aux voleurs : au premier larcin, ceux-ci recevaient des coups de fouets. S'ils recommençaient, on leur coupait les oreilles, pour qu'on les identifie par la suite comme malfaiteurs. Au troisième délit, ils étaient condamnés à être pendus.

Estar hecho unos zorros

EN: To be a load of foxes
FR: Être comme des renards

Estar cansado, maltrecho, deteriorado físicamente. *Más me vale hacer más deporte porque corro sólo cinco minutos y ya **estoy hecho unos zorros.*** Se denomina *zorros* al utensilio hecho de tiras de piel que, dispuestas en un mango, sirven para limpiar el polvo. Esas tiras, muy usadas y deterioradas, designan metafóricamente el pésimo estado físico de la persona en cuestión.

To be tired, injured or physically worn out. *Más me vale hacer más deporte porque corro sólo cinco minutos y ya **estoy hecho unos zorros*** (I should really do more exercise because if I run for just five minutes I'm **a total wreck**). *Zorros* is the name for an old-fashioned kind of feather duster, made of strips of animal skin tied to a handle. These worn out old strips metaphorically describe the dismal physical state of the person in question.

Être fatigué, épuisé, en mauvaise forme physique. *Más me vale hacer más deporte porque corro sólo cinco minutos y ya **estoy hecho unos zorros*** (« Je devrais faire plus de sport, parce que je cours cinq minutes à peine et que je me retrouve **sur les rotules** »). On nomme *zorros* l'ustensile en lanières de cuir qui, attachées à un manche, servent à faire la poussière. Ces lanières, très usées et détériorées, désignent métaphoriquement l'état physique très mauvais de la personne dont il est question.

Escurrir el bulto

EN: To wring out the lump
FR: Essorer le paquet

Desentenderse de una tarea o de una obligación. *Cada vez que hay un trabajo en grupo, intenta **escurrir el bulto** y que lo hagan los demás.* Término originario de la jerga taurina, donde se denomina *bulto* a la imagen que tiene el toro –que es corto de vista– del torero. Cuando éste quiere esquivar una embestida, se desliza para apartarse del toro.

To get out of a task or an obligation. *Cada vez que hay un trabajo en grupo, intenta **escurrir el bulto** y que lo hagan los demás* (Whenever we have to do any team work he tries **to pass the buck** and let everyone else do it). A term from bullfighting, in which the image the bull (a short-sighted creature) has of the matador is known as a *bulto,* or lump. When the matador wants to avoid being charged, he slips to one side and moves away from the bull.

Se désintéresser d'une tâche ou d'une obligation. *Cada vez que hay un trabajo en grupo, intenta **escurrir el bulto** y que lo hagan los demás* (« Chaque fois qu'il y a un travail en groupe, il essaie de **se défiler** pour que les autres le fassent »). Ce terme provient du lexique de la corrida, où l'on nomme *bulto* l'image qu'a le taureau – qui ne voit pas bien – du toréro. Lorsque celui-ci veut esquiver une charge, il s'écarte du taureau.

Estar frito

EN: To be fried
FR: Être frit

Estar dormido. *Después de todo el día corriendo, el niño **está frito** en el sofá.* Los verbos "freír", "asar" y "quemar" se han consagrado en el uso coloquial como sinónimos de "aburrir" o "cansar". El cansancio físico se ejemplifica aquí de manera hiperbólica, dejando a alguien aniquilado de sueño, como si hubiera sido sometido al efecto del aceite hirviendo.

To be asleep. *Después de todo el día corriendo, el niño **está frito** en el sofá* (After running around all day, now the little boy is **sleeping like a log** on the sofa). The verbs *freír* (to fry), *asar* (to roast) and *quemar* (to burn) are firmly established in colloquial usage as synonyms of "to be bored" or "to tire out." Physical exhaustion is portrayed here in an exaggerated way, leaving someone wiped out from tiredness, as if they had been subjected to the effects of burning oil.

Être épuisé. *Después de todo el día corriendo, el niño **está frito** en el sofá* (« Après avoir couru toute la journée, le petit **est cuit,** il est avachi sur le canapé »). Les verbes *freír* (« frire »), *asar* (« griller ») et *quemar* (« brûler ») se sont spécialisés dans le langage parlé comme synonymes de « lasser » ou « fatiguer ». La fatigue physique se reflète ici de manière hyperbolique, laissant quelqu'un abruti par le sommeil, comme s'il avait été plongé dans de l'huile bouillante.

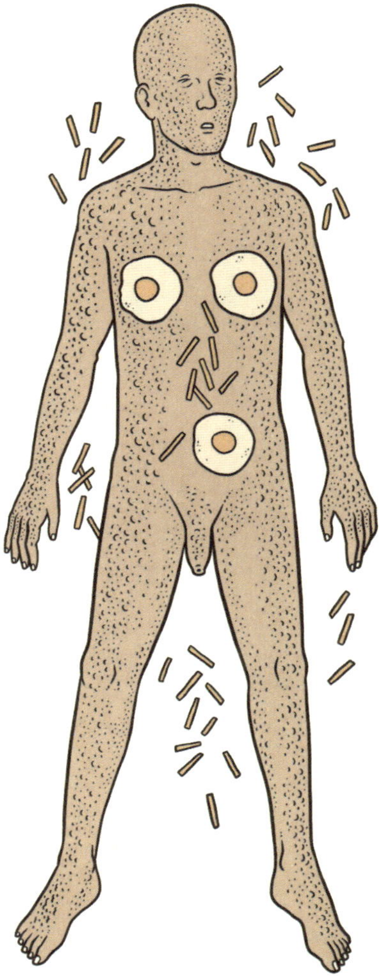

Éramos pocos y parió la abuela

EN: There were very few of us and then Grandma gave birth
FR: Nous étions peu nombreux et la grand-mère a accouché

Aplícase irónicamente a una situación, ya negativa, que empeora aún más y de manera imprevisible. ***¡Éramos pocos y parió la abuela!*** *Llego con retraso a la reunión y encima me he dejado los apuntes en casa.* El presente sarcasmo caricaturizaba la concurrencia masiva en algún sitio, como si de repente hasta las ancianas se hubieran puesto a dar a luz hasta rebosar el lugar por completo.

Used to refer sarcastically to a situation that is already bad and which gets worse in ways one couldn't have predicted. ***¡Éramos pocos y parió la abuela!*** *Llego con retraso a la reunión y encima me he dejado los apuntes en casa* (That's **the last straw!** I'm late for the meeting and I've left my notes at home). This sarcastic phrase is a caricature of somewhere that's full of people, as if even old women had started to give birth until the place is completely overflowing.

S'applique ironiquement à une situation, déjà malheureuse, qui empire encore, et de manière imprévisible. ***¡Éramos pocos y parió la abuela!*** *Llego con retraso a la reunión y encima me he dejado los apuntes en casa* (« **Il ne manquait plus que ça !** J'arrive en retard à la réunion et en plus, j'ai oublié mes notes à la maison »). Expression sarcastique dépeignant de manière caricaturale l'excès de gens en un lieu, comme si, tout à coup, les vieilles femmes s'étaient mises à y enfanter tant et plus.

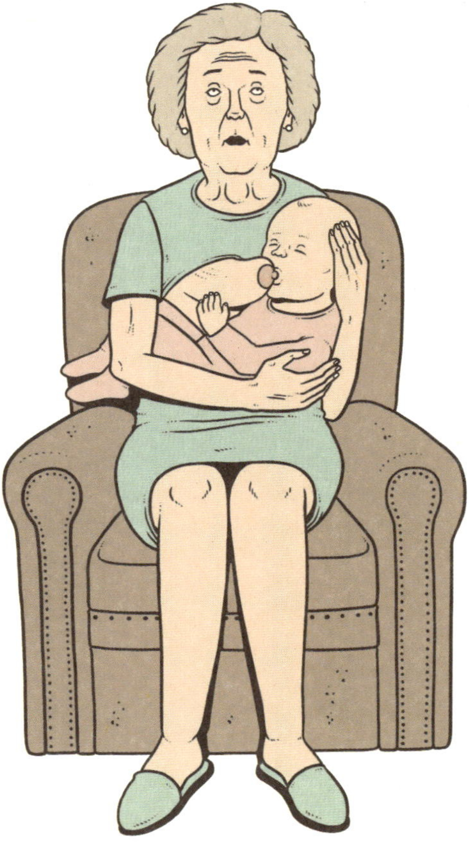

Irse por los cerros de Úbeda

EN: To go off round the hills of Úbeda
FR: Partir dans les collines d'Úbeda

Perderse en divagaciones o estar fuera de propósito. *Le pregunté por su luna de miel y* ***se fue por los cerros de Úbeda,*** *acabó contándome toda su vida.* Su origen se remonta a la reconquista de la ciudad de Úbeda (Jaén) en 1234: uno de los capitanes desapareció y llegó a la ciudad una vez tomada. Se cuenta que aseguró haberse perdido en la montaña –por los cerros de Úbeda–, lo que fue interpretado como cobardía.

To digress, to go off topic. *Le pregunté por su luna de miel y* ***se fue por los cerros de Úbeda,*** *acabó contándome toda su vida* (I asked him about his honeymoon and **he went off on one** and ended up telling me about his whole life). This saying goes back to the Muslims' reconquest of the city of Úbeda (in Jaén) in 1234: one of the captains disappeared and arrived at the city once it had been taken. It is said he claimed to have got lost in the mountains – in the hills around Úbeda – which was interpreted as cowardice.

Se perdre en divagations ou être hors de propos. *Le pregunté por su luna de miel y* ***se fue por los cerros de Úbeda,*** *acabó contándome toda su vida* (« Je l'ai interrogé sur sa lune de miel et **il s'est lancé dans de longs discours,** il a fini par me raconter toute sa vie »). Son origine remonte à la reprise aux musulmans de la ville d'Úbeda (Jaén), en 1234 : l'un des capitaines les plus importants disparut avant les combats et ne revint dans la ville que lorsque celle-ci fut prise. On raconte qu'il assura s'être perdu dans la montagne, dans les collines qui entouraient Úbeda, ce qui fut interprété comme de la lâcheté.

Hostias como panes

EN: Communion wafers like loaves of bread
FR: Des hosties comme des pains

Golpes o bofetadas muy fuertes. *Empezaron a discutir y acabaron dándose* ***hostias como panes.*** El término *hostia,* en su primera acepción, designa la fina y redonda hoja de pan ácimo con la que se comulga en la misa; en la segunda, se define como un golpe. El citado ejemplo amalgama ambas significaciones mediante un paralelismo hiperbólico: si una hostia es un golpe, por pura lógica un pan se convierte en un golpazo.

Very hard punches or blows. *Empezaron a discutir y acabaron dándose* ***hostias como panes*** (They started to argue and ended up **beating the crap out of each other**). The term *hostia* (host), in its primary meaning, refers to the thin, round wafer of unleavened bread with which one receives communion at Mass; its second meaning is that of a blow or punch. The phrase here amalgamates both meanings by way of an exaggerated correspondence: if the host is a blow then, through sheer logic, a loaf of bread becomes a very hard blow.

Coups ou gifles très fortes. *Empezaron a discutir y acabaron dándose* ***hostias como panes*** (« Ils se disputaient puis **se sont mis à se tabasser** »). Le terme *hostia,* dans sa première acception, désigne la tranche de pain azyme très fine et ronde avec laquelle on communie à la messe ; dans la seconde, il a le sens de coup. Le segment qui nous occupe fait l'amalgame des deux significations par un parallélisme hyperbolique : si une hostie est un coup de poing, il est parfaitement logique qu'un pain soit un « gros » coup de poing.

Índice alfabético

Bibliografía

Buitrago, Alberto.
Diccionario de dichos y frases hechas

Celdrán Gomariz, Pancracio.
Dichos, comparaciones y frases populares

Celdrán Gomariz, Pancracio.
Inventario general de insultos

Doval, Gregorio.
Del hecho al dicho

Luján, Néstor.
Cuento de cuentos. Origen y aventura de ciertas palabras y frases proverbiales

Moliner, María.
Diccionario de uso del español

Seco, Manuel, et ál.
Diccionario fraseológico documentado del español actual. Locuciones y modismos españoles

David Sánchez (Madrid, 1977). Su primera novela gráfica, *Tú me has matado* (Astiberri, 2010), le valió el premio al autor revelación en el Salón Internacional del Cómic de Barcelona. Su siguiente obra, *No cambies nunca* (Astiberri, 2012), fue nominada a mejor obra de autor español en el mismo salón. También es el autor de *Videojuegos* (Astiberri, 2012), de *La muerte en los ojos* (¡Caramba!, 2012), e ilustró los dos glosarios de jerga española *Con dos huevos* (Astiberri, 2014) y *Cagando leches* (Astiberri, 2015), con textos de Héloïse Guerrier. Sus dos últimas novelas gráficas son *Un millón de años* (Astiberri, 2018) y E*n otro lugar, un poco más tarde* (Astiberri, 2019). Es el responsable del diseño de las cubiertas de la editorial Errata Naturae y ha ilustrado para la misma editorial el libro *Paul está muerto* (2014) y *Kubrick en la luna* (2016).

Héloïse Guerrier (Châtenay-Malabry, 1981). Estudió filología hispánica en la Universidad de la Sorbona de París, donde le enseñaron el castellano como Dios manda. Posteriormente se estableció en Madrid, donde fue descubriendo el verdadero idioma de Cervantes, y donde nació su gusto por esas expresiones tan castizas. Ha trabajado en el sector editorial del cómic en Francia y en España.

Otros títulos de la colección Astiberri Pop

Papel y plástico 1, 2 y *3*
Oscar Lombana

Los colores del underground
Joan S. Luna

Monstruos modernos
Jordi Costa y Darío Adanti

¡Escucha esto!
Manuel Bartual

Cortocuentos 1 y *2*
Borja Crespo y Chema García

Toyland Made in Spain
Toyland Made in USA
Toyland Made in Asia
Guillem Medina y Núria Simón

Con dos huevos
Héloïse Guerrier y David Sánchez

Amo los uniformes
Blanca Lacasa y Cristóbal Fortúnez